Essays on Microeconomics and Industrial Organisation

Contributions to Economics

http://www.springer.de/cgi-bin/search_book.pl?series=1262

Sven-Morten Mentzel
Real Exchange Rate Movements
1998. ISBN 3-7908-1081-9

Lei Delsen/Eelke de Jong (Eds.)
The German and Dutch Economies
1998. ISBN 3-7908-1064-9

Mark Weder
Business Cycle Models with Indeterminacy
1998. ISBN 3-7908-1078-9

Tor Rødseth (Ed.)
Models for Multispecies Management
1998. ISBN 3-7908-1001-0

Michael Carlberg
Intertemporal Macroeconomics
1998. ISBN 3-7908-1096-7

Sabine Spangenberg
The Institutionalised Transformation of the East German Economy
1998. ISBN 3-7908-1103-3

Hagen Bobzin
Indivisibilities
1998. ISBN 3-7908-1123-8

Helmut Wagner (Ed.)
Current Issues in Monetary Economics
1998. ISBN 3-7908-1127-0

Peter Michaelis/Frank Stähler (Eds.)
Recent Policy Issues in Environmental and Resource Economics
1998. ISBN 3-7908-1137-8

Jessica de Wolff
The Political Economy of Fiscal Decisions
1998. ISBN 3-7908-1130-0

Georg Bol/Gholamreza Nakhaeizadeh/
Karl-Heinz Vollmer (Eds.)
Risk Measurements, Econometrics and Neural Networks
1998. ISBN 3-7908-1152-1

Joachim Winter
Investment and Exit Decisions at the Plant Level
1998. ISBN 3-7908-1154-8

Bernd Meyer
Intertemporal Asset Pricing
1999. ISBN 3-7908-1159-9

Uwe Walz
Dynamics of Regional Integration
1999. ISBN 3-7908-1185-8

Michael Carlberg
European Monetary Union
1999. ISBN 3-7908-1191-2

Giovanni Galizzi/
Luciano Venturini (Eds.)
Vertical Relationships and Coordination in the Food System
1999. ISBN 3-7908-1192-0

Gustav A. Horn/Wolfgang Scheremet/
Rudolf Zwiener
Wages and the Euro
1999. ISBN 3-7908-1199-8

Dirk Willer
The Development of Equity Capital Markets in Transition Economies
1999. ISBN 3-7908-1198-X

Karl Matthias Weber
Innovation Diffusion and Political Control of Energy Technologies
1999. ISBN 3-7908-1205-6

Heike Link et al.
The Costs of Road Infrastructure and Congestion in Europe
1999. ISBN 3-7908-1201-3

Simon Duindam
Military Conscription
1999. ISBN 3-7908-1203-X

Bruno Jeitziner
Political Economy of the Swiss National Bank
1999. ISBN 3-7908-1209-9

Irene Ring et al. (Eds.)
Regional Sustainability
1999. ISBN 3-7908-1233-1

Katharina Müller/Andreas Ryll/
Hans-Jürgen Wagener (Eds.)
Transformation of Social Security: Pensions in Central-Eastern Europe
1999. ISBN 3-7908-1210-2

continued on page 192

Pablo Coto-Millán (Editor)

Essays on Microeconomics and Industrial Organisation

With 19 Figures and 36 Tables

Physica-Verlag

A Springer-Verlag Company

Series Editors
Werner A. Müller
Martina Bihn

Editor
Professor Pablo Coto-Millán
University of Cantabria
Department of Economics
Avda. Los Castros s/n.
39005 Santander
Spain

ISSN 1431-1933
ISBN 3-7908-1390-7 Physica-Verlag Heidelberg New York

Cataloging-in-Publication Data applied for
Die Deutsche Bibliothek – CIP-Einheitsaufnahme
Essays on microeconomics and industrial organisation: with 36 tables / Pablo Coto-Millan. –
Heidelberg; New York: Physica-Verl., 2002
   (Contributions to economics)
   ISBN 3-7908-1390-7

Physica-Verlag Heidelberg New York
a member of BertelsmannSpringer Science+Business Media GmbH

© Physica-Verlag Heidelberg 2002
Printed in Germany

Softcover Design: Erich Kirchner, Heidelberg

SPIN 10794059   88/2202-5 4 3 2 1 0 – Printed on acid-free and non-aging paper

Table of Contents

Introduction

The aim of *Essays on Microeconomics and Industrial Organisation* is to serve as a source and work or reference and consultation for the field of Microeconomics in general and of Industrial Organisation in particular.

Traditionally, Microeconomics is essentially taught as theory and, although handbooks illustrate the various microeconomic theories with examples and practical cases, they hardly ever offer an estimation of a demand, production and cost function. In fact, Microeconomics is explained with self-contained theories without empirical tests. The editor of these Essays has taught Microeconomics for ten years in the traditional way; for the last eight years –in advanced courses and doctorates- he has offered a selection of empirical applications, which have complemented the traditional theoretical teaching. These applications have emerged from various research projects managed by the author during the last ten years with the financial support of several institutions (DGICYT, DGESIT, CICYT, and R&D National Plan). The success in this type of teaching and the availability of recent original applications from authors usually collaborating with the editor has led the later to compose this text.

This text combines microeconomic theories with appropriate empirical tests. The standardised microeconomic analysis of demand, production and costs (supply) is set forth along with appropriate econometric techniques. Moreover, it should be pointed out that over the last two decades Microeconomics has greatly broadened its field of application. On the one hand, this has been due to the fact that the conditions required for existence, unicity and stability of the general competitive equilibrium have been met. This was the prevailing focus of Microeconomics in the Sixties and part of the Seventies. On the other hand, as big samples of inter- and intra-industrial data were increasingly available, a neo-classical Microeconomics branch emerged in the mid Seventies traditionally called in Britain New Microeconomics or Industrial Organisation, which on the structure-behaviour-results paradigm, binds together the earlier and new works on structural change and technical progress and applies new techniques -mainly panel data- which enable us to observe how the behaviour of the new agents affects industrial structure.

Demand, production and costs are parts of Microeconomics which are greatly active at present. Industrial structure and regulation, markets and failures of market constitute central nuclei of Industrial Organisation. Therefore, the second part of the title of these essays records this expression. Although I dare not give it a Roman numeral, a new volume will foreseeably emerge in the future recording new advances both in the expression of ideas and in the econometric cointegration and panel data techniques used here.

The text consists of four parts: Demand, Production and Costs (Supply), Market and Industrial Structure and Failures of Market and Industrial Regulation. Each part has three chapters.

Section I deals with demand and starts with a paper that studies industrial demand. Chapter 2 offers a study on air transport demand with respect to the remaining modes of transport. To conclude, this section presents the behaviour of the consumer's with respect to the introduction of a new product.

Section II deals with supply. In Chapter 4 a production function is estimated with panel data for the hospital industry and the results corresponding to asignative efficiency are presented. In Chapter 5 economic efficiency is analysed for the case of road transport firms. Finally, Chapter 6 offers the productor's behaviour with technological innovation and structural change.

Section III studies the market and industrial structure. Chapter 7 covers the problems of measurement of inter- and intra-industry trade. The following chapter presents a typical model of Industrial Organisation in which intra-industry activity is explained by industrial structure and the behaviour of the agents. To conclude, this section presents a paper on economic integration in which the link between structural adjustment and horizontal and vertical intra-industry trade is analysed.

Section IV starts with a chapter on structure and regulation in electrical industry. In Chapter 11 the effects of a regulation of working time on labour market are studied. The last chapter includes a theoretical model which explains how the lack of co-ordination in the input and output of agents in industry may generate complex situations and presents an application.

Acknowledgements:
The editor thanks the DGICYT for the financial support, project number APC1998-0124, to the edition of this book.

PART I. DEMAND

1 Modeling Seasonal Integrated Time Series: the Spanish Industrial Production Index

José Luis Gallego-Gómez
Department of Economics
University of Cantabria (Spain)

In this paper the Box-Jenkins approach to the building of seasonal time series model is extended so that it is adequate to model seasonally integrated time series. To this end, the class of multiplicative ARIMA models is broadened in such a way that it allows to describe time series integrated at a few of the seasonal frequencies. Thus, tests for seasonal unit roots are not considered as a rival modeling approach, but can be used in the identification stage to decide the transformation inducing stationarity. The fit model is used to generate forecasts and to estimate unobservable components. The enhanced Box-Jenkins approach is illustrated modeling the Spanish Industrial Production Index.

1.1
Seasonal Time Series Models

The Box and Jenkins approach to the seasonal time series analysis can be sketched as follows. Firstly, the non-seasonal $1 - B$ and seasonal $1 - B^s$ differencing operators are used to convert a non-stationary series z_t into a stationary series w_t. It is usually necessary to use d-order non-seasonal and D-order seasonal differencing, that is,

$$w_t = (1 - B)^d (1 - B^s)^D$$

Then, the stationary series w_t is expressed, according the Wold decomposition theorem, as a weighted sum of current and past values of a white noise process

$$w_t = a_t + \sum_{j=1}^{\infty} \psi_j a_{t-j} = \psi(B)a_t$$

where

$$\psi(B) = 1 + \sum_{j=1}^{\infty} \psi_j B^j$$

Finally, to achieve parsimonious models the polynomial $\psi(B)$ is approximated by the rational polynomial

$$\psi(B) = \frac{\theta(B)\Theta(B^s)}{\phi(B)\Phi(B^s)}$$

where $\phi(B) = 1 - \phi_1 B - \dots - \phi_p B^p$ and $\theta(B) = 1 - \theta_1 B - \dots - \theta_q B^q$ are the non-seasonal autoregressive and moving-average polynomials which describe the dependence between consecutive data, and $\Phi(B) = 1 - \Phi_1 B - \dots - \Phi_P B^P$ and $\Theta(B) = 1 - \Theta_1 B - \dots - \Theta_Q B^Q$ are the seasonal autoregressive and moving-average polynomials describing the dependence between data which are s periods apart. Therefore, the nonstatinonary seasonal time series z_t is described by the general multiplicative model

$$\phi(B)\Phi(B^s)\nabla^d \nabla_s^D z_t = \theta(B)\Theta(B^s)a_t$$

(1.1)

The choice of the seasonal differencing to induce stationarity is based on the fact that seasonal time series show a cyclical behaviour with period s ($s = 4$ for quarterly data and $s = 12$ for monthly data). In the extreme case $z_t = z_{t-s}$, we have a homogeneous difference equation whose general solution is a linear combination of the s roots, $e^{-i2\pi j/s}$ ($j = 0, 1, \dots, s-1$ and $i = \sqrt{-1}$), of the characteristic equation $1 - B^s = 0$,

$$z_t = \sum_{j=0}^{s-1} a_j e^{i2\pi j/s} = \alpha_0 + \sum_{k=1}^{[s/2]} (\alpha_k \cos(\frac{2\pi k}{s}t) + \beta_k \sin(\frac{2\pi k}{s}t))$$

where $\alpha_k \cos(\frac{2\pi k}{s}t) + \beta_k \sin(\frac{2\pi k}{s}t)$ is a harmonic oscillation with period $p_k = s/2\pi k$ and constant amplitude $A_k = (\alpha^2 + \beta^2)^{1/2}$, generated by the pair of conjugate complex roots $e^{-i2\pi k/s}$ and $e^{-i2\pi(k-s)/s}$; the harmonic with frequency $s/2$, $\alpha_{s/2}\cos(\pi t)$, only arises when s is even and is generated by the negative unit real root; $[s/2] = s/2$ if s is even and $[s/2] = (s-1)/2$ if s is odd. Hence, it is seen the key role played by the seasonal difference in representing the seasonal pattern.

Although the 1 - Bs filter has been commonly used in the Box-Jenkins approach, Abraham and Box (1978) pointed out that sometimes some of its factors could be sufficient to handle the seasonality. Such factors are found by expresing 1 - Bs in terms of its roots

$$1 - B^s = \prod_{j=0}^{s-1} (1 - e^{i2\pi j/s}B)$$

and joining each pair of complex roots into a second-order factor

$$(1 - e^{i2\pi k/s}B)(1 - e^{i2\pi(s-k)/s}B) = 1 - 2\cos(2\pi k/s)B + B^2$$

Thus, the seasonal difference can be factored as follows

$$1 - B^s = \prod_{k=0}^{[s/2]} S_k(B) \tag{1.2}$$

where

$$S_k(B) = \begin{cases} 1 - B & k = 0 \\ 1 - 2\cos(2\pi k/s)B + B^2) & k = 1, \cdots, [(s-1)/2 \\ 1 + B & k = [s/2] = s/2 \end{cases} \tag{1.3}$$

Hylleberg, Engle, Granger and Yoo [HEGY] (1990) developed unit root tests to identify the simplifying operators $S_k(B)$ in the underlying time series model. These authors extend the notion of integration to cover the seasonal frequencies. Thus, a time series z_t is integrated of order d at the frequency k, denoted by $z_t \sim I_k(d)$, if its autoregressive representation contains the factor $S_k(B)^d$. Empirical evidence based on the HEGY test reveals that most of the monthly and quarterly economic time series are integrated of order one at a few seasonal frequencies (see, e. g., Osborn 1990, Beaulieu and Miron 1993, Hylleberg, Jorgensen and Sorensen 1993).

In contrast, the empirical evidence found using the Box-Jenkins methodology has revealed that most of the monthly and quarterly seasonal time series can be adequately described by the IMA(0,1,1)(0,1,1)$_s$ model,

$$(1 - B)(1 - B^s)z_t = (1 - \theta B)(1 - \Theta B^s)a_t$$

implying that z_t is $I_0(2)$ and $I_k(1)$ for $k = 1, \ldots, [s/2]$.

Gallego and Treadway (1995) have shown why the empirical results obtained with the HEGY test cannot be found with the conventional multiplicative ARIMA class, and how to broaden such a family to allow for unit roots at a few seasonal frequencies. Consider for example the seasonal IMA(1,1)$_4$ model for quarterly time series

$$(1 - B^4)z_t = (1 - \Theta B^4)a_t \tag{1.4}$$

It is interesting to write (1.4) as

$$(1 - B)(1 + B^2)(1 + B)z_t = (1 - \Theta^{1/4}B)(1 + \Theta^{1/2}B^2)(1 + \Theta^{1/4}B)a_t \tag{1.5}$$

The three nonstationary factors on the left-hand side of (1.5) contribute to "spectral peaks" at the frequencies 0, 1 and 2, respectively. So, under the condition of invertibility $\Theta < 1$, z_t is integrated of order one, $z_t \sim I_k(1)$, at $k = 0$, 1 and 2. However, if the MA parameter Θ is positive and strictly noninvertible, $\Theta = 1$, then the model contains three common factors whose cancellation implies that z_t is integrated of order zero, $z_t \sim I_k(0)$, at $k = 0$, 1 and 2. In contrants, let the seasonal MA(1)$_4$ polynomial in model (1.4) be replaced with a nonseasonal MA(4) polynomial. Then, the resulting IMA(1,4)(1,0)$_4$ model

$$(1 - B)(1 + B^2)(1 + B)z_t = (1 - \theta_1 B - \theta_2 B^2 - \theta_3 B^3 - \theta_4 B^4)a_t \tag{1.6}$$

enables the description of a richer class of integrated series. Here, the case $z_t \sim I_k(0)$ arises when the model contains a common factor with frequency k, that is, when $\theta(B) = \theta^*(B)S_k(B)$. But, if the factor $S_k(B)$ is not included in the MA structure, then $z_t \sim I_k(1)$. In (1.6) the order of integration of the process is not necessarily the same at all frequencies. In fact, $z_t \sim I_k(d_k)$, being $d_k = 0$ or 1 for $k = 0$, 1, and 2.

When investigating the order of integration of quarterly time series, it is convenient to express the IMA(1,4)(0,1)$_4$ in such a way that it shows more clearly the presence of common factors. Thus, in the constrained IMA(1,4)(1,0)$_4$ model

$$(1 - B)(1 + B^2)(1 + B)z_t = (1 - \theta_0 B)(1 + \theta_1 B^2)(1 + \theta_1 B)a_t \tag{1.7}$$

where $0 < \theta_k \leq 1$, one can readily to see that $z_t \sim I_k(1)$ if $0 < \theta_k < 1$ and $z_t \sim I_k(0)$ if $\theta_k = 1$. The MA(4) polynomial has been constrained so that it has roots at the frequencies $k = 0$, 1 and 2. This constraint is especially relevant when modeling monthly time series because the replacement of a seasonal MA(1)$_{12}$ polynomial by a nonseasonal MA(12) polynomial leads to a nonparsimonious model, whose estimation could be problematic. In such a case, the constrained MA(12) polynomial can be expressed as the product of the following seven factors

$$(1 - \theta_0 B), \ (1 - \sqrt{3\theta_1}\, B + \theta_1 B^2), \ (1 - \sqrt{\theta_2}\, B + \theta_2 B^2), \ (1 + \theta_3 B^2) \, ,$$

$$(1 + \sqrt{\theta_4}\, B + \theta_4 B^2), \ (1 + \sqrt{3\theta_5}\, B + \theta_5 B^2), \ (1 + \theta_6 B)$$

where $0 < \theta k \leq 1$. In general, a MA(s) polynomial can be constrained so that it has s roots at the frequencies $k = 0, 1, \ldots, [s/2]$, which correspond to the following factors with real coefficients

$$\vartheta(B) = \prod_{k=0}^{[s/2]} \vartheta_k(B) \tag{1.8}$$

where

$$\vartheta_k(B) = \begin{cases} 1 - \vartheta_0 B & k = 0 \\ 1 - 2\cos(2\pi k / s)\sqrt{\vartheta_k}\, B + \vartheta_k B^2) & k = 1, \cdots, [(s-1)/2] \\ 1 + \vartheta_{s/2} B & k = s/2 \text{ and s even} \end{cases} \tag{1.9}$$

The subscript k of the coefficient ϑ_k indicates the number of cycles in a period of s time instants. Comparing (1.8)-(1.9) with (1.2)-(1.3) it can be clearly seen the one-to-one correspondence between the factors $\theta_k(B)$ of the constrained MA(s) polynomial and the simplifying factors $S_k(B)$ of the seasonal difference. Thus, each MA factor acts as an indicator for overdifferencing.

In summary, seasonal integrated time series can be described by the generalized multiplicative ARIMA model

$$\phi(B)\Phi(B^s)\nabla^d \prod_{k=1}^{[s/2]} S_k(B)^{d_k} z_t = \theta(B)\Theta(B^s)\vartheta(B)a_t \tag{1.10}$$

which is compactly written as $\varphi(B)z_t = \eta(B)a_t$.

1.2
Forecasting

In this section the implications that the generalisation of the conventional multiplicative ARIMA model has on the forecasting function are examined; in particular, those derived from the relaxation of the assumption that time series are integrated at all seasonal frequencies. To this end, two specifications for the model (1.10) are used: (i) the difference equation representation

$$z_{t+l} - \varphi_1 z_{t+l-1} - \cdots - \varphi_p z_{t+l-p} = a_{t+l} - \eta_1 a_{t+l-1} - \cdots - \eta_q a_{t+l-q} \tag{1.11}$$

which is useful to recursively compute point forecasts, and (ii) the specification in terms of innovations

$$z_{t+l} = a_{t+l} + \psi_1 a_{t+l-1} + \psi_2 a_{t+l-2} + \cdots \tag{1.12}$$

or

$$z_{t+l} = \psi(B)a_{t+l} = (1 + \psi_1 B + \psi_2 B^2 + \cdots)a_{t+l}$$

which is more convenient to calculate interval forecasts and to update forecasts as new data become available.

The minimum mean square error forecast of z_{t+l} at origin t, for lead time l, is the conditional expectation $\hat{z}_t(l) = E[z_{t+l} / z_t, z_{t-1}, \cdots]$. Thus, taking conditional expectations at time t in (1.11) we obtain for $l > q$ the difference equation

$$\hat{z}_t(l) - \varphi_1 \hat{z}_t(l-1) - \cdots - \varphi_p \hat{z}_t(l-p) = 0, \quad l > q \tag{1.13}$$

whose general solution is

$$\hat{z}_t(l) = b_1^{(t)} f_1(l) + b_2^{(t)} f_2(l) + \cdots + b_p^{(t)} f_p(l), \quad l > \max(q-p,0) \tag{1.14}$$

To compute the p coefficients $b_i^{(t)}$ we need p initial conditions or pivotal values $\hat{z}_t(r+1)$, $\hat{z}_t(r+2)$, ..., $\hat{z}_t(r+p)$, where $r = \max(q-p,0)$. Let the column vector $\mathbf{b}^{(t)}$ be the p coeficients $b_i^{(t)}$, $i = 1, \ldots, p$, then

$$\mathbf{b}^{(t)} = (\mathbf{F}^T \mathbf{F})^{-1} \mathbf{F}^T \hat{\mathbf{z}}_t$$

where $\mathbf{F} = [f_i(j)]$ is a $p \times p$ matrix of fitting functions, $\hat{\mathbf{z}}_t = [\hat{z}_t(j)]$ is an $p \times 1$ column vector, and $j = r+1, \ldots, r+p$.

From (1.12), it follows that

$$\hat{z}_t(l) = \psi_l a_t + \psi_{l+1} a_{t-1} + \psi_{l+2} a_{t-2} + \cdots$$

Therefore, the forecast error l steps ahead

$$e_t(l) = a_{t+l} + \psi_1 a_{t+l-1} + \cdots + \psi_{l-1} a_{t+1}$$

has zero mean and variance

$$V[e_t(l)] = \sigma_a^2 (1 + \psi_1^2 + \cdots + \psi_{l-1}^2)$$

The coefficients ψ_j of the polynomial $\psi(B) = \eta(B)/\varphi(B)$ satisfy the difference equation

$$\psi_j - \varphi_1 \psi_{j-1} - \cdots - \varphi_p \psi_{j-p} = 0, \quad j > q$$

whose general solution is

$$\psi_j = c_1 f_1(j) + c_2 f_2(j) + \cdots + c_p f_p(j), \quad j > \max(0, q - p)$$

It is convinient to write

$$\psi = \mathbf{Fc} \tag{1.15}$$

where $\psi = (\psi_{r+1}, \ldots, \psi_{r+p})^T$ and $\mathbf{c} = (c_1, c_2, \ldots, c_p)^T$. The ψ_j weights are also used in updating the forecasts. As the forecasts of the future observation z_{t+l} made at origins t and $t-1$ are

$$\hat{z}_t(l) = \psi_l a_t + \psi_{l+1} a_{t-1} + \psi_{l+2} a_{t-2} + \cdots$$

$$\hat{z}_{t-1}(l+1) = \psi_{l+1} a_{t-1} + \psi_{l+2} a_{t-2} + \psi_{l+3} a_{t-3} + \cdots$$

the updating formula is

$$\hat{z}_t(l) = \hat{z}_{t-1}(l+1) + \psi_l a_t$$

Hence, it follows that

$$\mathbf{Fb}^{(t)} = \mathbf{Gb}^{(t-1)} + \psi a_t$$

where $\mathbf{G} = [f_i(j+l)], j = r+1, \ldots, r+p$. Solving for $\mathbf{b}^{(t)}$ we have that

$$\mathbf{b}^{(t)} = (\mathbf{F}^T \mathbf{F})^{-1} \mathbf{F}^T \mathbf{Gb}^{(t-1)} + \mathbf{c} a_t$$

Now we can see the role played by the constrained MA operators. While the roots of the autoregressive operator determine the form of the eventual forecast function and the pattern of the ψ_j weights, the moving average coefficients are relevant to provide initical conditions. Since that the replacement of the seasonal MA(1)$_s$ operator by the nonseasonal MA(s) operator does not change the orders of the extended ARMA model, neither the form of the forecast function nor the number of pivotal values are modified. Obviously to the extent the ψ_j weights changes, the pivotal values will change and also the position of the the eventual forecast function. However, the main implications arise when some of the MA roots are close to unit and cancel with some common simplifying operators, that is, when the series is $I_k(0)$ at a few k. In such a case, some coefficients c_i will be zero and, therefore, the forecasting function will contain non-updated or deterministic components and the squares sum of ψ_j weights, $V[e_t(l)] = \sigma_a^2 c^T \mathbf{F}^T \mathbf{F} c$, will be smaller.

1.3
Unobservable Components

Several procedures have been proposed to estimate the trend T_t, seasonal S_t and irregular I_t components of a time series described by an ARIMA model (see, e. g. , Gallego 2000). I addopt an variant of the approach based on the eventual forecasting function. Equation (1.14) can be written as

$$\hat{z}_t(l) = \sum_{k=1}^{p_1} b_k^{(t)} f_k(l) + \sum_{k=p_1+1}^{p} b_k^{(t)} f_k(l) = \hat{T}_t + \hat{S}_t \qquad (1.16)$$

where it has been assumed that the first p_1 fitting functions, $f_k(l)$ $(k = 1, ..., p_1)$ are nonseasonal, and $f_k(l)$ $(k = p_1+1, ..., p)$ are seasonal functions; $\hat{T}_t$ and $\hat{S}_t$ are the estimates for the trend and seasonal components.

Assuming that the unobservable components are described by ARIMA models, then it follows that

$$z_t = \hat{z}_{t-1}(1) + a_t, \quad T_t = \hat{T}_{t-1}(1) + b_t, \quad S_t = \hat{S}_{t-1}(1) + c_t, \quad I_t = \hat{I}_{t-1}(1) + d_t$$

where b_t, c_t, and d_t are white noise innovations. Hence, it is clear that the estimation of each unobservable component involves the calculation of its one-step-ahead predictor and error. While the quantities $\hat{T}_{t-1}(1)$, $\hat{S}_{t-1}(1)$, and $\hat{I}_{t-1}(1)$ can be obtained easily by breaking down $\hat{z}_{t-1}(1)$, the remaining problem is how to estimate the shocks b_t, c_t, and d_t.

For the additive seasonal model

$$z_t = T_t + S_t + I_t$$

it follows that

$$\hat{z}_{t-1}(1) = \hat{T}_{t-1}(1) + \hat{S}_{t-1}(1) + \hat{I}_{t-1}(1)$$

and

$$a_t = b_t + c_t + d_t$$

It is now apparent that the difficulty inherent to the decomposition of seasonal time series is how to isolate the three component innovations of the residual series a_t. As in other approaches, the identification problem also arises here. Nonetheless, the class of observationally equivalent decompositions is readily obtainable from the different allocations of white noise series among the one-step-ahead predictors

$$T_t^* = \hat{T}_{t-1}(1) + e_{1t}, \quad S_t^* = \hat{S}_{t-1}(1) + e_{2t}, \quad I_t^* = \hat{I}_{t-1}(1) + a_t - e_{1t} - e_{2t}$$

where e_{1t} and e_{2t} are white noise process. Hence, the canonical decomposition is

$$T_t^C = \hat{T}_{t-1}(1), \quad S_t^C = \hat{S}_{t-1}(1), \quad I_t^C = \hat{I}_{t-1}(1) + a_t \qquad (1.17)$$

The $\hat{I}_{t-1}(1)$ component will be zero for models with $p \le q$, since none of the AR roots generates an irregular movement. In such a case, the irregular component is equal to the residuals of the model fit to the data. In contrast, for top-heavy models $p < q$ the eventual forecast function for $\hat{z}_{t-1}(1)$ includes moving average terms, which are allocated to the irregular component. This result is consistent with the observation by Burman (1980) that top heavy models lead to irregular components with moving average structure.

1.4
Empirical Analysis

In this section, I embed the seasonal integration notion into the Box-Jenkins iterative modeling strategy. Although this can be made in several ways I follow a "general to specific" approach by assuming that times series, when showing seasonality, are integrated of order one in all of the seasonal frequencies. This general assumption does not imply a big change in the Box-Jenkins practice, in which the airlines models arises often as a tentative representation for many seasonal time series. Then, a more specific model is arrived at by looking for overdifferencing at single frequencies. The specific model, which can be thought of as a mixed regression-ARIMA model or transfer function model, is used to generate forecast and to estimate unobservable components.

Figure 1 displays several identification tools for the Spanish Industrial Production Index from January 1986 to January 2000, 169 monthly observations.

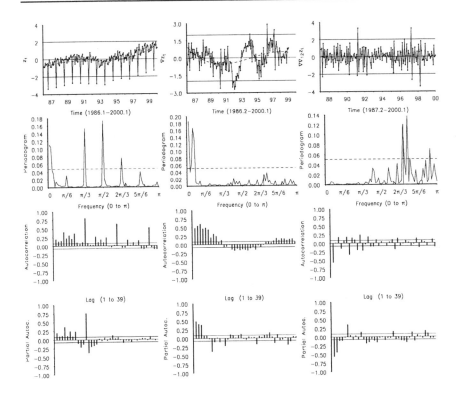

Fig. 1.1. Plot, Periodogram, Correlogram and Partial Autocorrelation Function for the series: z_t, ∇z_t y $\nabla\nabla_{12}z_t$

Following the Box-Jenkins approach it is concluded that $\nabla\nabla_{12}z_t$ seems to be a stationary series. On the other hand, its periodogram, column 3 in Figure 1, peaks at the calendar frequency 0. 348 (close to $\pi/3$, indicating a trading day variation which can be modelled (see, e. g. , Bell and Hillmer 1983) as

$$TD_t = \sum_{i=0}^{6} \beta_i td_{it}$$

where td_{it} ($i = 0, \ldots, 6$) are, respectively, the number of Sundays, Mondays, . . . in month t. Since $lom_t = \sum_{i=0}^{6} td_{it}$, where lom_t is the length of month t, an alternative specification for the trading day variation is

$$TD_t = \beta_0' lom_t + \sum_{i=1}^{6} \beta_i^* td_{it}^*$$

where $\beta_0' = (1/7)\sum_{i=0}^{6}\beta_i$ $td_{it}^* = td_{it} - td_{0t}$, and $\beta_i^* = \beta_i - \beta_0'$ measures the difference between the i-th day effect and the lom effect. Also it is expected that the production decreases due to holidays such as Easter. The Easter effect here is modeled as

$$E_t = \alpha \xi_t^{Easter}$$

where ξ_t^{Easter} is the proportion of Easter days falling in the month t. Here, it is assumed that the length of the Easter is four days.

Since the sample autocorrelation function (SACF) and the sample partial autocorrelation function of $\nabla\nabla_{12}z_t$ can be distorted by the calendar and Easter effects, instead of identifying a tentative multiplicative ARMA structure, the airline model with deterministic variables

$$z_t = \beta_0' lom_t + \sum_{i=1}^{6} \beta_i^* td_{it}^* + \alpha \xi_t^{Easter} + N_t$$

$$\nabla\nabla_{12}N_t = (1 - \theta B)(1 - \Theta B^{12})a_t$$

is estimated as starting point. The exact maximum likelihood estimates obtained with the AMB program (Gallego 2000b) are

$$z_t = -6.93\xi_t^{Easter} + 2.74 lom_t + 0.15 td_{1t}^* + 0.23 td_{2t}^* + 0.76 td_{3t}^*$$
$$\quad (0.68) \qquad (1.10) \qquad (0.33) \qquad (0.34) \qquad (0.32)$$

$$+ 0.73 td_{4t}^* + 0.57 td_{5t}^* - 1.35 td_{6t}^* + N_t$$
$$\quad (0.32) \qquad (0.33) \qquad (0.33)$$

$$\nabla\nabla_{12}N_t = (1 - 0.47B)(1 - 0.83B^{12})at$$
$$\qquad\qquad (0.07) \qquad (0.08)$$

$$a = .054(.175), \sigma_a = 2.19, \max(\rho_{ij}) = -.58,$$

$$Q(39) = 58, LLF = -343.4, AIC = 1.69 \tag{1.18}$$

Some of the usual diagnostic checks reveal model inadequacies: (i) the Q-statistic for the first $n/4$ residual autocorrelations is greater than the 5% point for χ^2 with 37 degrees of freedom, 52. 192320; (ii) the SACF and SPACF take large values compared with the $\pm 2/\sqrt{n}$ bands at some lags. While it is not clear how to reformulate this model with conventional operators, some improvement is obtain by replacing the MA(1)$_{12}$ i by a constrained MA(12) polynomial and including an AR(2)$_{12}$ polynomial to describe the annual dependence structure indicated by lags 12, 24 and 36. The estimated model is

$$z_t = -7.23\xi_t^{Easter} + 2.21 lom_t + 0.25 td_{1t}^* - 0.10 td_{2t}^* + 1.26 td_{3t}^*$$
$$\quad (0.53) \qquad (0.91) \qquad (0.26) \qquad (0.27) \qquad (0.26)$$

$$+ 0.28 \mathrm{td}^*_{4t} + 1.35 \mathrm{td}^*_{5t} - 1.95 \mathrm{td}^*_{6t} + \mathrm{N}_t$$
$$ (0.26) \qquad (0.26) \qquad (0.26)$$

$$(1 - .40 B^{12} + .21 B^{24}) \nabla \nabla_{12} \mathrm{N}_t = (1 - .34 B)(1 - .99 B)(1 - 1.71 B + .97 B^2)$$
$$ (.14) \qquad (.09) \qquad\qquad (.09) \qquad (.06) \qquad\qquad (.04)$$

$$(1 - 1.0 B + 1.0 B^2)(1 - .97 B^2)(1 + .97 B + .93 B^2)(1 - 1.73 B + .99 B^2)(1 + .96 B) a t$$
$$ (-.-) \qquad\quad (.05) \qquad\qquad (.06) \qquad\qquad (.15) \qquad\quad (.03)$$

$$a = .033(.174), \sigma_a = 2.18, \max(\rho_{ij}) = -.58,$$

$$Q(39) = 50, \mathrm{LLF} = -342.8, \mathrm{AIC} = 1.79 \qquad\qquad\qquad (1.19)$$

where the presence of a common factor $1 - B + B^2$ on both sides of the model equation is discovered. This is indicative of the presence of a single deterministic seasonal component with a period of six months or a frequency of two cycles per year. Thus, the common factor can be removed, but a pair of trigonometric variables c_{2t} and s_{2t} are added to the model (see,e. g. , Box, Jenkins and Reinsel 1994). Futermore, the simplifying factors $1 - B$ and $1 - \sqrt{3} B + B^2$ of the seasonal difference are nearly canceled by the associated MA operators, indicating that a constant term and a pair of trigonometric variables c_{1t} and c_{2t} must be included. Proceeding in this way we reach the estimated model

$$z_t = -7.06 \xi_t^{Easter} + 3.26 lom_t + .06 td^*_{1t} + .29 td^*_{2t} + .66 td^*_{3t} + .78 td^*_{4t} + .60 td^*_{5t}$$
$$ (0.54) \qquad (0.91) \qquad (.26) \quad (.27) \quad (.26) \quad (.26) \quad (.26)$$
$$ - 1.40 td^*_{6t} + 1.27 c_{1t} + 5.90 s_{1t} + 1.23 c_{2t} - 7.73 s_{2t} - 10.02 c_{3t} - 2.03 s_{3t}$$
$$ (.26) \qquad (.31) \qquad (.40) \qquad (.29) \qquad (.22) \qquad (.46) \qquad (.16)$$
$$ + 2.53 c_{4t} + 5.15 s_{4t} + 1.72 c_{5t} - 7.66 s_{2t} + N_t$$
$$ (.16) \qquad (.40) \qquad (.21) \qquad (.74)$$
$$(1 - .28 B^{12} + .23 B^{24})[\nabla(1 + B) N_t - .40] = (1 - .36 B)(1 + .96 B) a t$$
$$ (.08) \qquad\quad (.09) \qquad\qquad (.19) \qquad (.09) \qquad (.03)$$
$$a = .033(.174), \sigma_a = 2.18, \max(\rho_{ij}) = -.58,$$
$$Q(39) = 50, LLF = -342.8, AIC = 1.79$$

$$(1.20)$$

Now the main diagnosis checks do not reveal serious model inadequacies: the Q-statistics is less than the 50% point of the χ^2 with 40 degrees of freedom, and the residual plot, cumulative periodogram, correlogram and SPACF are consistent with the white noise hypothesis.

Several implications are derived from model (1.20). Firstly, the time series z_t is $I_k(1)$ at $k = 0$ and 6, but $I_k(0)$ at $k = 1, ..., 5$. Similar results are found with the Beaulieu and Miron test for seasonal unit roots showed in Table 1. Note that these results can not be indicated by the airlines model. Secondly, the trend component is described by a linear trend with stochastic ordinate, but deterministic slope. Thirdly, the seasonal component is the sum of five harmonic oscillations with deterministic amplitude and one oscillation with stochastic deterministic. Therefore, both the trend and seasonal component are a mixture of deterministic and stochastic terms. Finally, a damped cyclical component with period 4. 96 years is described by the annual $AR(2)_{12}$ polynomial. The estimates of three unobservable components, following the method described in the above section, are shown in Figure 2.

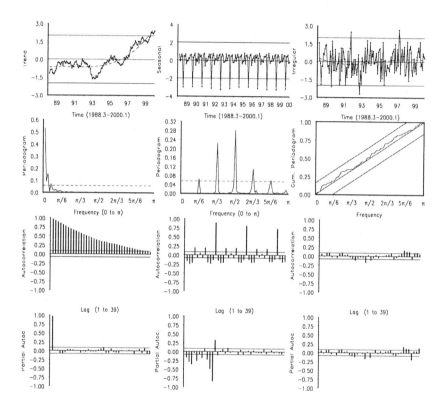

Fig. 1.2. Estimated trend, seasonal and irregular components for the Spanish IPI provided by model (1.20).

Table 1.1. Test for seasonal unit roots

	a_0	a_1	b_1	a_2	b_2	a_3	b_3	a_4	b_4	a_5	b_5	a_6
t	-1.49	-2.69	-3.80	-4.32	-248	-4.06	-1.12	-3.29	2.21	-2.93	.20	-2.68
F	.	10.4	.	14.4	.	9.10	.	8.48	.	4.34	.	

Lags: 5, 6, 7, 12, 15, 32. Deterministic inputs: Linear trend, seasonal dummies and calendar effects. Diagnostic checks: $\sigma_a = 1.8301$, $Q(31) = 33.01$, LLF = -252.91, AIC = 1.8327.

References

B. Abraham and G. E. P. Box. Deterministic and forecast-adaptive time-dependent models. Applied Statistics, 27:120 –130 (1978)

J. J. Beaulieu and J. A. Miron. Seasonal unit roots in aggregate U. S. data. Journal of Econometrics , 55:305 –328 (1993)

W. R. Bell and S. C. Hillmer. Modelling time series with calendar variation. Journal of the American Statistical Association, 78 (383):526 –311, September 1983

G. E. P. Box, G. M. Jenkins, and G. C. Reinsel. Time series analysis, forecasting and control . Prentice Hall, Engle Woods, New Jersey, 3rd edition, 1994

J. P. Burman. Seasonal adjustment by signal extraction. Journal of the Royal Statistical Society A , 143:321 –337 (1980)

H. S. Lee E. Ghysels and J. Noh. Testing for unit roots in seasonal time series. Journal of Econometrics , 62:415 –442 (1994)

J. L. Gallego. User guide for the arima model building package. Departamento de Economía, Universidad de Cantabria (2000b)

J. L. Gallego. Measuring seasonal variations wit regarima models. Departamento de Economía, Universidad de Cantabria (2000a)

J. L. Gallego and A. B. Treadway. The general family of seasonal stochastic processes. Departamento de Economía (1995)

D. R. Osborn. A survey of seasonality in uk macroeconomic variables. International Journal of Forecasting , 6:327 –336 (1990)

C. Jorgensen S. Hylleberg and N. K. Sorensen. Seasonality in macroeconomic time series. Empirical Economics , 18:321, 325 (1993)

C. W. J. Granger S. Hylleberg, R. F. Engle and B. S. Yoo. Seasonal integration and cointegration. Journal of Econometrics , 44:215 –238 (1990)

G. W. Schwert. Tests for unit roots: a monte carlo investigation. Journal of Business and Economic Statistics , 7:147 –160 (1989)

2 Passenger's Choice of Air Transport under Road Competition: the Use of Cointegration Techniques[*]

José Baños-Pino
Department of Economics
University of Oviedo (Spain)

Pablo Coto-Millán
Department of Economics
University of Cantabria (Spain)

Vicente Inglada-López de Sabando
Department of Economics
University Carlos III (Spain)

In this study, a theoretical model for the passenger transport demands in Spain is presented. Quarterly data have been used for the 1980.I-1992.IV period.

Cointegration techniques, which are subject to a wide range of tests, are used to obtain short and long run equations. Moreover, the product, price and cross elasticities of each mode of transport are obtained. These estimations may be used to analyse the effects of transport tariffs on income changes, as well as to predict short- and long run traffics.

2.1
Introduction

The initial models of passenger transport demand were the aggregate "modal split models". In these models, there has been an attempt to determine the number of

---

[*] This research was partly financed by the PS95-0095 research project from the DGICYT a body from the Spanish Ministry of Science and Education.

journeys by a given set of modes of transport for two towns, taking into account the characteristics of the passengers. Studies on modal split, such as Quandt and Baumol (1966), Boyer (1977), and Levin (1978), have been criticised by Oum (1979) and Winston (1985), among others, for the few variables used to account for the motivation in the user's behaviour, and for using very simple linear patterns in their estimations.

Several models of aggregate passenger transport demand based on the user's behaviour have been carried out in order to improve the previous ones. The user's utility is optimised in these models in line with the classic theory of consumer's behaviour and demand. The work by Oum and Guillen (1979) based on the user's behaviour is a typical example in which the passenger demand in Canada is analysed.

Some disaggregate research based on the user's behaviour has also been done on passenger transport demand. The most significant work on these models is McFadden (1973, 1974). In these works, the user takes a discrete choice of some of the different modes of transport (railway, air, road transport, etc.) and it is assumed that the mode chosen optimises the utility for the user.

Spanish interurban passenger transport was first studied in the "Elasticidad de la Demanda del Transporte Público de Viajeros" (Elasticity of the Passenger Public Transport Demand) by the Instituto de Estudios de Transportes y Comunicaciones (Institute of Transport and Communication Studies) (1978). This was analysed by Vázquez (1985) in a work carried out by the Secretaría General del Ministerio de Transportes (General Secretariat of the Ministry of Transport). In addition, other studies such as that by Inglada (1992), Coto-Millán and Sarabia (1994) and Coto-Millán, Baños and Inglada (1997) have been carried out on this issue. The elasticities of the modes of transport in the main regions were studied in IETC (1978) and Vázquez (1985). Price elasticities have been studied in Inglada (1992) for monthly data between 1980.01 and 1988.12, with time series in which the residues have been modelled with the Box-Jenkins techniques. Uniequational models have been carried out in Coto-Millán and Sarabia (1994) in order to estimate income elasticities, using the Industrial Production Index and the Electric Power Consumption, for the 1980.01-1988.12 period, and monthly data have been used in the estimations. In these works, the series is also modelled by the Box-Jenkins methodology.

An original model is offered in this paper in order to estimate price income and cross elasticities for the 1980.I-1992.IV period, applying cointegration techniques and using monthly data. Such techniques allow the estimation of short run elasticities, which add immediate responses to price and income changing, and the estimation of long run elasticities which allow to see the effects of the price and/or income changing produced later on.

This research offers a model according to the second proposal above, being based on a microeconomic analysis, which can be considered as classic. Its structure is very simple. Point number 2.2 presents the theoretical model for Spanish passenger transport demand. In the next point, the data used are described. Point number 2.4 presents the estimations of the different demands. Finally, the main conclusions are offered in point number 2.5.

2.2
The Model

Suppose a typical user whose preferences are weakly separable, then modelling passenger transport demand constitutes the second stage of a two-stage budget process. Therefore, the user's spending firstly falls into two large categories: passenger transport services and all other goods and services; secondly, the user's income is assigned to the goods and services contained in each of these two categories. That is to say, the utility function of the representative user is as follows:

$$U = U (X_1, X_2,..., X_k; X_{k+1},..., X_n)$$

where the vector $X_i = (X_1, X_2,..., X_k)$ with $i = 1, 2,..., k$ represents passenger transport services; the vector $X_j = (X_{k+1},..., X_n)$ with $j = k+1,...n$ represents goods and services except for those corresponding to passenger transport, and U represents a utility function which is continuous and differentiable, monotonic, increasing, and strictly quasi-concave.

The consumer balance is reduced to:

$$max\ U (X_i; X_j)$$

$$subject\ to:\ P_i \cdot\ X_i + P_j \cdot\ X_j = Y$$

where $P_i = (P_1, P_2,..., P_k)$ and $P_j = (P_{k+1},..., P_n)$ are the prices, and where Y represents the user's level of income.

First order conditions allow obtaining the following typical user's Marshallian demands:

$$X_i = X_i (P_i, P_j, Y) \tag{2.1}$$

$$X_j = X_j (P_i, P_j, Y) \tag{2.2}$$

Of these individual demand functions, function (2.1) is interesting for us since it corresponds with passenger transport services.

Equation (2.1) still presents some problems. First, functions such as (2.1) should be valid for any income distribution among the different economic agents. If this were not the case, this function would provide as many values as income Y distributions among the possible users and, therefore, such a function would not exist. Another assumption would be that income is distributed under a specific rule. Once this rule has been established, integrability conditions are verified and the existence of the aggregate Marshallian demand functions is guaranteed (Varian, 1992). However, there are no data to go along these lines. In order to solve this problem in this study we can assume that all the users have the same level of income.

Function (2.1) is general enough to analyse the passenger transport service demands -long-distance railway, air and road transport- identifying the different subindexes for the amounts demanded in each service.

From 1980.I to 1992.IV, passenger transport services in Spain have been provided under different regulation conditions. The government company RENFE and Iberia have the monopoly of railway and air national transport in Spain respectively, and road transport is provided by private companies which have exclusive routes under a system called "right of testing". It can be said that trump road passenger transport, which has a low incidence in quantitative terms, is the only mode of transport, which has not yet been regulated. However, given the impossibility to obtain quarterly statistical data on passenger road transport, and with the aim of adding interregional transport on the user's own vehicles, the premium petrol consumption variable has been used. The premium petrol consumption has also been regulated by the government during the period of this study. Under such regulatory conditions and with the aim of avoiding any problems arising from the supply-demand simultaneity, we assume that supply is exogenous in relation with prices and income and is determined by the decisions of the government.

2.3
The Data

Data on the series of passenger departures and arrivals of national fligths in Spanish airports (AERV) have been obtained from the series provided by the Informes de Coyuntura del Ministerio de Transportes, Turismo y Comunicaciones (Reports on the State of the Transport, Tourism and Communication Ministry) No data on road transport passengers are available and a "proxy" such as premium petrol consumption has been used in order to approximate the transport on the user's own vehicles. This variable, QGAS, has been obtained from the Dirección General de Previsión y Coyuntura del Ministerio de Economía y Hacienda (General Management of the Finance Ministry Forecast and State). The gas-oil consumption variable (QGLEO) has also been used with the aim of approximating the behaviour of regular and tramp passenger transport in public services. However, the results obtained are significantly anomalous and the reason for this may be that this variable shows the behaviour of road transport of goods (which is much more important in terms of consumption), rather than of passengers.

The data on the series of long distance railway prices (PF) and air transport fares (PA) have been obtained from the monthly series worked out from the fares of the Boletines Oficiales del Estado (Official State Reports), evaluated within the period in which each tariff is in force.

The data on the prices of premium petrol (PGAS) have been obtained from the Dirección General de Previsión y Coyuntura del Ministerio de Economía y Hacienda, as monthly data, also evaluated within the period in which each fare is in force.

Data on the prices of gas oil (PGLEO) have been obtained from CAMPSA until 1992. From then onwards, the data from the Compañía Logística de Hidrocarburos (Hydrocarbon Logistic Company) have been recorded for further studies.

The data on the income variable have been obtained considering the Spanish quarterly GDP as "proxy". The series used for the 1980.I-1989.IV period come from Contabilidad Nacional Española (Spanish National Accounting).

2.4
Marshallian or Non Compensated Demands of Interurban Passenger Transport: Air and Road Transport

In this paper we use cointegration analysis and error-correction modelling techniques to estimate transport demand functions. The analysis of cointegration offers a generic route to test the existence of long-term relationships, suggested by the economic theory, among various integrated variables, which has provided the most satisfactory results of the various approaches previously attempted (Inglada (1992), Coto-Millán and Sarabia (1994)). Engle and Granger (1987) formalize the equivalence between cointegration and error-correction.

Before an error-correction model can be constructed according to Engle and Granger's representation theorem, we need to establish that variables in demand equations are integrated, at most integrated of order 1, I(1), and are cointegrated. First of all, we examine the properties of individual time series by means of standard tests. The results of these tests suggest the presence of a single unit root in all series and this implies that the levels of these variables are nonstationary but the first difference is stationary.

The existence of a long run relationship among variables has been verified in this paper by applying the Engle and Granger (1987) technique and the Johansen (1988) and the Johansen and Juselius (1990) procedure. The Engle and Granger approach to test the existence of cointegration is characterized by a Dickey-Fuller statistic, which is used to test the existence of a unit root in the residual of static cointegration regressions. Johansen (1988) and Johansen and Juselius (1990) develop a maximum likelihood estimation procedure that has several advantages over the procedure suggested by Engle and Granger, because it eliminates the assumption that the cointegration vector is unique and it takes into account the error structure of the underlying process.

We have estimated some equations from the specifications in model (2.1) by adjusting the variables to each mode of transport. All variables headed by letter L are in natural logs and those headed by letter D are in differencess. The statistical "t" is presented within brackets under each coefficient.

2.4.1 Air Transport Demand

Long run

The estimated equation of long run balance cointegration has provided the following results:

$$LAERV_t = -1.88 \ -1.38 \ LPA_t \ + 1.48 \ LGDP_t$$

$$(-2.13) \ (-6.43) \qquad (21.14)$$

$$R^2 \text{ adjusted} = 0.91 \ ; \ S.E. = 0.04 \ ; \ D.W. = 1.25 \ ; \ D.F.^a = -4.14 \ ; \ D.W.^b = 1.79$$

[a] Indicates statistical significance at the 5% level.
[b] Is the Durbin-Watson from equation used to computed the DF (Dickey-Fuller) statistic.

Table 2.1 presents the results of cointegration tests applying the Johansen methodology. To test the null hypothesis of at most r cointegrating vectors, Johansen (1988) proposed the trace test . The critical value for these statistics has been generated by simulation by Osterwald-Lenum (1992) and the Pantula principle has been employed to determine the cointegration rank. Then, if Johansen technique is applied to a VAR along with three lags and a restricted constant, it is concluded that there is only one cointegration vector.

Table 2.1

Number of cointegration vectors			
Under H_0	Under H_1	Trace test	95% critical value (a)
$r = 0$	$r \geq 1$	41.14	34.91
$r \leq 1$	$r \geq 2$	19.60	19.96
$r \leq 2$	$r = 3$	6.83	9.24

(a) Critical values are from Osterwald-Lenum (1992)

After normalisation, the following long run solution is obtained:

$LAERV_t =$ -1.76 -1.41 LPA_t + 1.17 $LGDP_t$

In both estimated equations, the long run elasticity of air transport demand with respect to the GDP is close, somewhat higher than the unit ad takes 1.17 and 1.48 values as it would correspond to normal goods and particularly to "luxury" goods. The estimated long run own-price elasticity of goods is negative with values ranging from 1.38 to 1.41, which reflects a significant response of the demand to price changing.

Short run

All the demands of passenger transport have been specified, according to the Granger representation theorem, in the form of a model with error correction mechanism (ECM). This model incorporates the long run relationships, contained in the ECM, as well as the dynamics implied by the deviations from this equilibrium path and the adjustment process to recover it. The coefficients of the variables in differences represent short run elasticities. The joint non-linear estimation presents the following results:

$DLAERV_t =$ -0.51 ($LAERV_{t-1}$ + 2.24 + 1.12 LPA_{t-1} - 1.47 $LGDP_{t-1}$)

(-3.92)   (1.96)   (2.06)   (-9.8)

- 0.43 $DLPAERV_{t-4}$ + 0.45 $DLPGAS_t$ - 0.78 $DLPA_t$

(-3.07)   (2.14)   (-2.36)

R^2 adjusted = 0.95 ; S.E. = 0.048; F = 147.13; D.W. = 2.10

Serial Correlation: Ljung-Box: $Q(1) = 0.30$;

$$Q(2) = 0.19;$$

$$Q(3) = 1.36;$$

$$Q(4) = 2.44$$

Residual Normality: Bera-Jarque: $N(2) = 1.08$

Heteroscedasticity: ARCH (1-4) = 1.27

The long run elasticities obtained for this and the previous model do not differ from each other significantly. Then, long run income elasticity is now 1.47 in comparison with the former values 1.17 and 1.48, as it corresponds to luxury goods or services. The negative value of the own-price elasticity of goods is 1.12 in comparison with the former 1.38 and 1.41 values.

Short and long run elasticities are once more slightly different. Short run elasticities clearly present the inelastic feature of the demand, and a substitution effect of road transport, which has never been revealed before, is detected. Gross and net substitution relationships between air and road transport result once more from these estimations.

2.4.2 Road Transport Demand

Long run

In the inter-city road passenger transport demand equation, the dependent variable is the amount of premium petrol, in logs, LQGAS, and the independent variables are log real rpices of premium petrol, LPGAS and LGDP already defined. The equation of the long-term balance cointegration estimated, yielded the following results:

$$LQGAS_t = -3.80 - 0.13 \, LPGAS_t + 1.11 \, LGDP_t$$

$$(-3.21) \quad (-1.94) \qquad (8.29)$$

R^2 adjusted = 0.94 ; S.E. = 0.03 ; D.W. = 1.51; D.F.[a] = -5.52 ;D.W.[b] = 2.01

[a] Indicates statistical significance at the 5% level.
[b] Is the Durbin-Watson from equation used to computed the DF (Dickey-Fuller) statistic.

Table 2.2 presents the results of Johansen's cointegration test. This test strongly reject the null hypothesis of no cointegration ($r = 0$), but not the null hypothesis of at most one cointegrating vector, so there appears to be a single cointegrating vector, wich implies, after normalization, the following long run solution:

$$LQGAS_t = 2.85 - 0.47 \, LPGAS_t + 0.3611 \, LGDP_t$$

Table 2.2

Number of cointegration vectors			
Under H_0	Under H_1	Trace test	95 % critical value (a)
$r = 0$	$r \geq 1$	41.87	53.12
$r \leq 1$	$r \geq 2$	19.19	34.91
$r \leq 2$	$r = 3$	7.90	19.96

(a) Critical values are from Osterwald-Lenum (1992)

The results obtained from the long run estimations provide elasticities of 0.361 and 1.11 with respect to the GDP, relationships that characterise these services as basic goods rather than as luxury goods, always within the context of normal goods. The own-price elasticities of the goods take the negative values 0.13 and 0.47, once more referring to essential goods with inelastic demand and slight demand variations as a response to tariff changes (if we consider such changes as proportional to premium petrol price changing).the gas-oil demand equation QGLEO presents very similar values with respect to its price and to the GDP variable.

Short run

Finally, we estimate an error-correction model to integrate short run dynamics with long run equilibrium, which presents the following results:

$$DLQGAS_t = -0.69 (LQGAS_{t-1} + 3.88 + 0.15 LPGAS_{t-1} - 1.11 DLGDP_{t-1}) -$$
$$(-4.85) \qquad (2.20) \quad (1.68) \qquad (-6.19)$$

$$-0.36 DLPGAS_{t-4} + 0.34 DLPA_t$$
$$(-2.73) \qquad (2.23)$$

R^2 adjusted = 0.95 ; S.E. = 0.036 ; F = 212.45 ; D.W. = 2.13

Serial Correlation: Ljung-Box: $Q(1) = 0.28$;

$Q(2) = 1.91$;

$Q(3) = 4.81$;

$Q(4) = 4.82$

Residual Normality: Bera-Jarque: $N(2) = 4.16$

Heteroscedasticity: ARCH (1-4) = 1.17

The long run elasticities obtained for the ECM equation do not differ from the previous model. The value of the GDP long run demand elasticity is now 1.11, equal to the Engle and Granger approach, and the negative value of the long run own-price elasticity of goods is 0.15, while the former values were 0.13 and 0.47.

The estimated short run own-price elasticities of goods have the negative value 0.36 and a cross elasticity of 0.34 with respect to air transport price. In the short run, it is possible to speak about gross substitution relationships between road and air transport. However, it is not possible to meet any conclusion with respect to the net substitution or complementary relationships of these transport services without any further assumption.

2.5
Conclusions

A theoretical model of air passenger transport demand has been presented in this paper. With quarterly aggregated Spanish data, equations of inter-city passenger air and road transport demand have been specified for 1980.I and 1992.IV.

Moreover, different demand function estimations have been carried out using cointegration techniques, and have been subject to a wide evaluation which allows us to check the adequacy of this method with respect to others used in earlier works by Inglada (1992) and Coto-Millán and Sarabia (1994).

Each specific demand may require more detailed studies, especially road transport. However, having carried out the estimations, it is possible to draw conclusions as regards income, the own-price elasticity of goods and cross price elasticities:

- Long-term income elasticities are all positive and all the services are normal goods. Income elasticities are very close to the unit for air transport, and slightly below the unit for road transport.
- The own-price elasticities of goods increase parallel to the quality of the service, since they increase with fares, and present values close to the unit for air transport. They are clearly inelastic for road transport.
- All cross elasticities present positive values and they are below the unit. Gross and net long run substitution relationships between air and road transport and gross substitution relationships between road and air transport can be guaranteed, but net substitution relationships between these cannot.

References

Boyer, K.D.: Minimum Rate Regulations, Modal Split Sensitives, and the Railroad Problem. Journal of Political Economy 85(3), 493-512 (1977)

Coto-Millán, P., Sarabia, J.M.: Intercity Public Transport in Spain 1980-1988: Elasticities, Prices, Income and Time series. Mimeo. University of Cantabria, Department of Economics (1994)

Coto-Millán, P., Baños-Pino, J., Inglada, V.: Marshallian Demands of Intercity Passenger Transport in Spain: 1980-1992. An Economic Analysis. Transportation Research-E 33-2, 79-96 (1997)

Engle, R.F. and Granger, C.W.: Cointegration and error Correction: representation, estimation and testing. Econometrica, 55, 251-276 (1987)

I.E.T.C.: Elasticidad de la Demanda del Transporte Público de Viajeros. Ministerio de Transporte (Spanish Ministry for Transport) (1978)

Inglada, V.: Intermodalidad y Elasticidades Precio en el Transporte Interurbano de Viajeros. Revista TTC Transportes y Comunicaciones 54, 3-14 (1992)

Johansen, S.: Statistical Analysis fo Cointegration Vectors. Journal of Economic Dynamics and Control 12, 231-254 (1988)

Johansen, S., Juselius, K.: Maximum Likelihood Estimation and Inference on Cointegration with Applications to the Demand for Money. Oxford Bulletin of Economics and Statistics 52, 169-210 (1990)

Levin, R.C.: Allocation in Surface Freight Transportation: Does Rate Regulation Matter?. Bell Journal of Economics 9(1), 18-45 (1978)

McFadden, D.: Conditional Logit Analysis of Qualitative Choice Behaviour, Frontiers in Econometrics. In: Zaremka, P. (ed.). NY & London: Academic Press 1973

McFadden, D.: The Measurement of Urban Travel Demand. Journal of Public Economics 3, 303-28 (1974)

Ministerio de Transportes (Ministry for Transport): Informes de Coyuntura de los Transportes y Comunicaciones. Madrid, 1980-1993 (1994)

Osterwald-Lenum, M.: A Note with Fractiles of the Asymptotic Distribution of the Maximum Likelihood Cointegration Rank Test Statistics: Four Cases. Oxford Bulletin of Economic and Statistics 54, 461- 472 (1992)

Oum, T.H.: A Warning on the Use Linear of Logits Models in Transport Mode Choice Studies. Bell Journal of Economics 10(1), 374-387 (1979)

Oum, T.H., Gillen, D.: The Structure of Intercity Travel Demands in Canada: Theory, Tests and Empirical Results. Working Paper No 79-18.Queen's University (1979)

Quandt, R., Baumol, W.: The Demand for Abstract Transport Modes: Theory and Measurement. Journal of Regional Science 6(2), 13-26 (1966)

Varian, H.: Microeconomic Analysis. 3rd ed. W.W. Norton & Company, Inc. (1992)

Vázquez, P.: Un Estudio Limitado sobre Elasticidades de Demanda al Precio en el Transporte Interubano. Revista del Ministerio de Transportes, Turismo y Comunicaciones 15, 21-33 (1985)

Winston, C.: Conceptual Developments in the Economics of Transportation: An Interpretative Survey. Journal of Economic Literature XXIII, 57-94 (1985)

3 Introduction of an Innovative Product: the High Speed Train (AVE)

Vicente Inglada-López de Sabando
Department of Economics
University Carlos III (Spain)

Pablo Coto-Millán
Department of Economics
University of Cantabria (Spain)

3.1
AVE: Characterisation

The high-speed train (AVE) is mainly characterised by a new infrastructure, which uses the adequate mobile material to be able to obtain highly operating speeds. Moreover, its way of management is generally different from that typical of the conventional train. In line with this, Plassard (1992) proposes the following defining characteristics of this mode of transport:

- A high speed of 250-300 km/h.
- A high frequency as the traffic requires it.
- A weak capacity (lower than 400 people per train).
- Slightly higher fares than those of the conventional train.

With these operation conditions, he states that the AVE must be the link between two big cities, excluding every intermediate service, since this is the only way to combine the two requirements of high speed and satisfactory rates of utilisation.

Bonnafous (1987) agrees with this assumption and points out that the French TGV resembles more a plane than a conventional train if we consider some factors such as the distance covered, the capacity and the speed. He finally concludes that its structural effects essentially affect the urban poles with the highest population, as the air transport does.

In relation with the Madrid-Seville corridor, which is the object of our research, we carry out a more detailed analysis, which enables us, to distinguish between the following three clearly differentiated sub-products within the so-called high speed trains: the Shuttle, the Long Distance and the Talgo[1]. Chronologically, the first train used was the Long Distance. The Madrid-Seville route started to be operated on the 21st of April 1992 with intermediate stops in Ciudad Real, Puertollano and Cordoba. The demand for this sub-product had a great boom, especially the Madrid-Seville route due to the Universal Exhibition (EXPO) held at Seville in 1992. In October 1993, immediately after this event concluded, there was a fare reduction[2], which allowed this market to consolidate itself[3], thus compensating the decrease in the demand produced after the closure of EXPO. This also led to a rising tendency in the dynamics of the product to an aspect, which is always inherent to the stage of maturing of any new product.

Later, on the 18th of October 1992, a new train called "Shuttle"[4] was introduced. This train was characterised by the dramatic decrease in fares at rush hours, by the introduction of discounts and the addition of units with a greater number of tourist-class seats. The decrease in the average revenues of approximately 50% brought about an increase in demand of 275% and 115% in October and November of 1993 respectively. Therefore, this new offer, which had the initial aim of efficiently using the already existing units, was firmly consolidated.

Finally, the "Talgo" train started to operate in August 1992 from the introduction of the Cordoba gauge interchange service on the Madrid-Malaga route. This line was extended in the summer of 1993 by the introduction of the Majarabique (Seville) gauge interchange service, which offered the possibility of travelling from Madrid to Cadiz and Huelva on the new line without changing trains.

Table 3.1 presents the most significant features of each type of supply, which determine their differentiation from the High-Speed train. The primary differentiating factors between Shuttle and Long Distance are those of demand and fares. However, the Talgo differs essentially from the others for having to employ varied mobile material because it needs a track with different rail widths. This fact, along with the gauge interchange operation, leads to a lower average speed in this train and therefore, to a lower generalised cost reduction than that of the rest of the High Speed transport.

A more detailed analysis shows that the shuttle-service, which has low fares and in which discount tickets prevail, has generated a demand essentially for commuter journeys of day returns. This fact is mainly due to the reduction of the

---

[1] The new High Speed line has been built with UIC rail width, which is different from the Spanish rail width. The great advantage of the Talgo, is that, due to its variable axle system, both types of rail can be used with the minimum waste of time when one infrastructure is changed into the other.
[2] The average revenue fell from 19 ptas. to 14 ptas. per passenger-km.
[3] This is shown by the level of the load factor which exceeds 80%.
[4] In the Madrid-Ciudad Real, Ciudad Real-Puertollano and Madrid-Puertollano lines.

generalised cost of transport –especially in time[5] and fares -, which also leads to a reduction of the price of a supplementary commodity such as the housing.

Table 3.1. Discriminating factors of the different sub-products

	SHUTTLE	LONG DISTANCE	TALGO
Routes	Madrid-C.Real C.Real-Puertollano Madrid-Puertollano	Madrid-Seville Madrid-Cordoba Other routes[6]	Madrid-Malaga Madrid-Cadiz Madrid-Huelva Others[7]
Material	Gec-Alsthom	Gec-Alsthom	Talgo 200
Infrastructure	New High Speed Track	New High Speed Track	New and Conventional Track
Fares (Average revenue/ Passenger-Km) (PTAs. 1993)	10.5	15.4	10.2
Occupancy rate	0.65	0.84	0.68
Type of demand	Local train with a high percentage or commuters journeys	Long distance	Long distance

Source: Own elaboration

3.2
Qualitative Analysis

Table 2 records the results obtained from the successive surveys to the high-speed train passengers, both in the Long Distance and in Shuttle trains. These results refer to qualitative characteristics. The following conclusions can be reached from these data.

The Long Distance Train

- Education and professional level: The Long Distance passenger has higher education and professional level: almost 63% have University education. Of these, 22% hold University diplomas while 41% hold higher University

---

[5] For instance, the 171-km Madrid-City takes slightly longer than 50 minutes, virtually the same time as any city center-outskirts journey takes in Madrid. Moreover, we must take into account that the average price of housing in Ciudad Real is almost half that of Madrid.
[6] This includes the Cordoba-Seville, Ciudad Real-Cordoba, Ciudad Real-Seville, Puertollano-Cordoba, Puertollano-Seville lines.
[7] This would include lines such as Barcelona-Malaga.

degrees. As regards professions, 40% are executives and businessmen and 26% are technicians.

- Reasons for travelling: 58% travel for professional reasons, this is an especially significant motivation among the business class passengers (75%). As regards other reasons for travelling, 22% travel for tourism and 20% for family reasons.
- Fares assessment: A survey carried out before the fares were increased in September, 1993 reveals that 64% passengers think that the AVE fares are adequate. This fact led the company to raise the fares for the possibility, which such a measure offered of increasing returns.
- Level of and cause for satisfaction: There is an almost complete level of satisfaction (96%) and the main causes for satisfaction are: speed (29%), comfort (26%), good-quality service (11%), punctuality (8%), safety (4%) and good price (3%).

Table 3.2. Qualitative characterisation of the demand for high speed services

ATTRIBUTES	PERCENTAGES	
	Long Distance Train	Shuttle Train
Level of education		
Primary School	15	31
Secondary School	22	27
University Diplomas	22	16
Higher University Degrees	41	26
Professional occupation		
Executives	17	6
Businessmen	23	15
Technicians	26	23
Miscellaneous	14	19
Unemployed	19	37
Reasons for travelling		
Professional	58	37
Tourism	22	22
Family	40	41
Fares assessment		
Very high	5	6
High	30	25
Good	64	66
Low	1	2
Very low	0	1
Level of satisfaction		
Very satisfied	47	55
Satisfied	49	39
Indifferent	3	3
Unsatisfied	0	1
Very unsatisfied	1	2

Source: Own elaboration based on the RENFE surveys (1993)

The Shuttle Train

- Education and professional level: The passenger of this service has lower education in general, 42% of the passengers have University education. Of these 16% hold University diplomas and 26% hold higher University degrees. As regards professions, 21% are executives, 21% are businessmen, and 23% are technicians, which constitutes lower percentages than in the Long Distance train.

- Reasons for travelling: For those passengers using this service, business (37%) has stopped being the main reason for travelling. However, it is worth remarking that 41% of passengers travel for family reasons, which is much higher percentage than that for the Long Distance train.

- Fares assessment: As in the Long Distance train, the survey carried out before fares were raised in September, 1993, shows that an elevated percentage of passengers (69%) think that the AVE fares are appropriate or low. This percentage is even higher than that obtained in the Long Distance service, due to the multiple discounts made in this service. Therefore, the rise margin of fares also seems higher for the Shuttle train.

- Satisfaction causes and level: Almost all the passengers (94%) show a high level of satisfaction by their answers. The main causes for it are the following: speed (38%), comfort (30%), punctuality (9%), safety (4%), good-quality service (3%) and good fares (2%). It is worth remarking in this service that the highest values are for speed and punctuality for the great importance given to time, in connection with the clear commuter typology, which characterises this demand.

3.3
The Concept of Generalised Cost

As far as transport is concerned, the traditional concept of a product price must be replaced by a broader concept called the generalised cost of the respective transport mode. This cost includes other components apart from the purely monetary ones. Among these components, which correspond to the various attributes which characterise the transport product, the outstanding features, according to García-Alvarez (1998), are the frequency, time, punctuality, safety, comfort, reliability, intermodality and price. The importance of each one of these components when the user chooses a particular transport depends on the type of product.

If we analyse these components in detail, we can define the frequency in railway transport as the number of trains, which travel between two points at a particular period of time. The demand elasticity with respect to the frequency is positive, a fact due not only to the existence of more alternative schedules when frequency increases but also to a lower waiting time. The value of this elasticity naturally depends on extent of frequency since the more elevated this magnitude is the lower the elasticity will be[8]. In addition, one of the most important attributes of transport service is the travel time, especially in those journeys, which are not for leisure. Obviously, the time value varies depending on the individual and the reason for travelling. The total time includes not only the transport time but also the time of access and stay at departure or arrival terminals.

If we analyse fares or the monetary component within the framework of the generalised cost of transport, we observe a high demand elasticity with respect to price due to different reasons. Firstly, as in the case we are studying, we cannot consider the transport product as a first-necessity service, secondly, there are various substitutive products on the market we are analysing and finally, a large percentage of the population are car owners, a fact leading to the existence of a reference value of the marginal cost of car use, which enables a comparison of fares of the different modes of transport.

On the whole, the safety variable of a mode of transport does not significantly and directly conditions the decision of travelling or the choice of the mode of transport. In line with this, we only have to observe that the private car is the mode of transport with the lowest safety rate but it holds the highest passenger traffic rate all over the world. However, for certain individuals, this factor may be extremely important when choosing the mode of transport. Their decision is made from on a subjective point of view of the corresponding mode of transport rather than from an objective consideration. Thus, for example, in spite of the fact that the plane is much safer than the car, there are a great number of individuals who prefer any other means of transport to the air transport.

Along with the income level, comfort is increasingly important when choosing the mode of transport. This is a complex concept which includes, of course, a comfortable atmosphere, an adequate accommodation (dimensions and comfort of the seat) and the possibility of the minimum interruption in the passenger's day to day life during the journey. In connection with this, the availability of toilets, coffee and restaurant services, television or video significantly contributes to increase comfort.

The data appearing on table 3.3 refers to the reasons for the choice of the AVE in comparison with other Long Distance modes competing with it. We can reach several conclusions from these data about the importance of the various components of the AVE generalised cost. In short, we can state that the main causes for the choice of the AVE are, by order of importance, speed, comfort, price, novelty and safety.

---

[8] García-Alvarez et al. (1998) study the modal distribution and consider a coefficient due to the frequency of each operator measured in the number of services per day. This modal distribution coefficient increases when f increases, which reflects that the market share increases when the frequency increases. However, for high values of f, the additional growth of this coefficient is increasingly lower (for frequencies of more than 25 services per day the coefficient increases in a maximum 5%). For f=1 frequency, the coefficient value obtained is 1.187 while for f= infinite frequency, which may correspond for example to the car, the coefficient value is 4.55.

Table 3.3. Reasons for the choice of the AVE in comparison with other alternative modes of transport (% for the Long Distance Train)

	Plane	Car	Train	Bus	Total
Speed/Time	13	42	57	67	30
Punctuality	4	0	2	0	3
Comfort	31	35	19	13	29
Price	19	6	2	2	11
Novelty	11	3	9	3	9
Safety/Fear	6	10	0	0	5
City Centre	4	0	0	0	2
Schedules	6	0	8	10	5
Miscellaneous	6	4	3	5	6

Source: Own elaboration based on the RENFE surveys (1993)

A first result, certainly relevant, is the fact that the effect of the comfort component is virtually as important (29%) as that of time (30%) and it is even higher than the effect of price (11%). This result is especially significant within the group of air passengers, where the component of comfort is far more important (31%) than that of price (19%), a value which is even equal to the sum of the two "traditional" generalised cost components: price and time.

In a more detailed disaggregated analysis of each mode of transport, we can state that, the main reasons for the choice of the AVE with respect to the plane are comfort (31%), price (19%), speed (13%), novelty (11%) and safety (6%). With respect to the car, time is the most important reason (42%), followed by comfort (35%) and safety (10%). In relation to the conventional train, the reasons to choose the AVE are speed (57%), comfort (19%) and novelty (9%). Finally, with respect to the bus, speed (67%) and comfort (13%) are the essential reasons for the choice of the new product.

3.4
Comparison Among Different Competing Products

When we compare the different components of the AVE generalised cost with those of competing models, we can observe the great advantages of the former. In line with this, we can emphasise the fact that the AVE travel time is much lower than that of the remaining modes of transport except for the air transport. This time reduction is due not only to its high speed but also to the less time employed in accessing to the service, as well as to a decrease in the distances travelled thanks to the new infrastructure.

Table 3.4 presents the time the main routes take. We must point out that in the routes in which the new infrastructure is completely used[9], the time employed by the AVE is less than half that used by the remaining modes of transport, except for

---

[9] In other lines such as Madrid-Cadiz, Madrid-Huelva and Madrid-Malaga the Talgo is employed with High-Speed and conventional track.

the air transport. For example, in the Madrid-Seville route, the reduction of the travel time in the high-speed train is 2h 45' with respect to the car, 3h 55' with respect to the bus and 3h 20' with respect to the conventional train.

Table 3.4. Travel time for route

ROUTES	TRAVEL TIME				
	Air Transport	Car[10]	Bus	Conventional Train	AVE
Madrid-Seville	50'	5h 20'	6h 30'	5h 55'	2h 35'
Madrid-Malaga	55'	5h 40'	7h 15'	6h 50'	4h 45'
Madrid-Huelva	-	6h 20'	7h 50'	7h 40'	4h 40'
Madrid-Cadiz	55'	6h 30'	8h 10'	7h 45'	5h
Madrid-C. Real	-	2h 5'	2h 30'	1h 55'	55'
Madrid-Puertollano	-	2h 35'	3h	2h 45'	1h 15'
Madrid-Cordoba	-	3h 55'	5h	4h 25'	1h 45'

In addition, observing table 3.5, which shows the access time to the services of different modes of transport we see that the time used in the AVE is significantly lower than in that used in the conventional train and plane but it is equal to that used in the bus. The time of access used in the car, obviously null, is the only one, which is lower than that in the AVE. This is precisely one of the main advantages of this mode of transport since the user considers the access time more "lost time" than the travel time. Moreover, we must take into account that this concept includes delay penalties, safety, boarding time and access time to and from services. The advantageous aspects of the high-speed train vary depending on the mode of transport with which it is compared. For example, with respect to air travel, the new product has great advantages in relation to access - its stations are located in the city centre – and to delay since the AVE has a high punctuality rate. The advantage of this high punctuality rate is also apparent in the comparison of the AVE with conventional trains.

The use of a new infrastructure also adds a comparative advantage to the new product, which is the fact that the different distances travelled are quite lower as observed in table 3.6.

Finally, when comparing the prices of the different products appearing in table 3.7, we must remark that, on the whole, the AVE is – after air travel - the most expensive mode of transport. However, in some lines such as the short-distance ones, included in the segment of the Shuttle Train, differences with respect to the car and the conventional train are minimal. In every case the bus is the mode of transport with the lowest price.

---

[10] In order to obtain the V speed, the $V = 48 + 72\,(1-i/c)^{\frac{1}{2}}$ equation has been used for highways, while in the conventional road the $V = 90 - 22\,(i/c)$ alternative expression has been used, where i and c are the intensity and hour capacity respectively. Both expressions come from the "Highway Capacity Manual" from the Transportation Research Board (1985).

Table 3.5. Access time to service[11]

Plane	Car	Bus	Conventional Train	AVE
1h 55'	-	1h	1h 15'	1h

Table 3.6. Distances

	Road	AVE	Conventional Train
Madrid-C. Real	190	171	255
Madrid-Puertollano	228	210	293
Madrid-Cordoba	400	343	442
Madrid-Seville	538	471	565
Madrid-Malaga	544	528	627
Madrid-Cadiz	663	633	727
Madrid-Huelva	632	581	675

Table 3.7. Prices of different modes of transport (PTS. per passenger, 1993)

ROUTES	FARES						
	Plane[12]	Car[13]	Bus	Conventional Train		AVE	
				1^{st}cl.	2^{nd}cl.	Pref.	Tourist
Madrid-Seville	12650	7346	2210	7880	5450	10800	7900
Madrid-Malaga	13700	7655	2680	8750	6050	9200	6600
Madrid-Huelva	-	8630	2630	9450	6520	9700	6900
Madrid-Cadiz	13950[14]	9181	2600	10100	7250	10200	7300
Madrid-C. Real	-	2539	1440	3690	1425	2500	2000
Madrid-Puertollano	-	3080	1780	4280	1635	2900	2300
Madrid-Cordoba	-	5424	1650	6130	4480	7900	5800

[11] For the Madrid-Seville route. For other routes with departure or arrival in Madrid or Seville, the access time is reduced by 10 minutes for the bus, the conventional train and AVE. Moreover, for the remaining lines, the access time is reduced by 20 minutes. In planes, this concept includes 1h 15' for access, 30' for safety and boarding and 10' for delay penalty. In the bus and the AVE, this access times includes 15' for safety and boarding and 45' for the transport to and from the station. Finally, a 15' delay penalty has been considered for the conventional train respect to the AVE.
[12] Price for tourist class without weekend discounts.
[13] The occupation for vehicle is of 1.8 individuals and half the depretiation is due to the number of Kilometers travelled.
[14] Madrid-Jerez route.

3.5
Induction and Substitution Effects

The introduction of the AVE produces two clearly differentiated effects on transport demand viz. inducing and substitution effects. These effects correspond to those journeys which would have never been made if this new service had not existed and to those which would have been made but using a different mode of transport.

3.5.1 Induction Effect

Within the inducing or generation effect of new journeys, we must include not only those passengers who had never travelled on that route but also the component, which accounts for the increase in the travel frequency of those passengers who already used that route before the existence of the AVE. In table 3.8, we observe that the average journeys per year on the Madrid-Seville route have increased from 11 to 15 due to the introduction of the new product and that 28% of the users had never travelled on that route before. The inducting effect still continued, but at an increasingly lower rate, until 1996, which marked the end of the final period of maturing of the service. The results obtained show the importance of this effect, which, according to the studies made, once the period of maturing was completed, accounts for almost 45% of the AVE passengers[15].

Table 3.8. Travel frequency in the Madrid-Seville route

	Before the AVE	After the AVE
Twice of more a week	3%	6%
Once a week	6%	8%
Once a fortnight	7%	9%
Once a month	16%	16%
Once a quarter	18%	16%
Less	30%	17%
Did not travel	21%	-
Travelled on this route for the first time	-	28%
Average journeys per year	11.1	15.2

Source: Own elaboration based on the RENFE surveys (1993)

---

[15] A result similar to that indicated by Nash (1991) for the French Paris-Lyon line.

3.5.2 Substitution Effect

The reduction of the generalised cost in the new mode of transport in comparison with the substitutive modes[16] generates the change of part of the demand for these competitive modes of transport to the High Speed Train. Obviously, the intensity of this "substitution effect" is lower in the Talgo train because the reduction of the generalised cost is also lower.

The comparative analysis made in point 4 about the different components of transport generalised cost indicates that the high-speed train offers certain advantages in comparison with the remaining modes of transport. In line with this, as inferred from the reasons which lead to the choice of the AVE detailed in table 3, this new product is preferred to the air transport due to its lower price (19%) and higher comfort (31%) and safety (6%). Even a large number of passengers (13%) prefer this mode of transport for its reduced access time and waiting time, since these two aspects are considered a great time loss.

The large number of advantages presented by the AVE with respect to the conventional train, especially as regards time and comfort, causes such a high magnitude of the substitution effect that the demand for this mode of transport is virtually absorbed by the AVE. With respect to the car, the main causes for the choice of the AVE are the time (42%), comfort (35%) and safety (10%). Finally, in comparison with the bus, the main causes for substitution are time (67/%) and comfort (13%).

3.5.3 The Demand for the New Product

The demand for the AVE comes from the combination of the induction and substitution effects the above section. When we analyse the time evolution of these two effects, a period of maturing is observed during which the level of demand for that product adjusts and grows exponentially until it stabilises. This period of maturing is common to all new products. As a reference, we must remark that when the High Speed was introduced in the Paris-Lyon corridor, its period of maturing lasted 6 years. However, that period was lower – 4 years - in the Madrid-Seville case for various reasons[17]. A first reason for this time reduction was the demand shock generated by the EXPO, especially in the Madrid-Seville line. A second reason was the significant decrease in fares occurred in October 1992 at the end of the EXPO. This fall of prices, especially marked for the new shuttle-service, accelerated the rhythm of demand absorption by the new mode of transport. Consequently, the period of maturing was reduced[18].

---

[16] This reduction is mainly due to the decrease in fares and the increase in comfort with respect to the plane as well as by the reduction of time and the increase in comfort with respect to the bus, the conventional train and the car.
[17] This period lasted 6 years in the TALGO train.
[18] However, the TALGO fares were kept almost fixed so we cannot consider them as a reduction of the period of maturing.

3.6
Impact on Demand

Due to the high magnitude of the substitution effect, the introduction of the high-speed train causes very strong effects on the demand for the remaining modes of transport competing with it in the Madrid-Seville route. A more detailed analysis enables us to observe the highly strong effect particularly on the conventional train since this lost almost 78% of its traffic prior to the introduction of the AVE, which virtually produces the disappearance of this transport for the route. The introduction of the High-Speed train has led to an approximately 50% fall of the air transport demand in the Madrid-Seville route. Therefore, we can remark that the operating company has acted efficiently when it adjusted its supply to the demand fall by reducing the number of flights[19] and trying to keep the occupation percentage almost stable[20]. As regards the car, the losses are lower than in the previously mentioned modes of transport, approximately 30% in the Madrid-Seville route. Finally, in bus transport it seems that the impact on long-distance routes is not great (11% of demand fall) since both products are hardly substitutive. However, in the Madrid-Ciudad Real route, the demand fall, which reached 34%, is significant due to the low fares of the high-speed train.

Therefore, we can conclude that the introduction of the high-speed train causes a dramatic change in the modal distribution of the demand, and we can speak of a pre AVE transport market and a post AVE market. This effect is especially important in the long-distance segment, where the railway is the predominant mode of transport in the Madrid-Seville route, and where its use even exceeds the use of the private car, a most unusual situation in the Spanish transport market.

References

Bonnafous, A.: The Regional Impact of the TGV. Transportation 14, 127-137 (1987)

Inglada, V.: Análisis Empírico del Impacto del AVE Sobre la Demanda de Transporte en el Corredor Madrid-Sevilla. Revista de Estudios de Transportes y Comunicaciones 62, January-March, 35-51 (1994)

García-Alvarez, A.; Cillero-Hernández, A., Rodríguez-Jericó, P.: Operación de Trenes de Viajeros. Fundación de los Ferrocarriles Españoles 1998

Nash, C.A.: The Case for High-Speed Rail. Investigaciones Económicas 15(2), 337-354 (1991)

Plassard, F.: El Impacto Espacial de los Trenes de Alta Velocidad en Europa. Transporte y Medio Ambiente. Ministry for Transport and Public Works (MOPT) 1992

RENFE : Surveys Carried Out to the AVE Passengers. 1993

Transportation Research Board : Highway Capacity Manual. Special Report 209. 1985

---

[19] Other adjustment measures such as the reduction of fares have not been considered in detail.

[20] In fact, this percentage has bee reduced less than 10% due to the introduction of the High-Speed train.

PART II.   PRODUCTION AND COSTS (SUPPLY)

4 Technical and Allocative Inefficiency in Spanish Public Hospitals*

Carmen García-Prieto
Department of Foundations of Economic Analysis
University of Valladolid (Spain)

The OECD economies are undergoing an upward trend in health expenditure. The usual explanations for this tendency are based on such elements as the progressive ageing of population, the increasing use of technology in health procedures, and the fact that public health services become more extensive (cover more people) year after year.

All this has led governments to try to curb health spending by reducing the degree of inefficiency of public health services. Such inefficiency has been generally admitted by many studies carried out by experts in the area[1].

In Spain, health spending is mainly public and about 60% of this expenditure goes to hospitals. This draws attention to a sector that has continuously exceeded budgets in recent years, requiring extra money and generating a continuous pressure on costs.

There has been an attempt to deal with the situation from the point of view of prospective budgeting, through establishing *Program-Contracts*. This attempt, according to recent papers by González and Barber (1996) and Ventura and González (1999), has led to a significant decrease of inefficiency in hospitals directly managed by the national government. Ventura and González's study concentrates on technical efficiency by applying Data Envelopment Analysis. On the other hand, González and Barber follow a double approach: First, they analyse global inefficiency on the basis of the estimation of a parametric cost frontier.

* I wish to thank professors Guillem López-Casasnovas, Carlos Pérez Domínguez y José Miguel Sánchez Molinero for their comments, which I have found very helpful. However, I am responsible for any possible mistake.

[1] Undoubtedly, the "Dunning report" (1991) from Holland is the most renowned. In Spain, the Congress entrusted a committee headed by Abril Martorell with a study, and their conclusions were recorded in a document known as "Abril's Report" (1991).

Second, they use Data Envelopment Analysis to quantify the technical component of hospital inefficiency.

However, the allocative component of hospital inefficiency has not been given much attention in the literature. This is probably due to information problems concerning input prices. In spite of such problems, there have been some relevant papers on this matter, such as Eakin and Kniesner (1988) and Eakin (1991). These two papers use the same sample of 133 hospitals in the USA and concentrate exclusively on allocative inefficiency. Other papers, such as Morey, Fine and Loree (1990) and Byrnes and Valdmanis (1994), quantify allocative inefficiency for a set of hospitals in California by means of Data Envelopment Analysis.

For the case of Spain, only Puig-Junoy (2000) has studied allocative efficiency in hospitals, using a sample of both public and private hospitals in the region of Catalonia. Puig-Junoy's approach uses the Data Envelopment Analysis technique. This author finds an interesting negative association between the proportion of public funds in the total budget of each hospital and de degree of allocative efficiency.

The present paper studies the degree of efficiency of the Spanish hospitals managed by the *INSALUD,*[2] by quantifying the extent to which each of the two inefficiency components (technical and allocative) increases cost. We have used an econometric analysis based on the estimation of a system consisting of a cost frontier and a set of input share equations.

This paper is organised as follows: section 4.1 presents the theoretical model to be used; section 4.2 describes the variables and data to be used in the estimation; section 4.3 analyses the results, and section 4.4 summarises the final conclusions.

4.1
The Model

Empirical studies on economic efficiency have usually followed the frontier methodology, ever since Farrell (1957) set the bases for this approach[3]. Farrell's approach basically starts from the assumption that firms do not follow optimal behaviour patterns (they do not maximise profits) due to inefficiencies in the management of the production process.

When calculating a cost frontier, it must be taken into account that firms may fail in their attempts to minimise costs for two different reasons: On the one hand, firms may not manage to use the minimum quantity possible of each input for the obtained level of output; this causes technical inefficiency. On the other hand, the factor combination used by the firm may not be the cheapest one, given the input prices; this would lead to allocative inefficiency. Both behaviours are shown in figure 4.1 for the case of two inputs.

---

[2] *INSALUD* is the public agency which finances and administrates the Spanish hospitals in 11 out of the 17 autonomous regions existing in the country.
[3] Forsund, Lovell and Schmidt (1980), Bauer (1990), Greene (1993) and Coelli, Rao and Battesse (1998) are good surveys on this technique.

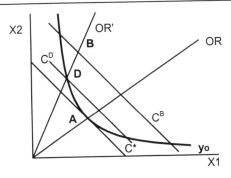

Fig. 4.1. Technical and allocative inefficiency

A firm operating at point B would present both types of inefficiency: allocative inefficiency, since the firm is using an input combination that is not optimal, and technical inefficiency, since both inputs are being used in quantities greater than those required by output level y_0, when production process OR' is chosen. The fact that OR' is chosen, instead of OR, results in allocative inefficiency, while the fact that input combination B is chosen, instead of D, results in technical inefficiency.

If the firm chose input combination D instead of B, there would be no technical inefficiency but there would be allocative inefficiency. This allows us to measure allocative inefficiency at point B by the ratio $AI_B = C^D/C^*$, where C^D stands for the total cost at point D and C^* stands for the minimum cost, reachable only when both sources of inefficiency have been eliminated (point A). The measure of technical inefficiency is given by the ratio $TI_B = C^B/C^D$ where C^B stands for total cost at point B. The product of these two measures ($TI_B * AI_B = C^B/C^*$) shows the proportion in which the actual cost is higher than the minimum cost. Therefore, we can state that C^B/C^* is a global measure of economic inefficiency.

Economic efficiency can be measured by the inverse ratio, C^*/C^B. It shows the proportion in which the minimum cost is lower than actual cost. This ratio is the product of two measures: that of technical efficiency and that of allocative efficiency:

$$\frac{C^*}{C^B} = \frac{1}{TI_B AI_B} = \frac{1}{TI_B}\frac{1}{AI_B} = TE_B AE_B$$

According to Aigner, Lovell and Schmidt (1977), the cost incurred by a firm may be outside the minimum cost function due to economic inefficiency (either technical or allocative) as well as to purely random elements (thus, the term "stochastic frontier"). This is shown by the expression:

$$C (y, w) = C^* (y, w, \beta) \ e^v \ TI \ AI \tag{4.1}$$

where C (y, w) is the effective cost of the firm and $C^* (y, w, \beta)$ is the minimum cost function which depends on production, y, input prices, w, and a number of parameters β, that must be estimated; the term e^{υ} is the random disturbance and the product TI AI, is the measure of economic inefficiency as stated earlier[4]. In logarithmic form:

$$\ln C (y, w) = \ln C^* (y, w, \beta) + \ln AI + \ln TI + \upsilon \tag{4.2}$$

While the random disturbance can make costs go up or down (υ may be either positive of negative), inefficiency always increases costs, as shown by the fact that lnAI and lnTI are both non-negative.

Expression (4.2) could be estimated directly. We would only need to postulate a particular functional form for the cost frontier and an adequate distribution for each of the error terms (ν, lnAI and lnTI). Nevertheless, this procedure would be subject to strong objections. The basic problem here is that allocative inefficiency (the lnAI term) is clearly related to input prices and this implies that estimators cannot be expected to be consistent.

In order to avoid this problem, we could estimate (4.2) together with the input share equations. This will be the procedure followed in this paper. Next, we will proceed to specify the input share equations, taking into consideration the fact that there may be allocative inefficiency.

The effective share of the jth input in total cost, $S_j (y, w)$, is given by the ratio:

$$S_j (y, w) = x_j w_j / C(y, w) \tag{4.3}$$

where x_j represents the amount of the jth input used by the firm, and w_i the price of that particular input. Now, if we take into account that $C(y, w) = \Sigma_j x_j w_j$, it follows that $\partial C(y, w)/\partial w_j = x_j$, which allows us to write:

$$\frac{\partial \ln C(y, w)}{\partial \ln w_j} = \frac{x_j w_j}{C(y, w)} \tag{4.4}$$

Hence, we may define the effective share of the jth input as:

$$S_j(y, w) = \frac{\partial \ln C(y, w)}{\partial \ln w_j} \tag{4.5}$$

and taking into account expression (4.2), it follows that:

$$S_j(y, w) = \frac{\partial \ln C^*(y, w, \beta)}{\partial \ln w_j} + \frac{\partial AI}{\partial \ln w_j} \tag{4.6}$$

since TI and υ do not depend on input prices.

Now, applying Shephard's lemma, we can identify $\partial \ln C^*(y,w,\beta)/\partial \ln w_j$ with the optimal share of the jth input; that is:

$$S_j^*(y,w,\beta) = \partial \ln C^*(y,w,\beta)/\partial \ln w_j \tag{4.7}$$

This expression allows us to write:

$$S_j(y,w) = S_j^*(y,w,\beta) + \varepsilon_j \tag{4.8}$$

where the error term, ε_j , would include the effects of allocative inefficiency plus a purely random element, ξ_j; that is:

---

[4] Subscripts have been removed with the aim of simplifying the expression.

$$\varepsilon_j = \partial \ln AI / \partial \ln w_j + \xi_j \qquad (4.9)$$

ε_j can have both positive and negative values, showing over or under-utilization of the jth input with respect to the optimum level.
In short, we will estimate the following system:

$$\ln C (y, w) = \ln C^* (y, w, \beta) + \ln AI + \ln TI + v$$

$$S_j (y,w) = S_j^*(y,w,\beta) + \varepsilon_j \qquad j = 1...n-1 \qquad (4.10)$$

It must be observed that the number of share equations is not n, but n-1. This is so in order to avoid the estimation problems derived from the fact that the sum of the n shares must be equal to one.

The relationship between the error terms of the input share equations and the lnIA term in the cost function is usually approximated[5] by a quadratic form. This quadratic expression accounts for the fact that both positive and negative deviations from optimality result in cost increases.

Schmidt (1984) proposed a specification in which the sum of error squares was weighed through a positive semi-definite matrix of parameters, F, such that $\ln AI = \varepsilon' F \varepsilon$. The problem here is how to chose such parameters. On this subject, Kumbakhar (1991) showed that the expression $\ln AI = \varepsilon' F \varepsilon$ cannot be taken without restrictions. More specifically, the integrability condition,

$$\partial \ln (\varepsilon' F \varepsilon) / \partial \ln w_j = \varepsilon_j \qquad j = 1...n \qquad (4.11)$$

must be fulfilled. As shown by Kumbhakar (1991), this integrability condition implies that the parameters in the F matrix are exact functions of the cost frontier parameters when a translog frontier is considered. To reach such a conclusion, he uses a rather restrictive specification of the share equations. In essence, he regards these equations as deterministic; that is to say, the error terms, ε_j's, are only due to allocative inefficiency and do not have any random component.

In a later paper, Melfi (1984) proposed simplifying F into an identity matrix. This would make allocative inefficiency take values systematically close to zero, since the absolute value of share deviations is lower than one. Faced with this problem, Bauer (1990) suggested weighing the identity matrix through a positive parameter, which, depending on the final value it takes in the estimation, enables us to avoid this systematic tendency. This paper will follow Bauer's suggestion. Hence, for us:

$$\ln AI = c \sum_{j=1}^{n} \varepsilon_j^2 \qquad (4.12)$$

In order to carry out the estimation of the system, some assumptions must be made about the distribution of the disturbances: lnTI, v and ε_j, taking into account that they are independent of one another. It will be assumed that v is independently and identically normal distributed with zero mean and variance σ_v^2 ; ε is distributed independently and identically as multivariate normal with constant mean μ and constant covariance Σ, where $\varepsilon = (\varepsilon_1...\varepsilon_{n-1})'$ and $\mu = (\mu_1,... \mu_{n-1})'$.

---

[5] The exact relationship for the restrictive Cobb-Douglas function has been proposed by Schmidt and Lovell (1979). It has also been obtained for the translog function –Kumbhakar (1997)- although, given its complexity, it has not yet been employed in any empirical study.

The fact that the mean of the errors in the share equations may be different from zero, as Schmidt and Lovell (1979) suggested, can be interpreted as evidence of systematic mistakes in the choice of the input combination. If the error mean is shown to be equal to zero, deviations with respect to optimal share levels will be merely random.

As far as technical inefficiency is concerned, we must propose a distribution over positive values. In this case, we have chosen an exponential distribution[6] with constant mean $1/\alpha$, although results show a high correlation with those obtained when the chosen distribution is a seminormal[7].

Once the errors of the input share equations have been estimated, lnAI can be obtained from expression (4.12). Therefore, the likelihood function of the system (4.10) is given by the product of two density functions: that of the composed error, lnTI + v, and that of the errors of share equations, ε, that is:

$$f\left[(lnTI + lnAI + v), \varepsilon\right] = g\,(lnTI + v)\,h\,(\varepsilon) \tag{4.13}$$

The maximum likelihood technique enables us to obtain a consistent and asymptotically efficient estimation of the cost frontier parameters and the allocative inefficiency of each firm. From the cost frontier residuals obtained, it is possible to estimate the mean technical inefficiency of all firms; particular estimates of technical inefficiency for individual firms can also be obtained using the procedure suggested by Jondrow et al. (1982). It must be observed, however, that the estimates of technical efficiency obtained by such a procedure are unbiased but non-consistent.

4.2
Definition of Variables and Functional Specification

Most of the data used in this estimation has been obtained from the EESRI, a survey of hospitals carried out by the INE (the Spanish Institute of Statistics). All data refer to 1994.

These data refer only to public hospitals managed by the *Insalud*. The very small hospitals (less than 80 beds) and the very large ones (more than 1000 beds) have been excluded from the sample. The reason for this is that small and large hospitals usually differ substantially in their endowments of technical equipment. They also differ widely in the type of cases attended. This fact could be a handicap for inefficiency estimation since the highest use of resources could be understood as inefficiency when, in fact, it could simply mean a more intensive attendance to very complex cases. A total of 67 hospitals have been studied.

Since we are dealing with a cross-sectional analysis, a short-run cost function has been specified, which depends on the output level, the input prices and the amount used of the fixed input, capital.

---

[6] The literature has mainly dealt with the following distributions: the seminormal, the truncated normal (only for positive values) and the exponential distributions: see, for instance, Greene (1993) for further details on this issue.

[7] In the case of a truncated normal distribution for positive values, the mean was not found different from zero.

4.2.1 Outputs

The first difficulty encountered when defining the variables involved in the cost function is how to measure the final output of hospital activity. Hospitals produce health and health improvement is difficult to measure. Nevertheless, since we do need a measure, we have to use some proxies. Such proxies could be the number of inpatient days or the number of cases attended. We have chosen the number of cases rather than the hospital stays. The problem with the number of stays is that many of them are presumably unnecessary and cost minimization may often lead the hospital to reduce the average length of the stay in each case by administering treatment in fewer days, all of which causes a cost increase per stay. To sum up, the accommodation services provided by hospitals may be considered as input in the "production of health" rather than an output.

When discussing hospital activity, it is convenient to distinguish between inpatient and outpatient attendance. This provides us with two basic output measures:

CASES : this variable accounts for inpatient hospital activity, and it is developed from the number of discharged patients adjusted by the casemix complexity. It is a weighed sum of discharges from the different hospital services. The weighs have been carried out using the coefficients defined by the *Insalud* in the UPA[8].

AMBU: this variable measures ambulatory hospital care: first and successive visits and emergencies with no hospitalization. In this case, weighing is also carried out with the coefficients fixed by the UPA.

4.2.2 Input Prices

Two inputs, labor and materials, have been considered. The variables that account for their respective prices are:

WAGE: The wage measure used in this paper is the average earnings of all hospital employees. *Insalud* wages are equal for all hospitals within each particular labor category (doctor, nurses, etc.), and wage data come from the BOE[9] (the Official State Bulletin).

According to the previous definition, differences in wages among hospitals basically show the existence of different mixes of labor inputs (that is, the fact that hospitals employ different proportions of doctors, nurses, etc.). In spite of everything, our wage variable can be regarded as a global measure of labor costs, which allows us to use it as a proxy for the price of labor. If instead of using this global measure, we were to use the "real" price of any particular labor category (doctors' salaries, for instance) we would observe identical values for all hospitals and that would make our estimation impossible.

---

[8] These coefficients have been determined by the *Insalud* in a study that estimated the relative consumption of resources of a one day stay in each service, outpatient visits and emergency attendance.

[9] 21/1993 Act of the *Presupuestos Generales del Estado* (National Budget Account) for 1994, December 29th.

PMAT: This variable accounts for the price of an aggregated input which includes the purchasing of varied health equipment, cleaning, food, energy supply..., all of which can be called materials. The diversity of components makes it difficult to estimate a particular price for this category. Hence, we have resorted to an approximation: the total spending in this category per day of stay[10].

The variability of PMAT may be related to both differences in prices and differences in the casemix of each hospital. This is indeed a drawback of the PMAT measure. Nevertheless, it can be argued that most elements included in this category (for instance: expenditure in food, clothes, cleaning, heating...) are unrelated to the casemix complexity.

4.2.3 Fixed Input

BEDS: The amount of fixed input (capital) used by each hospital is approximated by the number of beds. The justification for this is that the number of beds in the hospital reflects the stock of capital invested around them.

In order to use this proxy properly, it is necessary to have a homogeneous sample of hospitals. Therefore, we have focused the analysis on general hospitals[11], leaving out big hospitals with expensive modern technologies, and small hospitals with less sophisticated equipment. This leads us to consider that the hospitals in the sample have invested the same amount of capital per bed and, therefore, that the use of the bed variable seems adequate as an approximation to capital.

The statistical description of the variables defined above is summarized in table 4.1.

Table 4.1. Statistical description of the variables

VARIABLE	MEAN	STD. ERROR	MAX	MIN
COST	5,784,800	4,670,787	20,545,979	939,649
CASES	23,573	17,342	72,962	989
AMBU	119,038	92,075	533,145	7,530
WAGE	3,347,091	102,420	3,560,862	3,034,687
PMAT	19,870	12,925	95,672	12,088
BEDS	360	242	958	80

4.2.4 Functional Form

As regards the functional form, a translog cost function has been chosen for two reasons. On the one hand, for its flexibility, since it hardly places restrictions on technological features[12] from the beginning, but these restrictions can be tested

---

[10] Therefore, it is considered that the stays produced may be an adequate proxy of the amount of factor employed.

[11] Hospitals specialized in particular health services have not been included since they may show differences with respect to the rest for requiring either too much or too little capital investment.

[12] We should not forget that the translog function is the approximation to the real function in one point.

later. On the other hand, it enables us to introduce more than one output, thus accounting for the multiproduct character of hospital activity.
Then, the following system has been estimated:

$\ln(\text{Cost}) = \alpha_0 + \alpha_1 \ln(\text{CASES}) + \alpha_2 \ln(\text{AMBU}) + \beta_1 \ln(\text{Wage}) +$

$\frac{1}{2} \delta_{11} \ln(\text{CASES})^2 + \frac{1}{2} \delta_{22} \ln(\text{AMBU})^2 + \delta_{12} \ln(\text{CASES}) \ln(\text{AMBU}) +$

$\frac{1}{2} \gamma_{11} \ln(\text{Wage})^2 + \rho_{11} \ln(\text{CASES}) \ln(\text{Wage}) + \rho_{21} \ln(\text{AMBU}) \ln(\text{Wage}) +$

$\eta_{11} \ln(\text{BEDS}) + \ln\text{AI} + \ln\text{TI} + v$

$$S_1 = \beta_1 + \gamma_{11} \ln(\text{Wage}) + \rho_{11} \ln(\text{CASES}) + \rho_{21} \ln(\text{AMBU}) + \varepsilon_1 \qquad (4.14)$$

in which only the labor share equation[13] has been included; the usual symmetry restrictions have been imposed, and the theoretical requirement of homogeneity of degree one in input prices has been achieved by dividing costs and input prices by the price of the second input, which yields:

Cost = COST / PMAT,

Wage = WAGE / PMAT.

4.3
Estimation and Results

Maximum likelihood estimation has been carried out on deviations with respect to the mean. Therefore, the parameters of the first-order terms represent the respective cost function elasticities for the average hospital. All of them are positive and, except for the case of the AMBU variable, significant at 1%, as observed in table 2, which summarizes the results obtained.

On the whole, parameters are highly significant, except those associated with the AMBU variable and its cross products. This is due to the strong correlation between the AMBU and the CASES variables. However, the existing multicolinearity does not affect the precision of the parameters relevant for inefficiency; so, the conclusions still stand.

The significance of the exponential distribution parameter (α) confirms the existence of technical inefficiency, which explains 60% of the total variability of the composed error in the cost function[14].

As far as labor share is concerned, the mean error, μ_1, is significantly different from zero, indicating a systematic overutilization of labor. The estimated value of μ_1 means that hospitals, on the average, spend about 16.8 percentage points more on labor than required by minimum cost considerations.

---

[13] The share equation of the remaining factor has not been included because it does not provide any additional information (the sum of both equations is one).

[14] The composed error variability is explained by the variance of each one of its two components: lnTI and v. When the exponential distribution parameter, α, approaches infinity, the technical inefficiency variance tends to zero. In such a case, the variability of lnTI+v would be entirely explained by the random disturbance variance. Then, we would conclude that there is no technical inefficiency in that case.

Table 4.2. Estimation results

VARIABLE	COEFFICIENT	STD. ERROR
constant	-0.214891***	0.07496
ln (CASES)	0.596417***	0.11039
ln (AMBU)	0.052727	0.06816
½ ln (CASES)^2	-0.166184	0.14222
½ ln (AMBU)^2	-0.189554*	0.12799
ln (Wage)	0.549951***	0.07594
½ ln (Wage)^2	0.090459***	0.01210
ln (BEDS)	0.361394***	0.07057
ln (CASES) ln (AMBU)	0.143169	0.13046
ln (Wage) ln (CASES)	-0.034781***	0.00737
ln (Wage) ln (AMBU)	0.008727	0.00840
c	3.002640**	1.74996
α	12.97428***	4.59385
σ_v	0.063042***	0.01652
μ_1	0.168106**	0.07587
σ_ε	0.022380***	0.00246
Log likelihood		222.7361
Akaike info criterion		-6.171227

*** significant at 1%; ** significant at 5%; *significant at 10%.

The overutilization of labor implies underutilization of the other factor. Hence, we can state that the wrong input combination is been used, which is evidence of allocative inefficiency, and its overall impact on costs can be calculated through expression (4.12).

From these results, efficiency indexes, whose statistical description is summarized in table 4.3, are estimated for each hospital. In short, mean technical efficiency reached by the hospitals is considerably higher than mean allocative efficiency (with a difference of eight and a half points).

Table 4.3. Estimated economic, technical and allocative efficiency

	Economic ef.	Technical ef.	Allocative ef.
Mean	78.12	92.74	84.22
Std. Error	5.77	5.26	3.75
Min.	55.45	70.86	77.37
Max.	90.33	97.99	93.96

These indexes can be interpreted as follows: if *Insalud* hospitals were as efficient as the best ones, then their cost would be, on average, only 78.12% of their actual cost. If they used the least amount of resources possible, their cost would be around 92.7% of their actual cost, and if they chose factors in the right proportion (depending on prices), their cost would be 84.2% of their current cost.

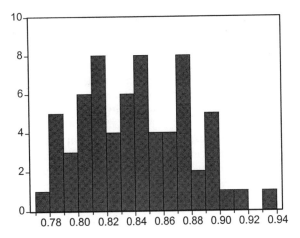

Fig. 4.2. Allocative efficiency distribution

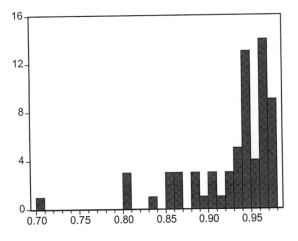

Fig. 4.3. Technical efficiency distribution

Figures 4.2 and 4.3 show the distribution of each of the two indexes among the hospitals. Both series are hardly correlative so it cannot be concluded that the most technically efficient hospitals also present the highest allocative efficiency.

Comparing the present paper with earlier works on Insalud hospitals, we may conclude the following: our technical efficiency index of 92.7% is slightly lower than the indexes estimated by González and Barber (1996). These authors use Data Envelopment Analysis and obtain estimates of technical efficiency for 1991, 1992 and 1993 of 95%, 96% and 97% respectively. However, our result is higher than the one obtained by Ventura and González (1999), who also used a non-parametric analysis. Ventura and González studied Insalud hospitals between 1993 and 1996, and obtained values that go from 80.7% in 1993 up to 84.7% in 1996.

As regards allocative inefficiency, we agree with Puig-Junoy (1999) in that this inefficiency represents a problem quantitatively more important than that of technical inefficiency. Puig-Junoy (2000) uses Data Envelopment Analysis on a sample including both public and private hospitals in the region of Catalonia and obtains a measure of allocative efficiency with a higher dispersion (mean 89.1% and standard error 9.5).

Table 4.4 shows the cost increase caused by both types of inefficiency. According to our previous results, allocative inefficiency has a much higher impact on costs than technical inefficiency (18.96% and 8.2% respectively). Hence, any study focussing exclusively on technical inefficiency ignores the quantitatively more important aspect of hospital inefficiency.

Table 4.4. Cost increase due to economic, technical and allocative inefficiency

	Economic inef.	Technical inef.	Allocative inef.
Mean	28.76	8.2	18.96
Std. Error	10.52	6.9	5.25
Min.	10.69	2.05	6.43
Max.	80.31	41.12	29.25

As shown in table 4.4, total inefficiency (both technical and allocative) accounts for a 28.76% increase in hospital costs above minimum cost. Previous estimates of global inefficiency in Spanish hospitals have shown a wide variety of figures ranging from 13% to 58%, -see for instance: González and Barber (1996), Wagstaff and López (1996), López and Wagstaff (1993)-.

4.4
Conclusions

The aim of this paper has been to quantify separately technical and allocative inefficiency in the Spanish public hospitals. Given that a separate estimation of the hospitals' cost frontier is not adequate, we have resorted to a joint estimation of the cost frontier together with the input share equations. On the basis of this joint estimation, we have obtained two separate measures of technical and allocative efficiency.

These measures allow us to conclude that total inefficiency accounts for a 28.7% increase in hospital costs above minimum cost. Previous estimates of global inefficiency in Spanish hospitals have shown a wide variety of figures ranging from 13% to 58%, -see for instance: González and Barber (1996), Wagstaff and López (1996), López and Wagstaff (1993)-.

Perhaps the most important aspect of the present paper is that it provides an estimate of allocative inefficiency, which is missing in previous papers. The present paper also identifies allocative inefficiency as the main component of economic inefficiency. More specifically, allocative inefficiency accounts for 65% of the total cost increase due to global inefficiency.

References

Aigner, D., Lovell C.A.K., Schmidt, P.: Formulation and Estimation of Stochastic Frontier Production Function Models. Journal of Econometrics 6, 21-37 (1977)

Bauer, P.W.: Recent Developments in the Econometric Estimation of Frontiers. Journal of Econometrics 46, 39-56 (1990)

Byrnes, P., Valdmanis, V.: Analysing Technical and Allocative Efficiency of Hospitals. In: Charnes, A., Cooper, W., Lewin, A.Y., Seiford, L.M., Data Envelopment Analysis: Theory Methodology and Application. Kluwer Academic Publisher 1994

Coelli, T., Rao, D.S.P., Battese, G.E.: An Introduction to Efficiency and Productivity Analysis. Kluwer Academic Publishers 1998

Comisión de Análisis y Evaluación del Sistema Nacional de Salud: Informe y Recomendaciones. Madrid 1991

Eakin, B.K.: Allocative Inefficiency in the Production of Hospital Services. Southern Economic Journal 58, 240-248 (1991)

Eakin, B.K., Kniesner, T.J.: Estimating a Non-Minimum Cost Function for Hospitals. Southern Economic Journal 54, 583-97 (1988)

Farrel, M.J.: The Measurement of Productive Efficiency. Journal of Royal Statistical Society 120, 253-281 (1957)

Forsund, F., Lovell, D.A.K., Schmidt, P.: A Survey of Frontier Production Functions and of Their Relationship to Efficiency Measurement. Journal of Econometrics 13, 5-25 (1980)

González, B., Barber, P.: Changes in the Efficiency of Spanish Public Hospitals after the Introduction of Program-Contracts. Investigaciones Económicas XX 3, 377-402 (1996)

Government Committee on Choices in Health Care: Report. Zoetermeer. The Nederlands 1991

Greene, W.H.: The Econometric Approach to Efficiency Analysis. In: Fried, H.O., Lovell, C.A.K., Schmidt, S.S., The Measurement of Productive Efficiency. Oxford University Press 1993

INE: Estadística de Establecimientos Sanitarios con Régimen de Internado. EESRI 1994

Jondrow, J., Lovell, C.A.K., Materov, I.S., Schmidt, P.: On the Estimation of Technical Inefficiency in the Stochastic Frontier Production Models. Journal of Econometrics 4, 23, 269-274 (1982)

Kumbhakar, S.C.: The Measurement and Decomposition of Cost-inefficiency: the Translog Cost System. Oxford Economic Papers 43, 667-683 (1991)

Kumbhakar, S.C.: Modelling Allocative Inefficiency in a Translog Cost Function and Cost Share Equations: An Exact Relationship. Journal of Econometrics 76, 351-356 (1997)

López, G., Saez, M.: Finance Versus Costs for Teaching Hospital in Spain. Working paper. CRES-UPF 1998

López, G., Wagstaff, A.: Eficiencia y Competitividad en los Servicios Públicos: Algunas Consideraciones Relativas a la Asistencia Sanitaria. Moneda y crédito 196, 181-231 (1993)

Melfi, C. A.: Estimation and Decomposition of Productive Efficiency in a Panel Data Model: An Application to Electric Utilities. Unpublished Doctoral Dissertation. University of North Carolina. Chapel Hill. NC 1984

Morey, R.C., Fine, D.J., Loree, S.W.: Comparing the Allocative Efficiencies of Hospitals. Omega 18, 71-83 (1990)

Puig-Junoy, J.: Partitioning Input Cost Efficiency Into Its Allocative and Technical Components. An Empirical DEA Application to Hospitals. Socio-Economic Planning Sciences, 34, 3, 199-218.

Schmidt, P.: An Error Structure for System of Translog Cost and Share Equations. Econometrics Workshop Paper 8309. Michigan State University 1984

Schmidt, P., Lovell. C.A.K.: Estimating Technical and Allocative Inefficiency Relative to Stochastic Production and Cost Frontiers. Journal of Econometrics 9, 343-366 (1979)

Shephard, R.W.: Cost and Production Functions. Princeton University Press 1953

Ventura, J., González, E.: Análisis de la Eficiencia Técnica Hospitalaria del Insalud GD en Castilla y León. Revista de Investigación Económica y Social de Castilla y León 1, 39-50 (1999)

Wagstaff, A., López, G.: Hospital Costs in Catalonia: a Stochastic Frontier Analysis. Applied Economics Letters 3, 471-474 (1996)

5 Technical Efficiency of Road Haulage Firms

Jose Baños-Pino
Department of Economics
University of Oviedo (Spain)

Pablo Coto-Millán
Department of Economics
University of Cantabria (Spain)

Ana Rodríguez-Álvarez
Department of Economics
University of Oviedo (Spain)

V. Inglada-López de Sabando
Department of Economics
University Carlos III (Spain)

This study justifies the contemporary importance of efficiency analysis. We put forward the theoretical concepts of technical, allocative, and economic efficiency. We then tackle problems of an empirical nature. In this way, different ways of measuring efficiency are presented, with their main disadvantages. To finish, a theoretical application is presented for haulage firms operating in Spanish roads in six different sub-sectors with panel data.

5.1
Introduction

The production theory of the firm, in most basic Microeconomics textbooks, starts from the premise that the manager behaves in an efficient manner, making the best possible use of the resources available. To begin with, there is the hypothesis that the firm, given the technology and the inputs available, produces the maximum output possible. This relationship is represented in the *production function*.

Secondly, the first order conditions for cost minimisation, given the factor prices, are introduced through the *cost function*. Finally, there is the assumption that the manager chooses that quantity of output which maximises profits, as represented through the *profit function*. However, in reality it may happen that some or none of these hypotheses are fulfilled. There are various reason for this, ranging from bad luck to the pursuit of objectives different to those outlined above. As a result, in the empirical estimation of these behavioural functions much research has been dedicated to testing firm behaviour by analysing the problem of inefficiency in the productive system.

5.2
Efficiency

We now distinguish between the different types of efficiency dealt with in the economics literature. We can distinguish between at least three types of efficiency: technical, allocative, and economic. We refer to *technical efficiency* when the optimality condition is defined by the production function. This means that the exact amount of inputs necessary are used in order to produce a vector of outputs, and hence there are no redundant (i.e. more than were strictly necessary) inputs. To estimate technical efficiency we need data about the quantities of inputs and outputs but it is not necessary to have data on prices.

Another concept is that of *allocative efficiency*, which occurs when the productive inputs are used in the proportions which minimise costs, that is, when the ratio of marginal products is equal to the ratio of their prices.

Finally, we talk about *economic efficiency* when both of the aforementioned kinds of efficiencies are achieved simultaneously. In Farrell (1957) this concept (he refers to it as productive or global efficiency) is defined as the product of technical efficiency and allocative efficiency (he refers to the latter as 'price efficiency').

We use Farrell's original ideas in order to provide a brief introduction to these concepts of efficiency. To begin, consider a firm employing two factors of production (x_1, x_2) to produce a single product. Under conditions of constant returns to scale, the technology of the company could be represented by a single isoquant, the unitary isoquant ($y = 1$), which can be drawn as in Figure 5.1.

According to the definition of technical efficiency used above, all the combinations of inputs lying on the curve $y = 1$ are technically efficient. The combinations below the frontier are unfeasible while the combinations which are above are technically inefficient. With reference to Figure 5.1, point A represents the situation of a company that employs (x_1^0, x_2^0) of inputs to produce the unit y. Now, according to the isoquant, $y = 1$ can be produced with $(OB/OA)x_1^0$ and $(OB/OA)x_2^0$. Alternatively, with (x_1^0, x_2^0) an efficient company can obtain $(OA/OB)y$ of the product. This means that technical efficiency (TE) can be measured using the ratio OB/OA. The maximum value of this index is one, which would mean that the firm is operating on the isoquant and is thus technically efficient. When a company is inefficient, then OB ≠ OA (as can be seen in Figure 5.1) and the index takes a value lower than one which informs us about the degree of technical efficiency achieved by the firm.

The definitions of allocative and economic efficiency can also be illustrated using Fig. 5.1. Allocative efficiency reflects the ability of a firm to use the inputs in the optimal proportions, given their respective prices and the production technology. Hence, if the relative prices of the factors of production are available it is possible to know the slope of the isocost line PP'. A company that allocates resources efficiently will thus produce with a input combination given by the slope of the isocost where it is equal to that of the isoquant, represented at point C. At this point, the firm is producing the output at minimum cost, given the technology and the input prices. Hence, the measure of allocative efficiency (AE) is derived from the ratio OD/OB.

It is also possible to compare the total cost of producing a unit y using the input combination at C with that of producing y using the combination at A. We can use the ratio OD/OA to derive a measurement of economic or global efficiency (EE). A producer is economically efficient if it minimises the cost of producing the output given the input prices and the technology. A producer is economically efficient if and only if it is technically and allocatively efficient. In addition, we can see that:

OD/OA = (OB/OA) (OD/OB)

That is to say:

EE = (TE) (AE)

Fig. 5.1

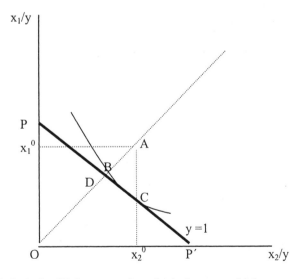

Technical efficiency as described above could be expressed in different ways depending on whether we use the output or the inputs as a reference. For example, we could take the production quantity as given and calculate the efficient quantity of inputs (input-oriented technical efficiency). Alternatively, we could take the quantities of inputs as given and calculate the efficient quantity of output (output-oriented technical efficiency). Only if the technology exhibits constant returns scale will the input-orientated technical efficiency index be the same that the output-orientated technical efficiency index (Färe and Lovell, 1978). Although constant returns to scale have been assumed in the explanation above, Forsund and Hjalmarsson (1979) generalises this for variable returns to scale.

It is important to point out that the concept of economic efficiency is very wide-ranging. For example, we could also define economic efficiency in terms of the objectives of the company or sector under study. If the objective is to maximise profits, the optimum is associated with a profit function, given the prices of outputs and inputs. If the objective is to minimise costs, the optimum is associated with the cost function, given the prices of inputs and the quantity of outputs. Economic efficiency may also be dealt with from other perspectives. For instance, when the price of production is not equal to the marginal cost of production, there will be economic inefficiency. Here we are referring to deviations with respect to the behaviour of a competitive industry, which generates inefficient allocations of resources in the long term.

5.3
Classification of Efficiency Frontiers

Measurements of companies' efficiency are obtained by comparing the observed values for each productive unit with the optimum defined by the estimated frontier.

The studies on functions of production frontiers (or those of costs or profits) can be classified in the following way:

i) Deterministic studies: the error term is composed of a single one-sided term, which captures inefficiency.
ii) Stochastic studies: the error term is composed of two parts - a component to capture "noise" and a one-sided component which captures inefficiency.

These give rise to two types of production frontier: deterministic or stochastic.

Either of these two production frontiers can be estimated using specifications that may be:

i) Parametric specifications: a concrete parametric function is specified (Cobb-Douglas, CES, Translog...)
ii) Non-parametric specifications: no function is specified.

In addition, to calculate efficiency measurements one can:

i) Use methods of mathematical programming to construct the frontier.
ii) Specify a statistical relationship to estimate the frontier.

From here eight possible combinations emerge in order to carry out empirical investigations. In the different empirical investigations stochastic frontiers are usually used with parametric specifications (for example, translog functions) and deterministic frontiers with non-parametric specifications (for example, Data Envelopment Analysis).

If we use *deterministic frontiers* (see for example Aigner and Chu, 1968), all the observed cases below the production frontier represent inefficiency. Then, if we have cross-sectional data with N inputs used to produce a single output, it is possible to define the production function as:[1]

$$y_i = f(x_i)\exp(-u_i)$$

where y_i is the output of producer i, x_i is the input vector of N inputs used by producer i, $f(x)$ is the production frontier and $u_i \geq 0$ $(0 \leq e^{-u_i} \leq 1)$. It is assumed that the observations on u_i are independently and identically distributed (iid) and that x is exogenous (independent of u). The technical efficiency index $TE_i = \exp(-u_i)$ will be:

$$TE_i = \frac{y_i}{f(x_i)}$$

In words, the technical efficiency index is the ratio of observed output to maximum output. However, the main disadvantage of this definition is that it attributes all of the deviation from the frontier to technical inefficiency.

Stochastic frontiers, proposed by Aigner, Lovell, Schmidt (1977) and Meusen and van den Broeck (1977), are also called frontiers of composed errors because to every frontier we add an error which is composed of two components: a random error, and another error which captures the degree of inefficiency in the company. That is:

$$y_i = f(x_i)\exp(v_i - u_i)$$

where v_i is a random error with some symmetric distribution to capture the random effects of measurement error and exogenous shocks, and $\{f(x_i)\exp(v_i)\}$ is the stochastic production frontier. In this way, technical inefficiency is captured by the one-sided error component $\exp(-u_i)$, $u_i \geq 0$. Hence, the technical efficiency index is defined as:

$$TE_i = \frac{y_i}{f(x_i)\exp(v_i)}$$

However, while this model is capable of revealing the average efficiency of the sample, it is unable to yield estimates of technical efficiecny for each observation.

A solution, proposed by Jondrow, Lovell, Materov and Schmidt (1982), was to specify the functional form of the distribution of the u_i component and to derive the conditional distribution $(u_i | v_i + u_i)$.

At first, empirical studies using frontier models used cross-sectional data. Schmidt and Sickles (1984) noted three difficulties with cross-sectional stochastic production frontier models:

i) It is necessary to make assumptions about the distribution of technical inefficiency (e.g., half-normal) and statistical noise (e.g., normal) in order to be able to decompose the error term. It is not clear how robust one's results are to these assumptions.

---

[1] Given the objectives of this study, the analysis will follow a production function focus.

ii) It is necessary to assume that the degree of inefficiency is independent of the regressors, although it is easy to imagine that if the firm knows the technical inefficiency level, this should affect its input choices.

iii) Technical inefficiency of a particular firm (observation) could be estimated, but not consistently.

Schmidt and Sickles (1984) formulated and estimated some methods with panel data that would overcome these disadvantages. If each producer is observed over a period of time, we can apply panel data techniques. A production frontier with time-invariant technical efficiency can be written as:

$$y_{it} = f(x_{it}) \exp (v_{it}\text{-}u_i)$$

where there are T time periods. We can then consider different panel-data models. The *fixed-effects model* treats the technical inefficiency component (u_i) as fixed effects, that is to say, as non-random. Thus, it is possible to allow for technical inefficiency to be correlated with regressors. However, if we assume that inefficiency indices are randomly distributed with a constant mean, we have the *random-effects model*. In this model it is necessary to assume that the technical inefficiency is uncorrelated with the regressors. To test this assumption, Hausman and Taylor (1981) created a test between individual effects (technical inefficiency) and explanatory variables (inputs vector in the case of the production function).

The development of the analysis of econometric models from the 1980s has led the way to applications to frontiers with panel data. The economic literature in the 1990s up to the present has gone in at least two directions: a) The first comes from the increasing use of data panels with a dynamic character. In models of efficiency there is an attempt to estimate indices of efficiency which vary with time. Studies by Cornwell, Schmidt and Sickles (1990), Kumbhakar (1990) and and Battesse and Coelli (1992) constitute and good example of the literature in this vein, b) The second direction has an empirical character. There have been efforts to compare research done on the same sector, using the same methods and concepts of efficiency, in different countries or groups of countries, and the most relevant conclusions are drawn. An excellent survey of stochastic frontier analysis since its beginnings was given by Kumbhakar and Lovell (2000).

5.4
A Theoretical Application to Goods Haulage Companies on Spanish Roads Using Panel Data

In this section, we calculate technical efficiency for goods haulage firms on Spanish Roads, considering six sectors (Full Load Transport, Grouppage-Service, Refrigerated Transport, Crane Transport, Special Transport and International Transport) over the period 1994-1997. We have chosen a translog functional form to estimate the production function. Thus, the econometric specification will be:

$$\text{Log GVA} = \beta_0 + \beta_1 \text{ LogCI} + \beta_2 \text{ LogK} + \beta_3 \text{ LogL} + \beta_4 (\text{LogCI})^2 + \beta_5 \text{ LogCI LogK}$$
$$+ \beta_6 \text{ LogCI LogL} + \beta_7 (\text{LogK})^2 + \beta_8 \text{ LogK LogL} + \beta_9 (\text{LogL})^2 + \beta_{10} T + \beta_{11} (T)^2$$
$$+ \beta_{12} \text{ LogCI T} + \beta_{13} \text{ LogK T} + \beta_{14} \text{ LogL T}$$

where GVA is the output, measured as the Gross Value Added of the different companies calculated as the sum of the Gross Operating Surplus (GOS) and the compensation to employees, where the GOS is calculated as the difference between the income and expenditures, excluding consumption of fixed capital; CI refers to the intermediate consumption, which in stock accounting is called provisions; K represents capital and is approximated by fixed assets dedicated to production; and L represents the number of employees.

All these variables except the variable L appear in millions of pesetas and are considered in constant pesetas. To achieve this, the variables VAB and K have been deflated by the Consumer Price Index (CPI), and the variable CI has been deflated by the Price of Energy Index to take into account that a very significant part of such consumption refers to the fuel of transport vehicles. In addition, all the variables are expressed in the form of deviations from their mean values, so that (at the mean) the first-order coefficients of the production function indicate how production varies with respect to the inputs.

In all the estimations a fixed-effects model was chosen, that is, a separate dummy is estimated for every firm and the constant term is suppressed. These effects will be interpreted as the indices of technical inefficiency for each firm (Schmidt and Sickles, 1984). According to this method, the most technically efficient firm takes the value one. To correct for endogeneity of inputs we have used an instrumental variables approach, using their lagged values as instruments. Though the generic expression of the production function takes into account a temporal trend to measure technical progress, it was finally decided not to include it since it either did not prove significant or, as in the case of international transport, it showed a coefficient of around 8%, which was not very credible.

In Tables 5.1 to 5.6, we summarise the results of the estimations. The estimations are quite satisfactory for most of the distinct sectors of haulage by road. In Table 5.7 the scale parameter and the technical efficiency parameter is measured for each sector. As can be observed, in haulage by road there is a sector such as Groupage-Service with increasing returns to scale, since the scale parameter is significantly higher than 1. In the other sectors there are decreasing returns to scale with an average scale parameter of 0.81, as in the case of Crane Transport and International Transport.

In Figures 5.2 to 5.7 the mean of the level of technical (in)efficiency and other statistics are summarised for each sector. The arithmetic mean of the indicators of technical efficiency relative to the sectoral mean is 0.80. The economic interpretation of this indicator is the following: in the haulage by road sectors, on average, the production could have been increased by 20% during the years 1994-1997 without increasing the quantity of inputs.

However, the average levels and the dispersion of the (in)efficiency show a great deal of sectoral heterogeneity. The average level varies from 92% in the sectors of Full Load Transport and Crane Transport to 44% in the sector of Groupage-Service. The sector in which the indicator of technical (in)efficiency presents the highest dispersion with respect to the average sectoral value is Groupage-Service. This sector also has an average level of efficiency that is quite low. The sectors with less dispersion in the grade of inefficiency of companies are International Transport, Full Load Transport and Crane Transport, which are mostly sectors with a high level of efficiency.

In developing this application we wanted to illustrate one of the many methods which have been developed and which are available for the empirical study of the relative technical efficiency of companies using the methodology of efficiency frontiers. As has been seen, the topic of relative efficiency is a fundamental part of the Microeconomics of the Theory of Production and it is a subject whose contribution is important in terms of its applications. There remains another important economic topic, which is the analysis of the causes of the differences between efficiencies across companies of the same sector. This is needed in order to identify allocation problems and to guide sectoral policies. This is important because, as is obvious, inefficiency is not only costly for the productive unit in question, but for the economy as a whole.

Table 5.1. Full load transport

	Coefficient	t-Student
β_1	0.3364	4.3769
β_2	0.7789	6.9367
β_3	0.0761	2.3175
β_4	0.5735	2.4592
β_5	-2.4978	-2.4874
β_6	0.3555	1.3071
β_7	1.2029	1.9595
β_8	0.6404	1.4513
β_9	-0.1562	-1.4568

Table 5.2. Grouppage-service

	Coefficient	t-Student
β_1	0.3854	6.7586
β_2	0.8036	10.744
β_3	0.0527	1.2349
β_4	0.3198	2.9957
β_5	0.2315	0.7376
β_6	-0.7004	-3.6098
β_7	0.2552	0.5308
β_8	0.2529	0.5032
β_9	-0.5415	-5.7813

Table 5.3. Refrigerated transport

	Coefficient	t-Student
β_1	0.1771	4.1177
β_2	0.1993	3.3153
β_3	0.7388	6.6673
β_4	0.2408	2.7204
β_5	-0.0363	-0.1296
β_6	-0.8211	-2.1997
β_7	-0.2916	-1.9447
β_8	0.4617	0.9723
β_9	0.0022	0.0059

Table 5.4. Crane transport

	Coefficient	t-Student
β_1	0.0635	1.6573
β_2	-0.0367	-1.3134
β_3	0.8261	10.678
β_4	0.0432	1.6237
β_5	0.0293	0.4857
β_6	-1.0788	-3.1990
β_7	0.0988	2.4034
β_8	-0.4035	-2.0788
β_9	1.8919	4.9323

Table 5.5. Special transport

	Coefficient	t-Student
β_1	0.2041	2.2994
β_2	0.0079	0.2239
β_3	0.5063	3.7002
β_4	0.3246	2.2737
β_5	0.4331	0.7951
β_6	-2.0812	-3.4231
β_7	0.1933	1.6674
β_8	1.2879	2.1186
β_9	-1.0610	-1.8020

Table 5.6. International transport

	Coefficient	t-Student
β_1	0.2336	5.9920
β_2	0.0865	3.7535
β_3	0.4440	10.449
β_4	0.2874	1.2973
β_5	0.2846	1.3142
β_6	-1.1295	-2.6446
β_7	-0.2230	-3.6819
β_8	-0.0015	-0.0064
β_9	0.9369	2.5462

Table 5.7. Summary of results

Sector	Scale Parameter	χ_1^2	Average Technical Efficiency
Full Load Transport	1.19	2.75	0.92
Groupage-Service	1.24	8.92*	0.44
Refrig Transport	1.11	0.98	0.80
Crane Transport	0.85	3.85*	0.92
Special Transport	0.72	3.21	0.80
International Transport	0.76	25.44*	0.89

*Statistically significant different from one at 5% level.

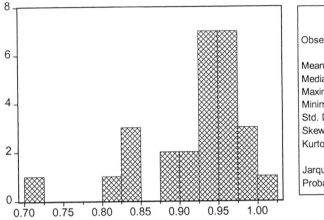

Fig. 5.2. Technical efficiency. Full load transport

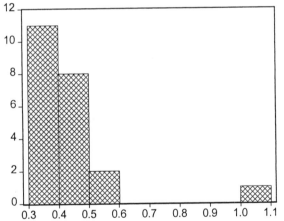

Fig. 5.3. Technical efficiency. Groupage-service

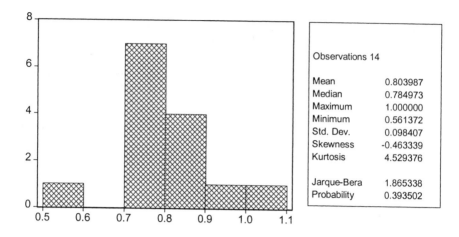

Fig. 5.4. Technical efficiency. Refrigerated transport

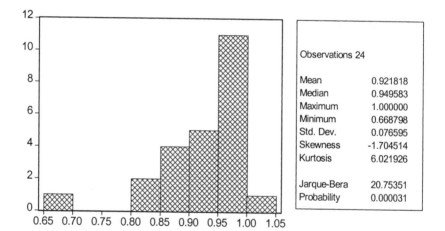

Fig. 5.5. Crane transport

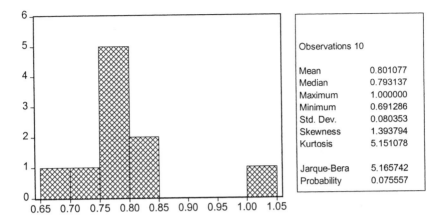

Fig. 5.6. Technical efficiency. Special transport

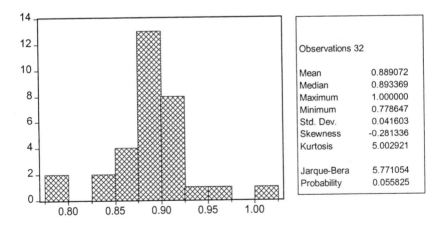

Fig. 5.7. Technical efficiency. International transport

References

Aigner, D. J. and Chu, S. F.: On Estimating the Industry Production Function. American Economic Review, 58, 826-839 (1968)

Aigner, D. J., Lovell, C. A. K. and Schmidt, P.: Formulation and Estimation of Stochastic Frontier Production Function Models. Journal of Econometrics 6, 21-37 (1977)

Battesse, G. and Coelli, T.: Frontier Production Functions, Technical Efficiency and Panel Data: with Application to Paddy Farmers in India. The Journal of Productivity Analysis 3, 153-169 (1992)

Cornwell, C., Schmidt, P. and Sickles, R. C.: Production Frontiers with Cross-Sectional and Times –Series Variations in Efficiency Levels. Journal of Econometrics 46,182-200 (1990)

Färe, R. and Lovell, C. A. K.: Measuring the Technical Efficiency of Production, Journal of Economic Theory, 19, 150-162 (1978)

Farrell, M. J.: The Measurement of Productive Efficiency. Journal of the Royal Statistic Society Series A 120, 253-281 (1957)

Forsund, F. R. and Hjalmarsson, L.: Generalized Farrell Measurement of Efficiency: An Application to Milk Processing in Swedish Dairy Plants. Economic Journal 89, 294-315 (1979)

Hausman, J. A. and Taylor, W. E.: Panel Data and Unobservable Individual Effects. Econometrica 49, 1377-1398 (1981)

Jondow, J., Lovell, C. A. K., Materov, I. S. and Schmidt, P.: On the Estimation of Technical Inefficiency in the Stochastic Frontier Production Function Model. Journal of Econometrics 19, 233-238 (1982)

Kumbhakar, S. C.: Production Frontiers, Panel Data and Time-Varing Technical Inefficiency. Journal of Econometrics 46, 201-211 (1990)

Kumbhakar, S. C. and Lovell, C. A. K.: Stochastic Frontier Analysis. Cambridge University Press (2000)

Meusen, W. and van den Broeck, J.: Efficiency Estimation from Cobb-Douglas Production Functions with Composed Error. International Economic Review 18, 435-444 (1977)

Schmidt, P. and Sickles, R. C.: Production Frontiers and Panel Data. Journal of Business & Economic Statistics vol. 2, 4, 367-376 (1984)

6 Technological Innovation and Employment: Intersectoral Appraisals of Structural Change in the Service Economy

Daniel Díaz-Fuentes
Department of Economics
University of Cantabria (Spain)

6.1
Introduction

One of the main structural changes in all OECD countries has been a shift in employment and total output towards services. This trend indicates that services are a dynamic part of the economy and make an increasing contribution to employment and economic growth. Thus it could be argued that the "service or tertiary society" is the stage towards which all industrialised countries are moving.

Although the share of services in the economy has increased, there is a lack of understanding about their industrial performance. Traditional views considered that employment in services was low-skilled and unproductive, while tertiary activities were considered neither dynamic nor innovative. In fact, several of the service activities require highly skilled jobs, show increasing productivity and are highly innovative and dynamic. Although services have been classified as non-tradable, they are increasingly exposed to competition and are becoming more tradable. The increasing importance of services in the so-called "industrialised countries" and the poor understanding of the process of services expansion require a review of the interpretations of the expansion of services.

The primary interpretation of the growth in services was the "theory of stages" (Kindleberger, 1958, Rostow, 1960) whose explanation was based mainly on the patterns of final consumption (Petty's Law and, specifically, Engel's Law: as income per capita increases, final demand shifts towards superior goods including services. This reflects a shift in consumer demand due to a high income elasticity of services). Furthermore, the growth of the service sector generated diverse interpretations about the "post-industrial societies" (Bell, 1974), according to which the service sector is gradually taking the place of industry as the new engine of growth. However, a different set of questions were raised about the growth in services with Baumol's (1967) "theory of unbalanced growth". Amongst the most important questions posed were those relating to the definition of the role of the pattern of consumption and the role of productivity differentials in relation to service output and employment growth. Fuchs (1968) showed that the pattern of consumption had a less important role than that of productivity differentials (relatively slow productivity growth in some services). As a consequence of the lower productivity growth of the service sector as a whole compared with the manufacturing sector, plus the low skilled labour intensive characteristics of many services ("cost disease of personal service"), a secondary set of questions appeared when the intersectoral comparisons are made in constant or current prices (Gershuny & Miles, 1983 and Kravis *et al.*, 1983, Baumol *et al* 1989). In general, the increase in the contribution of services to GDP during the last five decades has stemmed more from changes in relative prices than from an increase in output. In order to understand this trend, however, it is necessary to distinguish between different services.

One of the problems encountered when examining the "services" is how they can be most accurately defined. Since the service sector is highly heterogeneous, it must be broken down into different categories according to the functions performed, the transformation processes and to the market served: producer or consumer services; distributive, social, personal or business services; market or non-market services; and physical, person-centred or information services. Most of these branches have been incorporated gradually into the Systems of National Accounts to improve the classification of services for analytical purposes (CEC-EUROSTAT, IMF, OECD, UN & World Bank 1994 and OECD 1995a & B). In order to understand the shift towards the service economy, it is necessary to analyse *what* is being produced in the economic system and *how* it is being produced.

Classification of services is not the only difficulty, traditional analysis is too biased on manufacturing performance. The process that drives services activities in many cases is different to that of manufacturing. In the same way, the key factors in services have a different relevance to those in manufacturing (R&D, innovation, organisational change or human capital). Notwithstanding, several services activities are becoming similar to manufacturing and vice versa (standard process and mass production), while the differences among services are as varied as those among manufacturing. In fact, the focus on the different categories between manufacturing and services is becoming less interesting and it seems more relevant to analyse the interaction between sectors and activities (Tomlinson 1997).

Standard indicators of technology intensity show that services make a contribution to total R&D expenditures which is relatively limited compared with the size of the sector in total employment. Certainly there is a problem of measurement, since most countries have only recently covered services in R&D and innovation surveys because it was assumed that manufacturing was the source of technological change and traditional measures do not usually capture key factors of innovation in services (such as patent registration).

One advantage of macroeconomic analysis based on Input Output techniques is that it enables overall production to be disaggregated by sector and by sub-system. It then becomes possible to examine the growth of different services and industries in relation to the process of structural change of the economic system. Furthermore, since the evolution of a sector or sub-system is not independent of the rest of the economy, it is necessary to evaluate the links between sectors (intersectoral relations) in terms of changes of final demand and technical change (Diaz Fuentes1993).

With these general premises in mind, and with the specific methodological approach, the following sections of this paper aim to explore a number of key questions:

- What has been the extent of structural change in employment in services in the main "industrialised countries" over the past four decades?
- Which technological trends explain the directions of structural change in employment in manufacturing and services? Was there a relationship between direct technology intensity and employment growth by sector?
- What is the embodied contribution of R&D and innovation expenditures to total technology intensity in manufacturing and services? What is the sectoral importance of the acquisition of technology embodied in inputs generated by other industries?
- Is the growth of employment in services explained solely by the relative increase in the final demand of these services, or is it also necessary to consider the growth of intermediate demand of services? Has the growth of services been caused by a greater demand for their use in the production of manufactured goods?

While accepting that there is a positive correlation between economic growth and employment in services, this research departs from an optimistic point of view about services. This seeks to analyse the increasing integration between manufacturing and services in technological innovation. This integration includes the outsourcing of manufacturing to specialised services activities and services that were not performed previously by other firms.

The following sections discuss these questions and demonstrate the importance of detailed analysis of inter-industry performance. Part two considers the trends in employment in the main "industrialised countries" taking a global measure of the extent of structural change of the major sectors share from 1960 to 1980, and from 1980 to 1997 (OECD, 1992a & annual a). Part three discusses the relationship between conventional measurements of technology intensity and the trend's directions in employment in manufacturing and services since 1980 (OECD, annual b and 1998). Part four goes beyond examining the extent and direction of structural change in services and provides an inter-industry analysis of innovation which, on the basis of the most recently published input-output table, estimates technology flows and the acquisition of innovation by sector in 1994 (INE 1997a and 2000, EUROSTAT 1997). Part five presents the results of the changing composition of employment in services due to final and intermediate demand (Garcia et al. 1994, EUROSTAT 1987, 1992 and OCDE 1995c). These results have been obtained through the use of inter-industry analysis. This analysis is founded on the notion of vertical integration of the sub-systems and provides an enhanced view of the intersectoral relationships. Finally, some implications of the results are drawn in part six.

6.2
Extent of Structural Change in Services Employment

During the last four decades the world economy has exhibited extensive economic structural changes. At the same time, economic performance has varied significantly; the real increase in OECD GDP and productivity during the period from 1980 to 1997 was half that experienced between 1960 and 1980. The slow-down of economic growth in OECD countries since the end of the 1970s has been accompanied by three significant recessions, two oil shocks, growth of international trade, globalisation of financial markets and the diffusion of a set of new technologies (Freeman & Soete, 1994). As a consequence of these changes, the economic structures of these countries have been transformed markedly, reflecting structural, as opposed to cyclical, shifts in the composition of employment and production.[1] Notable economists consider that the reasons for this slow-down and higher unemployment are structural and are either caused by restrictions in markets,[2] or by the lack of technological innovative capabilities.[3]

Certainly, despite the considerable economic growth in the postwar period (GDP growth rates for OECD countries averaged around 4 per cent between 1960 and 1980 and 2 per cent between 1980 and 1990), labour absorption has been limited throughout the three decades, since employment average growth rates were around 1 per cent in both periods considered. This trend has been even more significant for EU countries, whose GDP growth averaged 4 per cent (1960-1980) and 2 per cent (1980-1997) while total employment growth rates were only 0.2 and 0.5 per cent for the respective periods. Considering the problems of labour absorption during the "golden age", it is interesting to explore employment trends since the turning point of the middle of the 1970s (OECD, annual a).

---

[1] "Whilst economic theory has pointed to compensation mechanism generating new employment to replace jobs which are lost through technical change, no one has claimed that this process is instantaneous or painless. Economists differ however on the extent to which they would rely on self-adjusting market-clearing mechanism or on active public investment and labour market policies". See Freeman & Soete (1994, pp. 17-38).

[2] Over the last decade the European unemployment rate has averaged 10 per cent, which is a much more serious matter than the fluctuations around the average. Conventional business cycles account for relatively little of the history of unemployment. Most of the annual variations in unemployment come from the long-frequency fluctuations between half decades rather than from the short-frequency fluctuations within half decades. This is because there are long term changes in social institutions, and the shocks (wars, oil or financial crisis) have long-lasting effects, see Layard et al. (1994, pp. 91-109).

[3] These Information and Communication Technologies, although they have a vast range of present and future applications, do not yet easily match the inherited previous skill profile, management organisation, industrial structure or institutional framework. See Freeman & Soete (1994, pp. 47-66).

Taking a global measurement of the extent of structural change of the major sectors shares for the main industrialised countries including Spain (Table 6.1), it is clear that there are basic similarities in the patterns of structural change among countries during the whole period: agriculture is declining while services are increasing as a share of overall employment and in all the three areas the sectoral changes were shifting towards services. However, in the period 1960-80 the rising share in employment services was mainly correlated to the declining share of agriculture rather than in manufacturing or industry as in the period 1980-97. Additionally, countries differ widely in the sectoral composition of employment, in the proportion of structural adjustment, and in the degree of flexibility which work organisation displays in response to changes. On the one hand, from 1960 to 1980, some countries showed an increase in structural changes and industrial employment (Japan, Spain and Italy) and GDP shares (Japan and Spain), implying a significant catching-up in comparison with the leader country. On the other hand, from 1980 to 1997, the contribution of services to GDP has declined in the two countries with higher productivity growth (Japan and Germany). Furthermore, structural change can be considered as a source of growth. This applies, in particular, to countries in which employment is high in agriculture and productivity is low, since labour can be reallocated to other sectors of higher productivity.[4]

Table 6.1. Structural trends in employment 1960-97

	Agriculture		Industry		Services		Wholesale & retail trade, restaurants & hotels	Transport, storage & commun - ications	Finance, insurance, real estate, business services	Community, Social & Personal services
	1960-80	1980-97	1960-80	1980-97	1960-80	1980-97	1980-97	1980-97	1980-97	1980-97
USA	-4.9	-0.9	-4.0	-7.4	8.9	8.3	1.2	-1.3	7.5	1.1
Canada	-7.8	-1.5	-4.2	-5.3	12.0	6.8	1.1	-0.9	3.4	3.5
UK	-2.1	-0.7	-10.1	-10.7	12.2	11.4	0.3	-0.7	4.6	1.9
Germany	-8.4	-2.4	-2.9	-7.6	11.3	10.0	2.9	-0.6	1.4	3.0
France	-13.8	-4.2	-1.7	-10.3	15.5	14.5	1.7	-0.7	4.2	10.1
Italy	-18.3	-7.5	4.0	-5.9	14.3	13.4	3.3	0.6	0.8	11.5
Spain	-19.5	-10.8	5.9	-6.2	13.7	16.9	5.7	-0.1	1.9	7.6
Japan	-19.8	-5.1	6.8	-2.3	13.0	7.4	-1.1	-0.6	1.7	6.9
Australia	-4.5	-1.3	-8.0	-8.8	12.5	10.1	1.8	-0.6	5.5	1.7

Source: OECD (annual a & b).

---

[4] There is some evidence, based on 30 countries for the period 1960-90, that the GDP growth rates correspond negatively to increasing services shares. See Chenery (1986).

Within services, the share of finance, insurance, real estate and business services (FIREBS) and community, social and personal services (CSPS) increases proportionally in all cases while that of transport, storage and communications (TSC) and, in certain cases, wholesale and retail trade, restaurants and hotels (WRTRH) lose their share in total service employment. Breaking down these figures shows that, from 63 to 85 per cent of growth was due to service sectors and that among these activities FIREBS and CSPS have the greatest impact. The increasing share of business and other intermediary services makes it gradually more difficult to measure compositional change, since it becomes necessary to look at structural links among sectors instead of showing only change in employment or GDP shares by sector.

6.3
Innovation and Employment Trends in Structural Change

The classification of the main sectors into three parts is a conventional but limited method of measuring the extent of structural change. A more accurate approach would be to disaggregate the sectoral evolution of GDP and employment in relation to the different trends in each individual sector, so it becomes possible to distinguish growing, medium and declining growth activities.[5] A complementary measurement of structural change in terms of direction could be obtained by classifying the branches according to their technology intensity.[6]

Contemporary theories of economic growth and international trade have stressed the role of innovation as a fundamental source of growth, employment and productivity, the capacity to innovate depends on multiple factors (Grossman, G. & Helpman, E. 1994). Technology investments are developed in a few manufacturing industries, however, the overall performance of the economic system depends on putting technology to work by using ideas and products developed in other activities. However, most firms and industries, in particular

---

[5] In OECD (annual b) the industries were classified according to their annual growth rate (1974-90) in the main industrialised countries as: **High-Growth**: 1. Computers and office machinery, 2. Aerospace, 3. Communications, 4. Finance and insurance, 5. Business service, 6. Government, 7. Rubber plastic, 8. Pharmaceutical, 9. Social and personal service, 10. Instruments. **Medium-Growth**: 11. Chemical, 12. Trade, 13. Transport, 14. Agriculture, 15. Electrical machinery, 16. Paper and printing, 17. Electricity, gas and water, 18. Non-ferrous metals, 19. Food, drink and tobacco, 20. Motor vehicles, 21. Hotels and restaurants. **Low-Growth**: 22. Mining, 23. Non-electrical machinery, 24. Construction, 25. Fabricated metals, 26. Stone, clay and glass, 27. Textiles, 28. Petroleum refining, 29. Wood and furnitures, 30. Ferrous metals, 31. Shipbuilding.

[6] In OECD (annual b) the 21 manufacturing branches across 11 industrialised countries are ranked according to the R&D expenditures to gross output as a rough estimate of technological sophistication, with the following scheme: **High-Tech**: 1. Aerospace, 2. Computer and office machinery, 3. Communication equipment, 4. Pharmaceutical, 5. Instruments, 6. Electrical machinery. **Medium-Tech**: 7. Motor vehicles, 8. Chemical, 9. Non-electrical machinery, 10. Rubber and plastic, 11. Non-ferrous metals, 12. Other transports. **Low-Tech**: 13. Stone, clay and glass, 14. Food, drink and tobacco, 15. Shipbuilding, 16. Petroleum refining, 17. Ferrous metals, 18. Fabricated metals, 19. Paper and printing, 20. Wood and furnitures, 21. Textiles, footwear and leather.

services such as FIRBS, acquire technology by purchasing and assimilating capital embodied technology machinery. This fact has changed the EU attitude to science, technology and innovation: "Support to innovation should be broadened from "mission-orientated" projects with specific research outcomes, such as a new combat aircraft, to "diffusion-orientated" programmes, such as educating small firms about new products and process" (Working Group on Innovation and Technology Policy 1999).

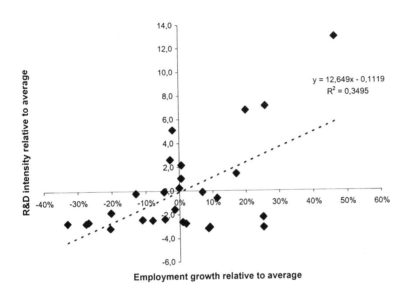

Fig. 6.1. R&D intensity and employment growth 1980-95

Source: OECD (annual b & c, 1998)

Technology intensity concerns the degree to which technology is produced and used within different industries. Activities with relatively high R&D or innovative expenditures per unit of output or value added are classified as high technology industries or technology intensive industries. However, technology generation and use are hard to measure, the roughest estimation is R&D intensity that measures the expenditure directly incurred by an industry, while technology use is estimated by R&D expenditures incurred by the acquisition of intermediate and capital goods. While the shares of manufacturing in employment and output have declined over the last two decades, the share of high technology industries in manufacturing output has increased steadily. However, employment shares of high technology industries have risen less than output shares, which means that labour productivity has risen in these industries. Fig. 6.1 provides some evidence of R&D effort and relative employment growth in the manufacturing industries for the period 1980-1995 for 15 OECD countries. The graph shows a correlation between high technology industries and employment. This indicates that technological change has accompanied structural change, favouring the emergence of employment in high technology sub-sectors such as Aircraft, Office and computing machinery, Drugs and medicines, and Professional goods.

In the services, the evidence shows that the most rapidly growing sectors in both output and employment terms are FIREBS and CSPS; in certain cases WRTRH has noted a significant expansion (in particular in countries specialised in tourism). Although the service sectors are increasingly recognised as being important innovators, the existing indicators of technological intensity do not reveal their significance (Andersen & Howells 1998). Innovation in services is less based on R&D and more linked to acquired technology and changes in process, markets and organisation. In the past many countries focused R&D surveys on manufacturing because it was assumed that this was the source of technological change and innovation (Young 1996).

The latter approach would be useful in helping to evaluate the direction of structural change, but would fail to identify the transformations taking place between industries below the aggregate levels. The economies are also undergoing a different structural change, as the firms change the organisation of their production and source inputs. These changes affect the linkage between and within firms, industries and sectors. These sorts of structural changes can be analysed by looking at the structure of production in each industry and sector. These can be done applying input-output techniques, which provide a picture of inter-industry relations and linkages. Additionally, it could not connect the change in the structure to other factors such as shifts in domestic demand, foreign trade, technical change or input productivity.

6.4
Embodied Technology and Technology Diffusion in Services

Input-output techniques make it possible to analyse the economic system based on intersectoral relations of innovation expenditures that represent the technology flow of embodied R&D or innovation. This methodology applied to technology diffusion allows the measurement of total innovation intensity by sectors (Sakurai et al.1996).

In order to understand the shift towards the service economy it is important to examine the principal factors affecting both what is produced in the whole economy and how it is produced. This means that, when examining the service sector, it is not enough to look at this sector alone, since structural changes in the patterns of final demand, the intermediate demand and technical change must also be considered.

Services form a network through which economic activity takes place. The process of structural change can influence the degree to which services are required throughout the whole economic system. The supply of services, in turn, makes it possible to attain greater specialisation and division of labour. These factors are essential in reinforcing the observed shift towards services employment.

In order to present the methodology, a sector will be defined as a cluster of branches (firms) producing commodities in agreement with a standard classification (NACE), and a sub-system as a group of different activities which are required in the economic system to produce a specific product or service. In the context of inter-industry relations, a sub-system consists of activities of different branches, all of which directly and indirectly contribute to the production of a specific final output.

The balance equation of output in an input-output table can be defined as:

$$x = A\,x + f \tag{6.1}$$

$$X = L\,F \tag{6.2}$$

where x is the vector of output by branch, A is the matrix of technical coefficients whose typical elements $a_{ij} = x_{ij} / \Sigma\, x_{ij}$ represent the value of the ith input needed to produce one unit of industry j's output; $L = (I-A)^{-1}$, known as the Leontief inverse, represents the total requirements per unit of final output in terms of gross output; X is the diagonalised vector x; and F is the diagonalised vector f of the final demand by industry. The intersectoral relationships presented in equation (6.1) for an open static economic system can be written as:

$$X = A^d x + f^d + e$$

$$X = L^d\,F \tag{6.3}$$

where A^d is the matrix of domestic coefficients, f^d is the domestic final demand vector for domestic outputs, e is the foreign demand or exports vector and the inverse $L^d = (I-A^d)^{-1}$ represents the total requirements per unit of final domestic output whose typical element is $l^d{}_{ij}$.

Technology intensity for each industry can be defined as the R&D or innovation directly incurred expenditure per output for industry i : $r_i = r_i / x_l$, whose diagonalised vector is R. Thus, the vector of technology or innovation embodiment ti can be expressed in diagonalised form as:

$$TI^d = R\,L^d\,F \tag{6.4}$$

This equation connects innovations to final domestic and foreign demand and the multiplier of total innovation embodiment per unit of final demand is $mi = \Sigma\, r_i\, l^d{}_{ij}$. Finally, in an open economy, imports are a source of technology diffusion, while production for exports induces demand for imported inputs.

$$m = A^m x + f^m = A^m L^d\,F + F^m = M(4)$$

$$TI^m = R* [A^m L^d\,F + F^m] \tag{6.5}$$

As was noted in the third section, conventional indicators of R&D or innovation intensity such as direct R&D per unit of output or value added, distort the measurement of total R&D and innovation of industries. Indicators that estimate total innovation embodiment per unit of output or (such as $mi = \Sigma\, r_i\, l^d{}_{ij}$ and $R^m A^m$) are more appropriate measures.

Table 6.2. Re-estimation of embodied technology intensity indicators by sector 1994

High technology sectors	R&D direct	Total R&D intensity	Innovation direct	Total Innovation intensity
28 Communications	15,9	16,5	80,6	83,1
13 Other transport n.e.c.	36,2	40,8	55,3	64,8
11 Electrical Machinery and electronic equipment	24,4	27,1	37,3	43,5
12 Motor vehicles	8,4	12,5	31,2	43,5
Medium technology sectors				
21 Rubber & Plastic Products	5,1	9,1	15,5	25,7
20 Publishing, Printing & Reproduction or recording media	0,4	3,6	12,7	24,5
30 Finance and insurance intermediation	*0,0*	*3,1*	*0,0*	*13,6*
10 Office and Computing Machinery	5,3	8,5	7,0	12,5
24 Recovery and repair	*0,0*	*4,7*	*0,0*	*12,4*
17 Leather products and footwear	0,6	2,9	3,4	11,5
29 Electricity, gas & water supply.	*2,8*	*4,2*	*5,2*	*10,5*
Lower technology sectors				
1 Agriculture, fishing	0,0	2,3	0,0	8,0
23 Construction	*0,0*	*2,2*	*0,0*	*7,3*
26 Hotels & restaurants	*0,0*	*1,4*	*0,0*	*7,0*
15 Tobacco products	2,0	2,6	4,5	6,9
27 Transport	*0,0*	*2,3*	*0,0*	*6,4*
33 Public services	*0,0*	*1,9*	*0,0*	*5,0*
32 Private social and personal services	*0,0*	*1,3*	*0,0*	*3,4*
31 Business services & real state	*0,0*	*0,6*	*0,0*	*2,8*
25 Wholesale & retail trade	*0,0*	*0,7*	*0,0*	*2,7*

Sources: Elaborated by the author based on R&D and innovation data (INE 1997 & 1999) and Input-Output tables for 1994 (INE, 2000).

Considering that R&D and innovation direct expenditures are reduced in most services with the exceptions of communications and electricity, gas and water distribution, the classification by sectors is blurred when considering the purchase of R&D and innovation inputs. The change is of particular significance for R&D users such as financial and insurance intermediaries and recovery and repair, and to a lesser extent for the rest of the services. In terms of innovation, table 6.2 shows similar results but the contribution of acquired innovation is relatively larger in sectors such as construction, hotels and restaurants and transport.

R&D expenditures are widely considered as indicators of technology intensity and the main determinant of economic growth and productivity. In Spain as well as in other "industrialised countries" these expenditures mainly originate in a few manufacturing industries such as: electronic machinery and electronic equipment, chemical products (including pharmaceutical) and other transport (including aerospace) (Papaconstantinou *et al*. 1996). A large share of the outputs of these "high technology" manufacturing sectors are demanded as intermediate inputs into the production process by different sectors and are also sold to final demand. In this way the direct R&D expenditures of the provider industries become embodied in products, process and services across the economic system.

The estimation of performed and acquired technology is estimated using input-output techniques and R&D and innovation expenditures. The shares of R&D and innovation are expressed in relative terms to the total indirect expenditures embodied in output using the methodology explained above (equations 6.4 and 6.5 for **TI**).

Table 6.3. Technology clusters of R&D and innovation. The 7 largest sectors in Spain in 1994

R&D providers	share	R&D users	share
11 Electrical machinery and electronic eq	18,05	24 Recovery and repair	6,8
7 Chemical products	15,92	21 Rubber & Plastic Products	6,4
13 Other transport n.e.c.	12,09	12 Motor vehicles	6,1
12 Motor vehicles	11,85	7 Chemical products	4,5
28 Communications	11,01	32 Private social and personal services	4,1
9 Machinery n.e.c.	6,90	4 Basic Metal Ferrous	4,1
29 Electricity, gas & water supply.	3,45	30 Finance and insurance int.	3,4
	79,28		35,3
		Total services	28,3

Innovation providers	share	Innovation users	share
28 Communications	17,31	1 Agriculture, fishing	6,2
12 Motor vehicles	13,76	24 Recovery and repair	6,0
14 Food & beverages	13,23	12 Motor vehicles	5,7
7 Chemical products	10,43	26 Hotel & restaurants	5,6
11 Electrical Machinery and electronic eq.	8,59	21 Rubber & Plastic Products	4,8
13 Other transport n.e.c.	5,74	30 Finance and insurance int.	4,6
9 Machinery n.e.c.	4,14	32 Private social and personal services	4,5
	73,21		37,4
		Total services	35,1

The picture that emerges in terms of R&D is, on the one hand, a concentrated cluster of "high technology" industries providing most of the R&D in the manufacturing sector and in certain services such as communication and electricity, gas and water distribution. On the other hand, the cluster of users is more disperse and includes different services and manufacturing activities, such as recovery and repair services, private and personal services and finance and insurance institutions.

In terms of innovation expenditures the picture that emerges is slightly different. The cluster of providers is still concentrated and includes some of the same industries than in R&D but also others such as food and beverages. The bulk of innovation is in communication and motor vehicles rather than in "high technology" manufacturing providers. Last but not least, the cluster of innovative users includes services that are not usually considered "high or medium technology intensive" such as: agriculture, forestry and fishery; recovery and repair services; hotels and restaurants; finance and insurance; and private social and personal services. Thus, many services industries act as the main users of technology and innovation and constitute significant R&D and innovative clusters.

6.5
Compositional Structural Change in Employment (Final and Intermediate Demand for Services)

In the second section the extent of the structural change has been examined and, in the third section, the direction of these changes in the face of technology intensities. A more precise definition of compositional structural change considers changes in the sectoral integration of an economy: output and employment shares reported for different sectors, and the changes in the inputs used by them. The advantage of this method is that it provides a detailed image of how the structure of an economic system and its linkages are at one moment, and how they have unfolded over time. The evaluation of both the extent and direction is connected to the broad sources of change for each sector, namely: final demand, import substitution and pattern of inter-industry linkages in the economy (referred to as technical change), and this represents the path of change followed to reach a specific sectoral structure.

The Input-Output (IO) technique enables changes in output and employment to be estimated, and it is also useful in helping to evaluate the relationship between employment and technology. The temporal variations of IO intermediate coefficients themselves reveal significant information about the technical change that operates in an economic system. In so doing, they represent an extension of previous measurements of structural change. A complementary IO analysis of employment and innovation is based on the concept of the sub-system and the notion of a vertically integrated sector, which was introduced by Sraffa (1960) and Pasinetti 1981) for theoretical purposes, but can also be used in applied terms (Sakurai 1993, Diaz Fuentes 1999).

The intersectoral relationships between branches and sub-systems from an IOT will be represented in a single table as matrix operator **B**. The last two terms on the right hand side of (6.2) $L^d F$ correspond to the actual amount of all domestic input that is directly and indirectly required for the production of a final commodity (column $_j$). When **X** is multiplied by the matrix $L^d F$ the operator **B** is obtained:

$$B = X L^d F \qquad (6.6)$$

This is the matrix of shares of production or **B** operators, the elements of which (b_{ij}) shows the share of total output x_i which is required in the sub-system j. The sum of these elements is one. The results of matrix operator **B** can be utilised to re-analyse variables associated with the production by branch such as employment, R&D and innovation. This can be disaggregated to the highest level (Terleckyj 1974, Barker 1990 and Sakurai 1997). In this case, the diagonalised vector of employment **û** by branch has been used to calculate the matrix of employment **U**:

$$U = û \, B$$

U shows, by rows, the amount of employment that each branch contributes to each sub-system (and of which the sums are the same total of **u**), and the columns of U show the employment of each sub-system. These matrices **B** and **U** disclose the direct and indirect shares of output and employment by sector and sub-system, and the indirect shares of output can be separated by replacing the Leontief inverse in (6.3) and (6.6) by **L - I**. With this methodology, employment in services can be separated by final and intermediate requirements.

Table 6.4

Employment in intermediate and final demand market services
(thousands of employees and percentage of total employment in services)

	1975	1980	1985	1989	1994
Intermediate	1.089	1.213	1.408	1.506	1.643
	26,0	*30,0*	*33,4*	*31,1*	*31,5*
Final	3.103	2.836	2.810	3.329	3.566
	74,0	*70,0*	*66,6*	*68,9*	*68,5*
	4.192	4.049	4.218	4.835	5.209

Employment in intermediate market services in manufacturing as a sub-system (thousands of employees and percentage of manufacturing sub-system)

	1975	1980	1985	1989	1994
Intermediate market service in Manufacturing	402	390	378	407	418
% of manufacturing subsystem	*16,1*	*18,0*	*19,1*	*22,1*	*28,1*

The general results that have been extracted can be summarised by the following two main points. First, Table 6.4 (top part) shows that the growth of market service employment in Spain was due mainly to an increase in intermediate demand; and this cannot be explained exclusively by the "stages of growth theory". This corresponds to the trends exhibited by the main advanced European countries that experienced constant growth in the share of employment due to intermediate market services since the 1960s. Therefore the growth of market service employment in the European economies is not directly, nor mainly, due to an increase in final demand, but rather to an increase in the intermediate demand of services. Second, Table 6.4 (bottom part) shows that the expansion in intermediate demand for services is accompanied by their increasing use in the production of manufactured goods in Spain, and this corresponds with the trends exhibited by the principal European economies throughout the considered period. This implies that the production of manufacturing goods goes beyond the industrial sector and requires increasing services.

6.6
Conclusions

This chapter has examined the expansion of employment in services that constitutes one of the most significant features of long term structural change in "industrialised economies". Four issues regarding structural change in employment in terms of innovation have been presented: structural change extension; direct technological intensity effects; embodied innovation; and the inter-industrial dimension in terms of the changes in the final and intermediate demand.

The most rapidly growing sectors in terms of employment in most "industrialised economies" have been services and in particular: FIREBS and CSPS. However, the increase in employment in WRTSRH has been significant in Spain, France and Italy, which have been at the same time the countries with the largest increases in service employment between 1980 and 1997. The observed patterns of the extension of structural change in employment do not indicate whether the growing role of services reflects a change in final demand, business demand or outsourcing to specialised services sectors.

Assuming the importance of technological innovation in international economic growth and productivity, and the fact that a few manufacturing industries concentrate most of the R&D surveyed expenditures, the correlation between direct technology intensity and employment was evaluated. It was observed that technological change determined structural change in employment in sub-sectors such as aerospace, office and computing machinery, telecommunications equipment, drugs and medicines and professional goods. Moreover, some services sectors such as FIREBS and CSPS acquire technology by purchasing and assimilating inputs embodied in innovation related to the previously mentioned high technology intensity manufacturing sub-sectors. However, it is notable that, although services are increasingly innovators, the existing indicators of R&D and technological intensity do not reflect the whole scope of innovation in services because traditional surveys have been designed for manufacturing.

One important element of innovation is the acquisition and not only the direct expenditures on R&D. To identify the inter-industrial flows of innovation taking place between sector below the aggregate levels input-output techniques were applied, in first instance, to analyse the embodied R&D and innovation technological flows with the purpose of measuring "total technology intensities" by sectors and sub-systems. Following a defined methodology it was noticed that the acquisition of technology was an important component of the innovation expenditures in services. Given the low level of direct technology intensity in services, the total innovation and R&D embodied intensity increased significantly in all services categories, but in particular in: finance and insurance, recovery and repair, electricity, gas and water distribution, hotels and restaurants and transport, which correspond with the aggregated trends envisaged in the second and third section. Moreover, given that a limited number of manufacturing sectors are the main providers of technology, the estimation of performed and acquired technology based on input-output techniques shows a concentrated cluster of high technology industries including communication services and a cluster of R&D and innovation users that includes recovery and repair, private and personal services, finance and insurance, and hotels and restaurants. Thus, many services act as the main users of technology and constitute a technology cluster which importance should be reconsidered in national survey on innovation (OECD 1995c).

This result points to the importance of policies of innovation diffusion in services. Although new technologies are concentrated in a small number of manufacturing industries that spend directly in R&D, the new process, products and services created in that industries generate benefits that become widespread through diffusion and use. The performance of an economic system depends on applying technology by using and adapting products, process and services generated elsewhere. This ability of the firms and industries is critical for the economic system's productivity and growth.

Finally, a more precise analysis of structural change was presented in the fifth section. This considered not only the extension and the technological direction component but also the broad sources of structural change from the intermediate and final demand side. Growth in service employment must be explained by considering the increasing integration between sectors (services and industry). This relationship can be explained by the following four factors. First, the increasing specialisation among sectors, which requires a complex network of services such as communications, transport, banks and insurance, recovery and repair, and after-sales services that link the different sub-systems. Second, the expansion in the foreign trade of goods and services, which is another perspective of specialisation. Third, the augmenting regulations (standards of quality or environment) which require specialised services (such as legal, tax, engineering, publicity, training, accounting, or finance and insurance). Fourth, the emergence of new economies of scale in the production of services, which induce a process of externalisation or outsourcing to specialised service sectors.

The application of intersectoral analysis in this research on Spain and other European countries has generated a different conclusion from that derived by the aggregated analysis, since the methodology allows the interpretation of the links between manufacturing and services, and the sets of innovation expenditures and employment that are directly and indirectly utilised in the productive systems.

References

Andersen, B. and Howells, J.: Innovation Dynamics in Services: Intellectual Property Rights as Indicators and Shaping Systems in Innovation. CRIC Discussion Paper No 8. Manchester, University of Manchester 1998

Barker, T.: Sources of Structural Change of the UK Service Industries 1979-1984. Economic System Research 2, 173-183 (1990)

Baumol, W.J.: The Macroeconomic of Unbalanced Growth. The Anatomy of the Urban Crisis. American Economic Review 57, 415-426 (1967)

Baumol, W. J., Blackman, S. A. B. and Wolf, E.: Productivity and American Leadership: The Long View. Cambridge MA, MIT Press 1989

Bell, D.: The Coming of Post-Industrial Society: A Venture in Social Forecasting. London, Heinemann 1974

CEC (Commission of the European Communities EUROSTAT), IMF (International Monetary Fund), OECD, UN (United Nations) and World Bank: System of National Accounts 1993. Brussels/Luxembourg, New York, EUROSTAT, IMF, OECD, UN and World Bank 1994

Chenery, H. B.: Growth and Transformation. In: H. Chenery, Robinson, S. and Syrquin, M. (Eds.), Industrialization and Growth. New York, World Bank-Oxford University Press 1986

Diaz-Fuentes, D.: Relaciones entre Cambio Tecnológico y Empleo a partir del Análisis Input-output: España 1980-1985. Revista de Economía y Sociología del Trabajo 19-20, 21-33 (1993)

Diaz-Fuentes, D.: On the Limits of the Post-Industrial Society: Structural Change and Service Sector Employment in Spain. International Review of Applied Economics 13(1), 111-24 (1993)

EUROSTAT (Statistical Office of the European Communities): European System of Integrated Economic Accounts, ESA. Luxembourg, EUROSTAT 1985

EUROSTAT (Statistical Office of the European Communities): Input-Output Tables, 1975-1980, (magnetic tape CEE IO TAB). Luxembourg, EUROSTAT 1987

EUROSTAT (Statistical Office of the European Communities): Coding System of the Input-Output Tables Database of Eurostat used on Magnetic Support (National Accounts Tables). Luxembourg, EUROSTAT 1992

EUROSTAT: The First European Innovation Survey. Luxembourg, EUROSTAT 1997

Freeman, C. and Soete, L.: Work for all or Mass Unemployment: Computerised Technical Change into the 21st Century. London, Pinter 1997

Fuchs, V. and Leveson, I.: The Service Economy. New York, National Bureau of Economic Research 1968

García-Perea, P. and Gomez, R.: Elaboración de Series Históricas de Empleo a partir de la Encuesta de Población Activa, D. 38668. Madrid, Banco de España 1994

Gershuny, J. and Miles, I.: The New Service Economy: the Transformation of Employment in Industrial Societies. London, Pinter 1983

Greenhalgh, C.; Gregory, M. and Ray, A.: Employment and Structural Change in Britain. Working Paper 44. Institute of Economics and Statistics. University of Oxford 1988

Grossman, G. and Helpman, E.: Endogenous Innovation and the Theory of Growth. Journal of Economic Perspectives 8(1), (1994)

INE (Instituto Nacional de Estadística): Encuesta sobre Innovación Tecnológica de las Empresas. INE, Madrid 1997a

INE: Estadistica sobre las Actividades en Investigacion Científica y Desarrollo Tecnológico (I+D) Indicadores Básicos 1994. INE, Madrid 1997b-annual

Kindleberger, C.: Economic Development. New York, McGraw-Hill 1958

Kravis, I. B., Heston, A. and Summer, R.: The Share of Service in Economic Growth. In: Adam, F. G. and Hickman, B. G. (Eds.) Global Econometrics. Essays in Honour of Lawrence R. Klein. Cambridge MA 1983

Layard, R., Nickell, S. and Jackman, R.: The Unemployment Crisis. Oxford, Oxford University Press 1994

OECD (Organisation for Economic Cooperation and Development): Historical Statistics 1960. Paris, OECD 1960 (annual a)

OECD (Organisation for Economic Cooperation and Development): Basic Science and Technology Statistics 1993. Paris, OECD 1960 (annual b)

OECD (Organisation for Economic Cooperation and Development): The OECD STAN database for Industrial Analysis OECD. Paris, OECD 1960 (annual c)

OECD (Organisation for Economic Cooperation and Development): Structural Change and Industrial Performance. Paris, OECD 1992

OECD (Organisation for Economic Cooperation and Development): The Measurement of Scientific and Technologic Activities: Proposed Standard Practices for Surveys of Research and Experimental Development (Frascati Manual 1993). Paris, OECD 1994

OECD (Organisation for Economic Cooperation and Development): ISDB Version 1995 - International Sector Data-base. Paris, OECD 1995a

OECD (Organisation for Economic Cooperation and Development): Services Innovation: Statistical and Conceptual Issues. Paris, OECD 1995b

OECD (Organisation for Economic Cooperation and Development): The Input-Ouput Database. Paris, OECD 1995c

OECD (Organisation for Economic Cooperation and Development): Oslo Manual, Proposed Guidelines for Collecting and Interpreting Technological Innovation Data. Paris, OECD 1997

OECD (Organisation for Economic Cooperation and Development): Science, Technology and Industry Outlook. Paris, OECD 1998

OECD (Organisation for Economic Cooperation and Development): Strategic Business Services. Paris, OECD 1999

Pasinetti, L.: Structural Change and Economic Growth. A Theoretical Essay on the Dynamic of Wealth of Nations. Cambridge, Cambridge University Press 1981

Papaconstantinou, G., Sakurai, N. and Wyckoff, A.: Embodied Technology Diffusion: an Emprical Analysis for ten OECD Countries. STI Working Paper 1966/1/OCDE/GD(96)26. OCDE 1996

Rostow, W. W.: The Stages of Economic Growth: a Non-communist Manifesto. Cambridge, Cambridge University Press 1960

Sakurai, N.: Structural Change and Employment: Empirical Evidence for Eight OECD Countries. Paper of the Helsinki Conference on Technology, Innovation Policy and Employment 7-9, October. Paris, OECD 1993

Sakurai, N., Ioannidis, E. and Papaconstantinou, G.: Impact of R&D and Technology Diffusion on Productivity Growth: Empirical Evidence for 10 OECD Countries. Economic System Research 9(1), 81-110 (1996)

Sraffa, P.: Production of Commodities by Means of Commodities. Cambridge, Cambridge University Press 1956

Tomlinson, M.: The Contribution of Services to Manufacturing Industry: Beyond the De-industrialisation. Debate, CRIC Discussion Paper 5. Manchester, University of Manchester 1997

Working Group on Innovation and Technology Policy: Promoting Innovation and Growth in Services. DSTI/STP/TIP(99)4. Paris, OECD 1999

Young, A.: Measuring R&D in the Services. STI Working Paper 1996/7. Paris, OECD 1996

PART III. MARKET AND INDUSTRIAL STRUCTURE

7 The Measurement of Intra-industry Trade and Specialisation: a Review

Gema Carrera-Gómez
Department of Economics
University of Cantabria (Spain)

The assessment of the relevance of the new theories of trade as opposed to the traditional theoretical approach, when it comes to explain real trade patterns, is essentially an empirical question. Nevertheless, there are two problems (which remain unsolved) which influence the results obtained when measuring intra-industry trade and specialisation. The first problem refers to the very existence of the phenomenon and is related to the definition of "industry" and the selection of the level of data dissagregation more appropriate to study such a phenomenon. The second problem, closely connected to the former, comes from the objective difficulty of finding a convenient quantitative measure.

This chapter is devoted to the analysis of the obstacles faced by empirical treatment of intra-industry trade. With this purpose, we present first in 7.1 a general critical overview of the main measurement indices proposed by the literature. We deal next in 7.2 with two important problems of measurement: the adjustment of global trade imbalance and the question of categorical aggregation. Finally, in 7.3 we offer a summary of the main conclusions reached regarding these aspects of intra-industry trade.

7.1
Measures of Intra-industry Trade and Specialisation

Intra-industry trade may be defined as simultaneously importing and exporting products belonging to a particular country and the same industry. This phenomenon comes usually accompanied by intra-industry specialisation, which is the concentration of production factors in particular groups of products inside an industry, at the expense of other production lines. Although both expressions are often indiscriminately used, they refer to two different aspects.

Therefore, at a conceptual level, it is possible to establish a distinction between intra-industry trade and intra-industry specialisation. According to that distinction and following the classification provided by Greenaway and Milner (1986) and Kol and Mennes (1983, 1986), we can differentiate two broad categories of indices regarding empirical measurement of the aforementioned concepts:

i) Indices determining the extension of intra-industry trade by measuring the level of overlap existing in trade flows.
ii) Indices of intra-industry specialisation, which are measuring the degree of similarity of trade patterns (relative structure of imports and exports).

We next present separately the main indices used for the measurement of both aspects. Later, a comparison is made among the diverse measures and a suggestion is proposed as to which may be more appropriate according to the purpose of the analysis to be performed. Finally, we summarise in subsection 7.1.4 the later developments on the measurement of intra-industry trade and mention the current unresolved issues on the subject.

7.1.1 Intra-industry Trade Indices

The question of intra-industry trade measurement and the inherent problems was first explicitly analysed in early works of Grubel and Lloyd (1971, 1975). Nevertheless, some previous papers (Verdoon, 1960; Michaely, 1962; Kojima, 1964; Balassa, 1966) already provided several procedures which could be applied to the measurement of intra-industry trade; although, that was not the main purpose of these works.

Verdoorn (1960) used the following indicator to examine changes in trade patterns in the Benelux:

$$S_j = \frac{X_j}{M_j}$$

where X_j and M_j are exports and imports of commodity j and S_j takes values inside the interval $[\ 0\ ,\ +\infty\ )$. When the value of the index comes closer to unity along time, it would be an indicator of increasing intra-industry specialisation.

The disadvantage of this measure, as Grubel and Lloyd (1975) already pointed out, is that any fraction and its inverse measure the same level of intra-industry trade, what makes it complicated to compare among industries. It can be seen that, except for the case where $S_j = 1$, this indicator does not measure directly the degree in which imports and exports overlap in a specific group of products.

Kojima (1964) solved this problem by defining the degree of "horizontal trade" in a group of products j between two countries A and B as follows:

$$D_j = \frac{X_j}{M_j} \ \text{if} \ M_j > X_j$$

and

$$D_j = \frac{M_j}{X_j} \quad \text{if } M_j < X_j$$

D_j takes values inside the interval $[0, 1]$, making it easier comparison among industries. The value of the index approaches unity as the degree of "horizontal trade" increases[1]. Although the index D_j represents an improvement compared to the Verdoorn (1960) measure, both indices share a problem: the use of ratios between trade flows is not giving a direct measure of intra-industry trade as a proportion of total trade.

Kojima (1964) also provided an aggregated indicator of "horizontal trade" between two countries. The aggregated index was a weighted sum of indices D_j using as weight the share of trade of commodity group j in total trade. This aggregated indicator was defined as follows:

$$\overline{D} = \sum_{j=1}^{n}\left(\frac{X_j}{M_j} \cdot \frac{X_j + M_j}{\sum_{j=1}^{n}(X_j + M_j)} \right) = \sum_{j=1}^{n} D_j \cdot w_j \,, \text{ if } M_j > X_j$$

$$\overline{D} = \sum_{j=1}^{n}\left(\frac{M_j}{X_j} \cdot \frac{X_j + M_j}{\sum_{j=1}^{n}(X_j + M_j)} \right) = \sum_{j=1}^{n} D_j \cdot w_j \,, \text{ if } M_j < X_j$$

where n is the number of groups considered and $w_j = \dfrac{X_j + M_j}{\sum_{j=1}^{n}(X_j + M_j)}$ [2].

In a work aimed at analysing the effects of the completion of the Common Market on international specialisation in EC countries, Balassa (1966) proposed the

---

[1] Note that D_j is equal to S_j when $M_j > X_j$ and it is equal to S_j^{-1} when $M_j < X_j$.

[2] Note that it is in fact a weighted mean since the sum of weights is unity.

$$\sum_{j=1}^{n} w_j = \sum_{j=1}^{n}\left(\frac{X_j + M_j}{\sum_{j=1}^{n}(X_j + M_j)} \right) = 1.$$

For this reason and from now on, we will call mean the type of weighted sums in which the sum of weights is 1.

following indices to measure the degree of overlapping between exports and imports:

$$A_j = \frac{\left|X_j - M_j\right|}{X_j + M_j} \text{ for commodity group } j,$$

and

$$\overline{A}_j = \frac{1}{n}\sum_{j=1}^{n}A_j \text{, as an aggregate index for } n \text{ groups of products.}$$

where $\overline{A}_j$ is an arithmetic mean of indices A_j for a specific level of disaggregation. Therefore, this procedure of aggregation has the following shortcoming: it gives the same weight $(1/n)$ to all industries independent of their share in total trade.

The A_j index is inversely related to the degree of intra-industry trade. It takes values from 1 (when all trade is inter-industrial) to 0 (when all trade is intra-industrial). It has the advantage compared to previous measures of giving information on the proportion of total trade that is of the intra-industry type.

Another important point to mention is that, as a result of expressing net trade as a proportion of total trade in a specific group of products, absolute values of imports and exports that may be quite different may produce the same value of the index[3].

Moreover, suppose that commodity group j is formed by a number of subgroups m (which will be denoted by the subindex i). In this case, A_j may be expressed as follows:

$$A_j = \frac{\left|\sum_{i=1}^{m}(X_{ij} - M_{ij})\right|}{\sum_{i=1}^{m}(X_{ij} + M_{ij})}$$

Assuming that either $(X_{ij}-M_{ij}) < 0, \forall i = 1, 2, .., m,$ or $(X_{ij}-M_{ij}) > 0, \forall i = 1, 2, .., m,$ then:

$$\left|\sum_{i=1}^{m}(X_{ij} - M_{ij})\right| = \sum_{i=1}^{m}\left|X_{ij} - M_{ij}\right|$$

and we can write:

---

[3] Note, for instance, that A_j is always 0 when X_j equals M_j, independent of the actual value of imports and exports.

$$A_j = \frac{\sum\limits_{i=1}^{m} \left| X_{ij} - M_{ij} \right|}{\sum\limits_{i=1}^{m} (X_{ij} + M_{ij})} = \sum\limits_{i=1}^{m} \frac{\left| X_{ij} - M_{ij} \right|}{(X_j + M_j)}$$

Multiplying and dividing by $(X_{ij} + M_{ij})$:

$$A_j = \sum\limits_{i=1}^{m} \frac{\left| X_{ij} - M_{ij} \right|}{(X_{ij} + M_{ij})} \cdot \frac{(X_{ij} + M_{ij})}{(X_j + M_j)} = \sum\limits_{i=1}^{m} A_{ij} \cdot w_{ij}$$

where $A_{ij} = \dfrac{\left| X_{ij} - M_{ij} \right|}{(X_{ij} + M_{ij})}$ is the correspondent index for subgroup i and where

$$w_{ij} = \frac{(X_{ij} + M_{ij})}{(X_j + M_j)} = \frac{(X_{ij} + M_{ij})}{\sum\limits_{i=1}^{m} (X_{ij} + M_{ij})}$$ is the weight for that subgroup i.

Therefore, A_j is a weighted average of the indices of the subgroups that form a group j only when the sign of trade imbalance is the same for all the subgroups. This weighting effect is lost, nevertheless, when there are trade imbalances of opposite sign.

In general, a weighted average may be more suitable when we want to obtain a *compendium* measure, which reflects the relative importance of intra-industry trade at a particular level of aggregation[4]. This is so specifically when such a *compendium* index refers to an economy in a wide sense, including all trade. On the other hand, if the level of aggregation that has been selected to calculate individual indices closely corresponds to the researcher's view of homogeneity inside a group or industry, weighting individual indices may be inappropriate.

Greenaway and Milner (1986) propose the following procedure to guarantee the weighting effect of the index:

$$A'_j = \frac{\sum\limits_{i=1}^{m} \left| X_{ij} - M_{ij} \right|}{X_j + M_j}$$

Note that multiplying and dividing by $(X_{ij} + M_{ij})$ we have:

$$A'_j = \sum\limits_{i=1}^{m} \frac{\left| X_{ij} - M_{ij} \right|}{(X_{ij} + M_{ij})} \cdot \frac{(X_{ij} + M_{ij})}{(X_j + M_j)} = \sum\limits_{i=1}^{m} A_{ij} \cdot w_{ij}$$

---

[4] For instance, if we want to show the relevance of intra-industry trade in subgroups i, we would want A_j to be a weighted average of indices A_{ij}.

where $w_{ij} = \dfrac{(X_{ij} + M_{ij})}{(X_j + M_j)}$.

Therefore, when all the subgroups trade imbalances have the same sign, the relationship $A_j^{'} = A_j$ holds.

Using the same procedure it is possible to obtain *global* weighted averages of all indices A_j, that is:

$$\overline{A}_j^{'} = \frac{\sum\limits_{j=1}^{n} \left| X_j - M_j \right|}{\sum\limits_{j=1}^{n} (X_j - M_j)} = \sum\limits_{j=1}^{n} A_j \cdot w_j$$

where $w_j = \dfrac{(X_j + M_j)}{\sum\limits_{j=1}^{n} X_j + \sum\limits_{j=1}^{n} M_j}$.

That is to say, the weight employed is the ratio volume of trade in industry j to total trade.

Grubel and Lloyd (1975) proposed an index according to which the share of intra-industry trade in total trade flows of an industry j can be computed by the following expression:

$$B_j = \frac{(X_j + M_j) - \left| X_j - M_j \right|}{(X_j + M_j)} = 1 - \frac{\left| X_j - M_j \right|}{(X_j + M_j)}$$

where $0 \le B_j \le 1$.

The average of indices B_j for a set of industries ($j=1, 2, 3, ..., n$) may be computed as follows[5]:

$$\overline{B}_j = \sum\limits_{j=1}^{n} w_j \cdot B_j = \sum\limits_{j=1}^{n} \frac{(X_j + M_j)}{\sum\limits_{j=1}^{n} (X_j + M_j)} \cdot \frac{(X_j + M_j) - \left| X_j - M_j \right|}{(X_j + M_j)} =$$

$$= \frac{\sum\limits_{j=1}^{n} (X_j + M_j) - \sum\limits_{j=1}^{n} \left| X_j - M_j \right|}{\sum\limits_{j=1}^{n} (X_j + M_j)} = 1 - \frac{\sum\limits_{j=1}^{n} \left| X_j - M_j \right|}{\sum\limits_{j=1}^{n} (X_j + M_j)},$$

---

[5] Note that the same weighting procedure as in index $\overline{A}_j^{'}$ is used.

where $\sum_{j=1}^{n} \left| X_j - M_j \right| \neq \left| \sum_{j=1}^{n} (X_j - M_j) \right|$ when the sign of trade imbalances is not the same for all industries.

The advantage of index $\overline{B}_j$ when compared to Balassa's $\overline{A}_j$ is that the latter gives the same weight to all industries, whereas the former takes into account the share of industry j trade in total trade.

A potential shortcoming of the aggregated G-L index $\overline{B}_j$ is that it introduces a downward bias in the measurement of intra-industry trade when total trade is not balanced, that is when $\sum_{j=1}^{n} X_j \neq \sum_{j=1}^{n} M_j$. In this case imports and exports cannot match exactly in all industries and therefore the index can never reach its maximum value 1. Grubel and Lloyd propose a correction procedure to deal with this problem, which we will discuss in section 7.2, totally devoted to trade imbalance adjustments.

On the other hand, it can be noted that index B_j is a modification of Balassa's A_j[6], sharing the same properties concerning the weighting effect. However B_j is directly related to the level of intra-industry trade. It reaches its maximum value when total trade is of the intra-industry type and its value is zero when there is no matching at all between exports and imports in a specific industry.

The same comments we have pointed out for the Balassa (1966) index concerning the trade imbalances opposite sign effects hold for the B_j index. If we consider the industry j composed of m subgroups i, we can rewrite the B_j index as follows:

$$B_j = \frac{\sum_{i=1}^{m}\left(X_{ij} + M_{ij}\right) - \left|\sum_{i=1}^{m}\left(X_{ij} - M_{ij}\right)\right|}{\sum_{i=1}^{m}\left(X_{ij} + M_{ij}\right)}$$

There is, however, an alternative aggregating procedure, which will provide the following index:

$$B_j^* = \sum_{i=1}^{m} w_{ij} \cdot B_{ij} = \frac{\sum_{i=1}^{m}\left(X_{ij} + M_{ij}\right) - \sum_{i=1}^{m}\left|X_{ij} - M_{ij}\right|}{\sum_{i=1}^{m}\left(X_{ij} + M_{ij}\right)}$$

---

[6] $B_j = 1 - A_j$.

where $w_{ij} = \dfrac{(X_{ij} + M_{ij})}{(X_j + M_j)} = \dfrac{(X_{ij} + M_{ij})}{\sum\limits_{i=1}^{m}(X_{ij} + M_{ij})}$ and $B_{ij} = 1 - \dfrac{\left|X_{ij} - M_{ij}\right|}{(X_{ij} + M_{ij})}$.

As $\sum\limits_{i=1}^{m}\left|X_{ij} - M_{ij}\right| \geq \left|\sum\limits_{i=1}^{m}(X_{ij} - M_{ij})\right|$, we have that $B_j \geq B_j^*$

As we commented before, the question to consider is which procedure is more suitable. If the trade flows to aggregate are not homogeneous from the intra-industry trade point of view (that is, if they are not belonging to the same *industry*) it doesn't seem desirable trade imbalance to cancel among themselves. In this case, B_j^* would be a more convenient measure to use. On the other hand, if trade flows to aggregate are homogeneous, the use of B_j would be preferable. Nevertheless, the problem in practice consists of finding out if a group of products included under a concrete level of aggregation by a classification system can be considered as homogeneous from the perspective of intra-industry trade. That is to say, if this commodity group constitutes an *industry*. International trade flows classification systems may include under the same group products with very different factor requirements. This gives rises to the denominated categorical aggregation problem, which will be treated in section 7.3.

Moreover, as B_j measures the degree of trade overlapping in a commodity group or industry j related to total trade in the industry, the behaviour of the index is affected by changes in total trade among industries and/or over time. For example, a high degree of trade overlapping may be registered in a specific industry in which the volume of trade is relatively small compared to total trade in manufactures. Besides, the volume of trade in an industry may or may not vary directly with the level of production or the level of sales.

Other features of index B_j are its simetry regarding X_j and M_j and its non-linearity[7].

A different way of addressing the question of intra-industry trade measurement is provided by Vona (1991). This author takes as elementary units the 5 digit SITC items[8] and points out that, for this high level of disaggregation, all trade is to be considered as intra-industry trade or inter-industry trade depending on the existence of two way flows[9]. Vona proposes the following intra-industry trade index for bilateral exports between two countries A and B in a commodity group i:

$$I_{A,B,i} = X_{A,B,i} + X_{B,A,i}, \text{ if } X_{A,B,i} \quad 0 \text{ and } X_{B,A,i} \quad 0$$

---

[7] For an illustration of these features of B_j see Carrera (1996).

[8] Standard International Trade Classification.

[9] According to this approach industries may be classified under two categories. A first group of industries is characterised by scale economies, product differentiation and imperfect competition, giving rise to intra-industry trade. A second group is formed by industries under perfect competition producing homogeneous goods (according to the H-O-S model), which leads to inter-industry trade.

$$I_{A,B,i} = 0 \text{ , if } X_{A,B,i} = 0 \text{ or } X_{B,A,i} = 0$$

where

$X_{A,B,i}$ = exports from country A to country B in commodity group i (5 digit SITC item)

$X_{B,A,i}$ = exports from country B to country A in commodity group i (5 digit SITC item)

Vona calculates an aggregated index for 3 digit SITC groups j from 5 digit SITC items i as follows:

$$I_{A,B,j} = \frac{\sum\limits_{i=1}^{n} I_{A,B,i}}{X_{A,B,j} + X_{B,A,j}} \cdot 100$$

where

$X_{A,B,j}$ = exports from country A to country B in commodity group j (3 digit SITC)

$X_{B,A,j}$ = exports from country B to country A in commodity group j (3 digit SITC)

Vona's indicator takes values in the interval $[0, 100]$. It is 0 when all $I_{A,B,i} = 0$ and there is no intra-industry trade and it is 100 when all $I_{A,B,i}$ 0 and all trade is intra-industry trade.

As a feature of this indicator Vona mentions that it is not affected by the existence of trade imbalances, as all trade (imports and exports) is considered intra-industry trade or inter-industry trade independent of the exact coincidence of the volumes of imports and exports[10]. Nevertheless, the problem of sensitivity of the index to the number of items included in every industry still remains unsolved. That is, the intra-industry index tends to decrease as the number of subgroups included in an industry increases.

7.1.2 Intra-industry Specialisation Indices

Michaely (1962) proposed the following indicator to measure the degree of overlapping between the share of exports and the share of imports in a commodity group j:

$$\overline{H} = 1 - \frac{1}{2} \cdot \sum_{j=1}^{n} \left| \frac{X_j}{\sum\limits_{j=1}^{n} X_j} - \frac{M_j}{\sum\limits_{j=1}^{n} M_j} \right|.$$

---

[10] According to this point of view it is not the degree of overlapping between imports and exports what matters, but the mere existence of exchange of products in both directions.

The indices ranges from 0 to 1[11], higher values suggesting a higher degree of similarity in the composition of exports and imports. A value of 0 would imply perfect inter-industry trade, with non-existence of simultaneous exports and imports in a specific commodity group for a country during the time period considered[12].

Balassa (1966) introduces the concept of "revealed" comparative advantage and proposes the following indicator to measure it:

$$RCA = \frac{X_j}{X_{gj}} \Big/ \frac{X}{X_g}$$

where $\dfrac{X_j}{X_{gj}}$ indicates the share of a country in world exports of commodity j and

$\dfrac{X}{X_g}$ is the share of a country in world exports of manufactured products.

When the value of the index tends to 0, it would be indicating a "revealed" comparative disadvantage for industry j, while a value above 1 would identify a comparative advantage in the correspondent industry[13]. From a general point of view, this index is measuring similarity in trade patterns and thus it can be employed to measure intra-industry specialisation[14]. As we will show later, the

---

[11] Note that it is feasible for $\overline{H}$ to reach unity without global trade balance ($\sum_{j=1}^{n} X_j = \sum_{j=1}^{n} M_j$) or without trade balance in industry j ($X_j = M_j$). Actually $\overline{H} = 1$ when the following condition is satisfied:

$$\frac{X_j}{\sum_{j=1}^{n} X_j} = \frac{M_j}{\sum_{j=1}^{n} M_j}.$$

[12] The index originally proposed by Michaely was actually the following:

$$D = \sum_{j=1}^{n} \left| \frac{X_j}{\sum_{j=1}^{n} X_j} - \frac{M_j}{\sum_{j=1}^{n} M_j} \right|.$$

This indicator ranges from 0 to 2. Index $\overline{H}$ (which ranges from 0 to 1) is just an adaptation of D in order to make it easier comparison to other measures.

[13] A value of RCA = 1.1, for example, would indicate that the share of a country in exports of commodity j is 10% higher than its share in total exports of manufactures.

[14] Aquino (1978) is using the standard deviation of Balassas's index as a measure of the intensity of inter-industry specialisation in a country. A deviation of 0 would indicate the absence of inter-industry specialisation while higher dispersion of the values of the index would point at higher inter-industry specialisation.

index is, in fact, equivalent to the measure proposed by Glejser, Goossens and Vanden Eede (1982) aimed at measuring intra-industry specialisation in foreign trade.

Finger and Kreinin (1979) develop an indicator that uses the share of every industry's exports in a country's total exports to measure the degree of similarity of export patterns from two countries (a and b) to a third market (c). The indicator was computed as follows:

$$S\ (ab,\ c) = \sum_{j=1}^{n} \min\ [X_j\ (ac),\ X_j\ (bc)],$$

where X_j (ac) is the share of industry j in the exports from country a to country c and X_j (bc) is the share of industry j in the exports from country b to country c. The indicator takes the same values than the index of Michaely (1962) and, in fact, both measures are equivalent, as it is shown in Kol (1988). For this reason, Michaely's index can be used to compare trade patterns from many points of view. It can be employed, for instance, to compare imports and exports patterns in a country, exports (or imports) patterns for two countries or a group of countries, among them or related to a third market.

Glejser, Goossens and Vanden Eede (1979) mark a break with previous methodology and propose a conceptually different approach to quantify the magnitude and variations of intra-industry trade. Unlike other measures that consider simultaneously imports and exports, these authors make a distinction between supply specialisation (exports) and demand specialisation (imports). The indicators are built on the assumption that a country is specialised in a specific industry when it exports (or imports) relatively more than a group of conveniently selected countries.

The comparative supply specialisation for a given time period can be computed as follows:

$$\xi = \frac{1}{n} \sum_{j=1}^{n} \log\left(\frac{X_j}{X} \Big/ \frac{X_{gj}}{X_g}\right) = \frac{1}{n} \sum_{j=1}^{n} \xi_j$$

where:

n = number of industries considered
X_j = exports from industry j made from a country to the group of countries considered
X = total exports from a country to the group of countries considered
X_{gj} = total exports from industry j made by the group of countries considered (except for the country that is being analysed)
X_g = total exports from the group of countries considered (except for the country that is being analysed)

The index of comparative demand specialisation is similarly computed as follows:

$$\mu = \frac{1}{n} \sum_{j=1}^{n} \log\left(\frac{M_j}{M} \middle/ \frac{M_{gj}}{M_g}\right) = \frac{1}{n} \sum_{j=1}^{n} \mu_j$$

where:

n = number of industries considered

M_j = imports from industry j made from a country to the group of countries considered

M = total imports from a country to the group of countries considered

M_{gj} = total imports from industry j made by the group of countries considered (except for the country that is being analysed)

M_g = total imports from the group of countries considered (except for the country that is being analysed)

A higher divergence between X_j/X and X_{gj}/X_g and between M_j/M and M_{gj}/M_g is to be expected with a higher degree of inter-industry specialisation. On the other hand, if intra-industry specialisation is dominating, the quotiens $(X_j/X)/(X_{gj}/X_g)$ and $(M_j/M)/(M_{gj}/M_g)$ approach unity in every industry j and, consequently, the unweighted means $\xi = \frac{1}{n} \sum_{j=1}^{n} \xi_j$ and $\mu = \frac{1}{n} \sum_{j=1}^{n} \mu_j$ approach zero.

The variability among industries, that is, the variances of ξ and μ can be computed as follows:

$$S_\xi^2 = \frac{1}{n} \sum_{j=1}^{n} \left(\xi_j - \xi\right)^2$$

$$S_\mu^2 = \frac{1}{n} \sum_{j=1}^{n} \left(\mu_j - \mu\right)^2$$

Kol and Mennes (1986) and Kol (1988) establish an equivalence between this indicator and the one introduced by Balassa (1966) to measure "revealed" comparative advantage based on the share of exports from every industry in total world exports[15]. Although the purpose of those authors was not the same, both indicators are able to measure "revealed" comparative advantage and intra-industry specialisation in the form the authors define such concepts.

7.1.3 Comparison of Measures

In previous subsections we have examined two groups or families of measures and evaluated the most commonly used indices of intra-industry trade and

---

[15] Operating in RCA we obtain the following relationship with the index of Glejser, Goossens and Vanden Eede:

$\xi_j = \log (RCA)$.

specialisation. The first group of indicators is mainly based on the degree of overlapping of imports and exports in every industry[16]. The second group of measures takes into account the degree of similarity in relative structure of imports and exports.

Concerning the first family of measures, the following considerations can be mentioned:

- The index S_j introduced by Verdoorn (1960) has the following shortcomings:

a) Every fraction and its inverse measure the same degree of intra-industry trade, making it complicated to compare among industries.

b) The index is not giving a direct measure of intra-industry trade as a proportion of total trade.
- The index D_j introduced by Kojima (1964) is solving the former problem in a) but the problem in b) remains unsolved.
- The measure A_j introduced by Balassa (1966) has, compared to the previous ones, the advantage that it gives information on the proportion of total trade that is of the intra-industry type. However, it has the unattractive feature of being inversely related to the degree of intra-industry trade. Moreover, the aggregated measure $\overline{A}_j$ is giving the same weight to all industries, independent on their share in total trade.
- Grubel and Lloyd (1975) introduce the index B_j, which is the most widely used in the empirical measurement of intra-industry trade. The B_j index shares some features of the A_j index of Balassa (1966) but has the advantage of being directly related to the level of intra-industry trade. Moreover, the aggregated measure $\overline{B}_j$ is preferable to $\overline{A}_j$ because it takes into account the share of every industry in total trade unlike the later, which gives the same weight to every industry.
- The index $I_{A, B, i}$ of Vona (1991) gives a different approach to the problem of intra-industry trade measurement. It has the advantage of not being influenced by trade imbalance. However, its use at the empirical level is complicated because the information on the high level of data disaggregation required[17] is not easily available and it is difficult to handle.

From the previous analysis it can be concluded that the indicators proposed by Grubel and Lloyd (1975) are the more convenient among those indices that form the first group of measures.

Concerning the second family of measures a distinction can be made among those that are using differences in relative shares of imports and exports in total respective flows (Michaely, 1962; Finger-Kreinin, 1979) and those, which are using quotients among such shares (Balassa, 1966; Glejser, Goossens y Vanden Eede, 1979). Following Kol (1988) and with the purpose of making it easier to compare both groups of measures we will first express the index of Balassa (1966) in terms of the indicator of Michaely (1962):

---

[16] Except for the index of Vona (1991).

[17] Vona proposes the 5-digit SITC level of aggregation.

$$RCA = \frac{X_j}{X} \Big/ \frac{M_j}{M}$$

This indicator has some shortcomings. First, it has to be corrected in case $M_j = 0$, a case not uncommon at high levels of data disaggregation. Second, while a total similarity of trade patterns gives a value zero for the index, in case of increasing dissimilarity the value of the indicator tends to zero or ∞. This unlimited range of values complicates the interpretation of results concerning the degree of dissimilarity of trade patterns. A third problem is the following: when changing numerator and denominator we obtain completely different values of the index (and the variance of the sample). The degree of similarity is however the same[18]. Finally, the use of quotients to compare trade patterns gives rise to a fourth problem. Imports and exports with a comparatively small value but very different shares in total respective flows may influence the value of the index in an undesirable way, by increasing it in case of high similarity of exports and imports patterns[19].

On the other hand, the index provided by Michaely (1962) has none of these disadvantages. Values of $X_j = 0$ or $M_j = 0$ are not a problem. The interpretation of results is easier because the index range from 0 (complete dissimilarity) to 1 (complete similarity). The third and fourth problems do not apply here because differences are used rather than quotients. Because of all these reasons it can be concluded that, when trying to measure the degree of similarity of trade patterns, it is preferable to use Michaely's index. As stated before, this indicator has a wide range of applications in numerous situations and it is suitable to compare trade patterns from diverse points of view.

Two criteria have been thus basically used when it comes to measuring intra-industry trade's intensity: the magnitude of trade flows and the similarity in relative structure of imports and exports. These two criteria give rise to two families of indices, which are not strictly comparable. However, Silber and Broll (1990) show that both types of measures[20] can be alternatively expressed as measures of distance or measures of similarity, deriving the corresponding family of indices. The empirical section of their work shows that, although the two groups of indices measure different types of distances or equalities, both are highly correlated.

---

[18] Using the logarithm of the indicator may solve this third problem. This is, in fact, what Glejser, Goossens and Vanden Eede are doing. In this case, when changing numerator and denominator, the indicator changes its sign but not its value. However, the aggregated index still ranges from 0 to . The second problem remains thus unsolved.

[19] Kol (1988) is giving an illustrative example of this feature.

[20] That is, those that are based on the degree of overlapping of trade flows and those based on the similarity of trade patterns.

7.1.4 Later Developments

In later years a great deal of work on IIT measurement has concentrated in two refinements of the traditional Grubel-Lloyd index. One of them is aimed at measuring what has been called marginal IIT, an issue related to the analysis of adjustment costs associated to trade liberalisation. The other one is targeted at adjusting IIT measures to disentangle vertical and horizontal IIT.

7.1.4.1 Measuring Marginal Intra-industry Trade

It is generally assumed that the costs of the adjustment process following trade liberalisation may differ depending on whether the new trade generated is classified as inter-industry or intra-industry trade. If emerging trade has an intra-industry nature the adjustment costs will be probably lower, because in this case reallocation is to take place within every industry rather than among different industries. When analysing the adjustment consequences of trade expansion, what is relevant is not the current level of IIT but the composition of changes in exports and imports. In other words, how IIT changes at the margin.

To capture this important issue, Hamilton and Kniest (1991) developed a measure, which calculated the share of IIT in new trade flows as follows:

$$MIIT = \begin{cases} \dfrac{X_t - X_{t-n}}{M_t - M_{t-n}} \text{ for } M_t - M_{t-n} > X_t - X_{t-n} > 0 \\[3mm] \dfrac{M_t - M_{t-n}}{X_t - X_{t-n}} \text{ for } X_t - X_{t-n} > M_t - M_{t-n} > 0 \end{cases}$$

where X_j and M_j refer to exports and imports of commodity group j and t and $t\text{-}n$ refer to the two points in time taken into consideration. The index is calculating the proportion of the increase in imports or exports that is matched. When all new trade is matched (the increase in imports totally matches the increase in exports for a particular industry) the index will be unity. When all new trade is inter-industry trade (there is no matching at all between new imports and new exports for a concrete industry) the index will be zero.

The Hamilton and Kniest measure, although being a considerable improvement for the analysis of adjustment issues, has some important shortcomings, as several authors have pointed out [see, for example, Brülhart (1994) and Greenaway, Hine, Milner and Elliot (1994)]. First of all, the index cannot be calculated when the change in exports or imports is negative. Second, the measure is unscaled, that is to say, it is not related to total amount of new trade or to the initial level of trade or to the value of production in the industry considered. Third, the index measures the changes in nominal terms rather than in real ones. To address these shortcomings the aforementioned authors have proposed several alternatives providing a menu of indices (which deal with the scaling problem and are always defined) to choice depending on the purpose of the job at hand.

The Brülhart (1994) index has been widely used in later works on adjustment issues. This *dynamic* measure can be expressed as follows:

$$A_i = 1 - \frac{|\Delta X_i - \Delta M_i|}{|\Delta X_i| + |\Delta M_i|} = 1 - \frac{|(X_t - X_{t-n}) - (M_t - M_{t-n})|}{|X_t - X_{t-n}| + |M_t - M_{t-n}|},$$

where X_j and M_j refer to exports and imports of commodity i and t and t-n refer to the two points in time taken into consideration. The index has values ranging from 0 to 1, a value of 0 indicating that new trade is entirely of the inter-industry type and a value of 1 showing complete matching between new exports and imports in industry j and so lower transitional adjustment costs. The measure is dynamic in the sense that it provides information on the proportion of changes in total trade flows that are of an intra-industry type.

Recent work by Thom and McDowell (1999) shows that the proposed marginal intra-industry trade indicators [such as Brülhart (1994)] may be underestimating the extent of intra-industry trade as they cannot distinguish between inter-industry trade and vertical intra-industry trade. These authors propose an alternative procedure of classifying marginal trade flows based on the joint application of the Brülhart's index and the aggregate measure defined as follows:

$$A_j = 1 - \frac{|\Delta X_j - \Delta M_j|}{\sum_{i=1}^{n}|\Delta X_i| + \sum_{i=1}^{n}|\Delta M_i|}$$

where A_j measures the extent of total intra-industry trade in industry j, which has n subindustries, aggregating vertical and horizontal intra-industry trade. The difference between A_j and Brülhart's index would give vertical trade and inter-industry trade would be given by the residual.

7.1.4.2 Disentangling Vertical and Horizontal Intra-industry Trade

The distinction between horizontal and vertical differentiation of product is an important one when dealing with adjustment issues. As several authors point out [see Greenaway, Hine and Milner (1994, 1995)] horizontal IIT is likely to lead to lower adjustment pressures than vertical IIT. This is so since different industry and country characteristics can be associated with the exchange of products depending on whether such products involve similar or different qualities (horizontal or vertical differentiation).

Greenaway, Hine and Milner (1994, 1995) propose a methodology to identify vertical and horizontal IIT built upon previous work of Abd-el-Rahman (1991). This approach assumes that quality is reflected in price and price can be proxied by unit values. The share of vertical and horizontal IIT in total trade is computed as follows:

$$
IIT_j^h = \left[1 - \frac{\sum_{i=1}^{n} \left| X_{ij}^h - M_{ij}^h \right|}{\sum_{i=1}^{n} \left(X_{ij}^h + M_{ij}^h \right)} \right] \cdot \frac{\sum_{i=1}^{n} \left(X_{ij}^h + M_{ij}^h \right)}{\left(X_j + M_j \right)},
$$

$$(7.1)$$

$$
IIT_j^v = \left[1 - \frac{\sum_{i=1}^{n} \left| X_{ij}^v - M_{ij}^v \right|}{\sum_{i=1}^{n} \left(X_{ij}^v + M_{ij}^v \right)} \right] \cdot \frac{\sum_{i=1}^{n} \left(X_{ij}^v + M_{ij}^v \right)}{\left(X_j + M_j \right)},
$$

$$(7.2)$$

where i refers to the 5th digit SITC products in a commodity group or industry j.
Total IIT is then decomposed in vertical IIT and horizontal IIT as follows:

$$
IIT_j^* = IIT_j^v + IIT_j^h
$$

$$
IIT_j^* = 1 - \frac{\sum_{i=1}^{n} \left| X_{ij} - M_{ij} \right|}{\sum_{i=1}^{n} \left(X_{ij} + M_{ij} \right)}
$$

Horizontal intra-industry trade (IIT_j^h) is given by (7.1) for the items i in commodity group j where the following condition holds:

$$
1 - \alpha \le \frac{UV_{ij}^x}{UV_{ij}^m} \le 1 + \alpha \,,
$$

where UV^x and UV^m refers to unit values of exports and imports and   is a given dispersion factor.

Vertical intra-industry trade (IIT_j^v) is given by (7.2) for the items i in commodity group j where the following condition holds:

$$
\frac{UV_{ij}^x}{UV_{ij}^m} < 1 - \alpha \qquad \text{or} \qquad \frac{UV_{ij}^x}{UV_{ij}^m} > 1 + \alpha \,.
$$

The dispersion factor α has been given several values in the diverse works where this procedure is employed[21] giving different price wedges within which IIT is considered as horizontal and outside of which it is defined as vertical. However, even when large price wedges have been used, vertical IIT has been found to be very significant in empirical studies. The results obtained suggest that the distinction between horizontal and vertical IIT should be taken into account in econometric models, as the determinants of both types of IIT may differ[22].

7.2
Trade Imbalance Adjustment

7.2.1 Grubel and Lloyd (1975)

One of the shortcomings of the aggregated index $\overline{B}_j$ is that, in case of global trade imbalance (that is, $\sum_{j=1}^{n} X_j$ $\sum_{j=1}^{n} M_j$), it can introduce a downward bias in intra-industry trade measurement. This is due to the fact that, under this assumption, $\sum_{j=1}^{n} |X_j - M_j| > 0$ and, therefore, $\overline{B}_j$ can never reach its maximum value unity.

To deal with this problem, Grubel and Lloyd (1975) proposed an alternative adjusted measure, which expresses intra-industry trade as a proportion of total trade minus the value of trade imbalance (in absolute terms), as follows:

$$\overline{C}_j = \frac{\sum_{j=1}^{n}(X_j + M_j) - \sum_{j=1}^{n}|X_j - M_j|}{\sum_{j=1}^{n}(X_j + M_j) - \left|\sum_{j=1}^{n}(X_j - M_j)\right|} = \frac{\overline{B}_j}{1-K}$$

$$\text{where } K = \frac{\left|\sum_{j=1}^{n}(X_j - M_j)\right|}{\sum_{j=1}^{n}(X_j + M_j)}$$

---

[21] Abd-el-Rahman (1991) uses $\alpha = 0.15$ and Greenaway, Hine and Milner (1994, 1995) employ both $\alpha = 0.15$ and $\alpha = 0.25$.

[22] Some work on this subject can be found in Menon, Greenaway and Milner (1999).

and where $0 \leq \overline{C}_j \leq 1$[23].

As it can be observed, $\overline{C}_j$ increases as the value of K (value of trade imbalance as a proportion of total trade) gets higher. On the other hand, the index refers to aggregated trade flows and it has no counterpart for individual industries. Moreover, when trade imbalance has the same sign in all industries, $\overline{C}_j$ reaches the value 1, independent of the size of such trade imbalances[24].

In short, the adjusted measure $\overline{C}_j$ intends to indicate what the level of intra-industry trade would be when no trade imbalance would exist. Nevertheless, Greenaway and Milner (1986), among others, argue that the need for the index to be adjusted when that is not the case should be based on wider theoretical grounds than the mentioned functional restriction of $\overline{B}_j$. Specifically, it has to be considered that a situation of global macroeconomic equilibrium may be compatible with the existence of trade imbalance for a group of industries. Moreover, in case we actually have a situation of disequilibrium, the direction of the adjustment may be different from the one proposed by Grubel and Lloyd. The restoring forces could imply an increase in trade balance and, in this case, $\overline{B}_j$ would be upwards biased.

Finally, it is worthy to mention that Grubel and Lloyd's argumentation on the need to correct in the presence of global trade imbalance implies the classification of trade flows in three categories: inter-industry trade flows, intra-industry trade flows and trade imbalances. The third of these categories is considered as a "disturbing" factor that has to be excluded of the analysis. Nevertheless, and if we take into account that most empirical works on intra-industry trade refer to the manufacturing sector, it is difficult to find a theoretical reason why trade in manufactured products should be balanced. A country may have, by instance, a deficit in this sector while having a superavit in other sectors. This matter becomes more evident if we consider bilateral trade flows, because it is not clear which

---

[23] Note that $\sum\limits_{j=1}^{n}(X_j + M_j) \geq \sum\limits_{j=1}^{n}\left|X_j - M_j\right| \geq \left|\sum\limits_{j=1}^{n}(X_j - M_j)\right|$.

[24] Note that, in this case, $\left|\sum\limits_{j=1}^{n}(X_j - M_j)\right| = \sum\limits_{j=1}^{n}\left|X_j - M_j\right|$.

The index reaches thus its maximum value unity even when not all trade is intra-industry trade in the analysed country. Vona (1991) points out that this problem is not, nevertheless, very important at the empirical level. The probability for this problem to appear is inversely related to the number of elementary items used to compute $\overline{B}_j$ or $\overline{C}_j$, what makes it difficult to happen when using a high level of data disaggregation.

bilateral position would be consistent with a situation of multilateral equilibrium.[25].

The critics to the Grubel and Lloyd's adjustment refer not only to the suitability of the proposed procedure [Aquino (1978)], but also to the very need to adjust global trade imbalance [Greenaway and Milner (1981, 1983), Kol and Mennes, 1983). Other contributions to the debate may be found in Greenaway (1984), Pomfret (1985), Greenaway and Milner (1986, 1987), Kol (1988), Kol and Mennes (1989) and Vona (1990, 1991).

7.2.2 Aquino (1978)

Aquino (1978) argues that, if $\overline{B}_j$ then there is a downwards biased when there exists a trade imbalance. It is precisely because individual indices B_j are themselves downward biased measures of intra-industry trade at the industry level. Consequently, this author proposes to adjust individual indices B_j under the assumption of equiproportional distribution of trade imbalance effects among all industries. The adjustment procedure begins by estimating the value of exports and imports in case no global trade imbalance would exist. For this purpose, the following expressions are computed:

$$X_{je} = X_j \cdot \frac{1}{2} \cdot \frac{\sum\limits_{j=1}^{n}(X_j + M_j)}{\sum\limits_{j=1}^{n} X_j} \qquad (7.3)$$

$$M_{je} = M_j \cdot \frac{1}{2} \cdot \frac{\sum\limits_{j=1}^{n}(X_j + M_j)}{\sum\limits_{j=1}^{n} M_j} \qquad (7.4)$$

Operating in (7.3) and (7.4) we have:

$$\sum_{j=1}^{n} X_{je} = \sum_{j=1}^{n} M_{je} = \frac{1}{2} \cdot \sum_{j=1}^{n}(X_j + M_j)$$

Using these "artificial" values the following intra-industry trade index for commodity group j can be computed:

---

[25] The equilibrium condition could be thus imposed only when measuring intra-industry trade including total exchange of goods and services between a country and the rest of the world (excluding, to simplify, capital flows).

$$Q_j = 1 - \frac{\left| X_{je} - M_{je} \right|}{(X_{je} + M_{je})} = 1 - \frac{\left| \dfrac{X_j}{\sum\limits_{j=1}^{n} X_j} - \dfrac{M_j}{\sum\limits_{j=1}^{n} M_j} \right|}{\left(\dfrac{X_j}{\sum\limits_{j=1}^{n} X_j} + \dfrac{M_j}{\sum\limits_{j=1}^{n} M_j} \right)}$$

Finally, based on individual indices Q_j the following aggregated index is computed:

$$\overline{Q}_j = \frac{\sum\limits_{j=1}^{n}(X_j + M_j) - \sum\limits_{j=1}^{n}\left| X_{je} - M_{je} \right|}{\sum\limits_{j=1}^{n}(X_j + M_j)} \tag{7.5}$$

Examining (7.5) it can be deduced that this indicator uses as a criterion for measurement the degree of similarity of relative shares of imports and exports. Taking into account this feature, an equivalence between $\overline{Q}_j$ and the Michaely's indicator $\overline{H}$ can be obtained as follows:

$$\overline{Q}_j = \frac{\sum\limits_{j=1}^{n}(X_j + M_j) - \sum\limits_{j=1}^{n}\left| X_{je} - M_{je} \right|}{\sum\limits_{j=1}^{n}(X_j + M_j)} =$$

$$= \frac{\sum\limits_{j=1}^{n}(X_j + M_j) - \dfrac{1}{2} \cdot \sum\limits_{j=1}^{n}(X_j + M_j) \cdot \sum\limits_{j=1}^{n}\left| \dfrac{X_j}{\sum\limits_{j=1}^{n} X_j} - \dfrac{M_j}{\sum\limits_{j=1}^{n} M_j} \right|}{\sum\limits_{j=1}^{n}(X_j + M_j)} =$$

$$= 1 - \frac{1}{2} \cdot \sum\limits_{j=1}^{n}\left| \dfrac{X_j}{\sum\limits_{j=1}^{n} X_j} - \dfrac{M_j}{\sum\limits_{j=1}^{n} M_j} \right| = \overline{H} .$$

The use of this adjustment procedure does not imply a variation in total trade flows as the following holds:

$$\sum_{j=1}^{n}(X_j + M_j) = \sum_{j=1}^{n}(X_{je} + M_{je}) \qquad (7.6)$$

Exports and imports patterns are also preserved after adjustment, that is:

$$\frac{X_{je}}{\sum_{j=1}^{n}X_{je}} = \frac{X_j}{\sum_{j=1}^{n}X_j}$$

and

$$\frac{M_{je}}{\sum_{j=1}^{n}M_{je}} = \frac{M_j}{\sum_{j=1}^{n}M_j} .$$

The above equality (7.6), however, does not hold necessarily at the industry j level. In fact, when total trade is not balanced, the fulfilment of $(X_{je}+M_{je} = X_j+M_j)$ implies that:

$$\frac{M_j}{\sum_{j=1}^{n}M_j} = \frac{X_j}{\sum_{j=1}^{n}X_j}$$

On the other hand, as Greenaway and Milner (1986) point out, the direction of the adjustment of B_j for every industry depends on the relationship between the sign of trade imbalance in the industry and total trade imbalance.

$$X_j > M_j \text{ and } \sum_{j=1}^{n}X_j > \sum_{j=1}^{n}M_j \text{ imply that } Q_j > B_j;$$

$$X_j > M_j \text{ and } \sum_{j=1}^{n}X_j < \sum_{j=1}^{n}M_j \text{ imply that } Q_j < B_j;$$

$$X_j < M_j \text{ and } \sum_{j=1}^{n}X_j > \sum_{j=1}^{n}M_j \text{ imply that } Q_j > B_j;$$

$$X_j < M_j \text{ and } \sum_{j=1}^{n}X_j < \sum_{j=1}^{n}M_j \text{ imply that } Q_j < B_j.$$

This variability in the direction of the correction affects the ranking of industries according to their intra-industry trade index. The election of the group of transactions, which will be the basis for the adjustment of trade imbalance, becomes thus critical, especially when the adjusted index is to be used in econometric analysis. Other critics to this procedure are the following: first, the fact that a trade imbalance in a group of industries is considered as a disequilibrium situation and, second, the assumption that the effects of restoring forces are equiproportionally distributed among industries[26]. For these reasons, it would be advisable, when analysing the determinants of intra-industry trade, a sensible selection of the time periods included in the sample rather than the use of adjusted indices. Another alternative proposed by the aforementioned authors is the use of an average measure of the indices corresponding to a carefully selected period of time.

7.2.3 Balassa (1979)

Balassa (1979, 1986) utilises a correcting procedure similar to the one used by Aquino (1978). However, while the latter is using as a basis for adjustment the group of transactions analysed (manufactured products, total trade or other sets of transactions), Balassa only takes into account total trade imbalance[27].

Technically, the Balassa adjustment is identical to Aquino's correction:

$$X_j^b = X_j \cdot \frac{1}{2} \cdot \frac{\sum\limits_{j=1}^{n}(X_j + M_j)}{\sum\limits_{j=1}^{n}X_j}$$

and

$$M_j^b = M_j \cdot \frac{1}{2} \cdot \frac{\sum\limits_{j=1}^{n}(X_j + M_j)}{\sum\limits_{j=1}^{n}M_j}$$

Like in the previous case, the correction is equiproportionally distributed among industries[28]. However, the election of a specific trade imbalance as the basis for the adjustment represents an improvement regarding the problem of ambiguity commented for Aquino (1978).

---

[26] Aquino (1981) argues that such a feature can be acceptable in absence of other elements that help to identify an alternative criterion.

[27] Balassa (1986) justifies this selection "in order to allow for inter-industry specialisation between primary and manufactured products".

[28] In case of a deficit (superavit), all exports are increased (diminished) in the same proportion. The same applies for imports.

7.2.4 Loertscher and Wolter (1980)

Loertscher and Wolter (1980) use the same correcting procedure as Aquino (1978). However, they apply it to bilateral trade flows of manufactured products instead of total trade of a country with the rest of the world. We have already mentioned, nevertheless, the lack of theoretical support for the existence of bilateral equilibrium with specific countries in a concrete set of transactions. Greenaway and Milner (1981) comment that, particularly, bilateral disequilibrium may be the result of factors leading to inter-industrial and intra-industrial specialisation. It may be thus inconvenient to adjust on the basis of bilateral disequilibria because it can hide the influences that one pretends to measure.

7.2.5 Bergstrand (1982)

Finally, Bergstrand (1982) considers total trade imbalance as the basis for adjustment, as in Balassa (1979), but, opposite to the later, he uses bilateral trade flows to measure intra-industry trade[29].

The indicator proposed for the measurement of bilateral intra-industry trade between countries i and j in products of industry k[30] is the following:

$$IIT_{ij}^{k*} = 1 - \frac{\left| X_{ij}^{k*} - X_{ji}^{k*} \right|}{\left(X_{ij}^{k*} - X_{ji}^{k*} \right)}$$

where

$$X_{ij}^{k*} = \frac{1}{2} \cdot \left[\frac{(X_i + M_i)}{2X_i} + \frac{(X_j + M_j)}{2M_j} \right] \cdot X_{ij}^k$$

$$X_{ji}^{k*} = \frac{1}{2} \cdot \left[\frac{(X_j + M_j)}{2X_j} + \frac{(X_i + M_i)}{2M_i} \right] \cdot X_{ji}^k$$

X_{ij}^k = value of exports from country i to country j of products in industry k

$X_i = \sum\limits_{k=1}^{n} \sum\limits_{j=1}^{m} X_{ij}^k$ = total exports of country i

---

[29] Bergstrand justifies this decision arguing that in a model with multiple countries, multiple goods, two factors of production and non equality of factor prices, the Heckscher-Ohlin theorem is always fulfilled for bilateral trade flows between pairs of countries and thus the focus of interest should be the presence of bilateral intra-industry trade, which is "non expected" according to the mentioned theorem.

[30] Adjusted on the basis of each country's multilateral trade imbalance.

$$M_i = \sum_{k=1}^{n} \sum_{j=1}^{m} X_{ji}^{k} = \text{total imports of country } I$$

Finally, X_{ji}^{k}, X_j and M_j are similarly defined.

Taking, for example, the case of exports of industry k from country i to country j it can be noted that the correcting factor $\dfrac{1}{2} \cdot \left[\dfrac{(X_i + M_i)}{2X_i} + \dfrac{(X_j + M_j)}{2M_j} \right]$ is an arithmetic mean of two elements. The first of them, $\dfrac{(X_i + M_i)}{2X_i}$, tends to increase exports from i when such country presents a global trade deficit $(X_i + M_i > 2X_i)$ and to reduced them in the opposite case. Regarding the second element, $\dfrac{(X_j + M_j)}{2M_j}$, it tends to increase exports from i to j when country j has global trade superavit $(X_j + M_j > 2M_j)$ and to reduce them in the opposite case. A similar analysis applies to X_{ji}^{k}.

In short, both elements of the correcting factor act in the same direction when one of the countries has a deficit and the other one has a superavit. However, both elements tend to offset when the sign of trade imbalance is the same in the two countries.

On the other hand, it can be noted that the correcting factors for X_{ij}^{k} and X_{ji}^{k} are independent on the industry considered k[31]. This means that the correction is equiproportionaly applied to all industries, the same as in Aquino's and Balassa's procedures.

The correcting procedure stops when countries i and j present a multilateral equilibrium (independent on the existence of bilateral disequilibria). It is thus an iterative procedure to compute X_{ij}^{k*} and X_{ji}^{k*} in which bilateral trade flows are changed until all countries reach a multilateral equilibrium. The amount of information required to apply this method is much higher than the one needed by the other indicators commented.

7.2.6 Comments and Conclusions

We have revised in previous subsections different methods, which can be applied to correct for trade imbalance, either in global trade or in specific sectors, for bilateral trade flows or multilateral exchanges.

---

[31] The exports of every industry k are multiplied by the same factor and the same applies for imports.

The correction of the index $\overline{B}_j$ was introduced to allow the indicator to reach its maximum value unity, even in the presence of trade imbalance. However, this argument has no theoretical foundations. Moreover, the adjusted index $\overline{C}_j$ has no counterpart at the industry level, as opposite to indices B_j and $\overline{B}_j$. Finally, we have to mention that, in case all trade imbalances have the same sign in all industries, the index $\overline{C}_j$ reaches its maximum value 1 independent on the size of such trade imbalances[32].

Concerning the Aquino (1978) index, although it is an improving compared to the previous one, it suffers from several shortcomings. In concrete, we have already commented that the ranking of industries according to their level of intra-industry trade experiments significant variations, depending on the trade balance of the set of transactions considered as a basis for the adjustment. On the other hand, the correction is equiproportionaly distributed among industries, what may imply the lost of important information on specific industry characteristics related to intra-industry trade. Moreover, the Aquino (1978) index always takes the same value when the share of imports and exports in every industry in total imports and exports, respectively, remains constant.

In Aquino (1978) and Loertscher and Wolter (1980) the adjustment is made on the basis of trade imbalance in manufactured products but, again, there is *a priori* no theoretical foundations for trade in a specific group of transactions to be balanced.

Loertscher and Wolter (1980) correct in terms of bilateral trade flows but the situations of bilateral disequilibrium may be consistent with multilateral equilibrium and, in fact, they may be reflecting a trend towards inter or intra-industry specialisation. For this reason, it is even more hazardous to use and adjustment procedure of the Aquino (1978) type on a bilateral basis because it may hide the very influences that one pretends to measure.

In our opinion, a convenient method to correct for trade imbalance should satisfy, at least, the following conditions: first, it should be applicable to several levels of data aggregation; second, it has to use total trade as a basis for the correction (and not only a particular set of transactions) and third, it has to simulate a situation of multilateral equilibrium. Taking all this into account, the methods proposed by Balassa (1979) and Bergstrand (1982) seem to be more suitable than the other procedures commented. Balassa's adjustment has, compared to Bergstrand, the advantage of its simplicity.

Nevertheless, none of the exposed procedures considers the causes underlying the disequilibrium situations considered, conveniently adjusting the procedure[33].

---

[32] This is due to the following:

$$\left| \sum_{j=1}^{n} (X_j - M_j) \right| = \sum_{j=1}^{n} \left| X_j - M_j \right|.$$

[33] The equiproportional distribution of the correction among industries reflects the lack of flexibility of the proposed procedures.

In fact, these methods could create more distortions than the ones they pretend to eliminate and have no clear relationship with theoretical foundations. However, in some cases, particularly when it comes to comparing among countries with different trade imbalances or for a country with very different trade imbalances along the time period considered, the use of adjusted indices may be convenient. Some alternative methods may be used [Greenaway and Milner (1981)]. A sensible selection of the years considered could be made, which avoids periods of evident global trade imbalance. On the other hand, an average of intra-industry trade indices may be used for a carefully selected time period.

In any case, the distortions that trade imbalance may introduce in the measurement of intra-industry trade are probably insignificant when compared with those brought about by the definition of "industry" and the consequent effects of categorical aggregation. We deal with this question in next section 7.3.

7.3
Categorical Aggregation

7.3.1 Definition of the Problem

One of the most important problems of intra-industry trade's measurement is the unknown influence of categorical aggregation. The identification and measurement of intra-industry trade clearly depends on the degree of homogeneity of the products classified under the same group in trade statistics and the nature of such homogeneity. The bias introduced by categorical aggregation on intra-industry trade measurement emerges when essentially heterogeneous products (that is, products than cannot be considered belonging to the same industry) are classified under the same group in trade statistics. In general, the existence of bi-directional trade flows for a commodity group will identify "genuine" intra-industry trade and statistical aggregation (simultaneous exchange of products classified under the same category but with different factor requirements).

The most convenient procedure to eliminate this problem seems to be, at first sight, the reclassification of data in a way that all resulting categories correspond as close as possible with the theoretical construction of an "industry". The problem is that there are multiple criteria or regrouping the data and, even is a specific criterion is systematically used, reclassification is an extremely arduous job[34].

International trade data may be classified according to different criteria. The most commonly used system is the SITC nomenclature[35], in which products are grouped at various levels of aggregation identified by digits. The alternative to reclassification would be the election of a specific level of data disaggregation in official classifications as the best approximation to the concept of industry. In this case, a double question emerges. On the one hand, the most convenient level of

---

[34] An additional problem would be the classification of pieces and components.

[35] Standard International Trade Classification.

data disaggregation has to be identified (that is, the level that more narrowly corresponds to the concept of "industry"). On the other hand, the influence of categorical aggregation for the selected level of data disaggregation has to be determined.

7.3.2 Categorical Aggregation Tests

Due to the difficulties of product reclassification under a systematic and coherent with the economic criterion, several alternatives have been proposed. Particularly, three alternative methods to assess the influence of categorical aggregation on intra-industry trade indices have been suggested[36]:

i) To perform measurement at higher levels of statistical disaggregation.
ii) To execute diverse measurements based on different classification systems.
iii) To compute an adjusted intra-industry trade index.

The first of these procedures has been the more widely employed. It is based on the consideration that a substantial fall in average intra-industry indices when descending from a specific level of aggregation to a higher one may be indicating the presence of categorical aggregation problem.

However, an important point has to be taken into account. There is no specific standard pattern to evaluate if the fall in the value of the index is significant and so the results of this test are not at all conclusive but have an indicative character[37].

Concerning the second type of categorical aggregation test mentioned, it is also instructive to observe the sensibility of indices B_j to classification systems based on different criteria (like processing characteristics of product features). The stability in the ranging of indices computed using different classifications may be illustrative but, like in the previous case, no conclusions can be obtained regarding the absolute significance of the categorical aggregation error. Moreover, the need to select a specific level of data aggregation for the indices' computation still remains.

The third type of categorical aggregation test involves a more systematic way of evaluating the categorical aggregation problem associated with trade imbalances of opposite sign in subgroups of products with different factor *ratios* and low degree of substitution[38]. If we considered commodity group *j* formed by *m* subgroups denoted by *i*, this procedure consists of computing an adjusted intra-industry trade index according to the following expression:

---

[36] Greenaway and Milner (1983).

[37] Usually, a fall in the value of the index of about 20% when passing from the 3-digit SITC to the 5-digit SITC level of aggregation, while maintaining a reasonably high volume of intra-industry trade for the 5-digit level, is considered to indicate that the main component of recorded intra-industry trade is not categorical aggregation.

[38] See subsection 7.1.1.

$$B_j^* = \sum_{i=1}^{m} w_{ij} \cdot B_{ij} = \frac{\sum_{i=1}^{m}(X_{ij}+M_{ij}) - \sum_{i=1}^{m}|X_{ij}-M_{ij}|}{\sum_{i=1}^{m}(X_{ij}+M_{ij})}$$

where $w_{ij} = \dfrac{X_{ij}+M_{ij}}{\sum_{i=1}^{m}(X_{ij}+M_{ij})} = \dfrac{X_{ij}+M_{ij}}{X_j+M_j}$ and $B_{ij} = 1 - \dfrac{|X_{ij}-M_{ij}|}{X_{ij}+M_{ij}}$.

The aggregation procedure to compute the intra-industry trade index for commodity group j consists of computing B_{ij} indices for the subgroups i and averaging them according to the share of every subgroup in total trade of j.

As $\sum_{i=1}^{m}|X_{ij}-M_{ij}| \ge \left|\sum_{i=1}^{m}(X_{ij}-M_{ij})\right|$ holds, we have $1 \ge B_j \ge B_j^* \ge 0$.

This means that, the more trade imbalances of opposite sign cancel between subgroups, the higher B_j will be related to B_j^* and, in case all trade imbalances in the subgroups have the same sign, we have $B_j = B_j^*$.

The adjustment is thus based on the assumption that categorical aggregation is associated with opposite sign trade imbalances in the subgroups i of which a commodity group j is composed. When this situation exists, a measurement of intra-industry trade at a higher level of data disaggregation generates a lower value of intra-industry trade and helps to correct for the influence of statistical aggregation.

7.3.3 Critics and Conclusions

The available evidence collected in the literature devoted to examine the influence of statistical aggregation on intra-industry trade measurement and, specifically, the existence of high volumes of intra-industry trade even at high levels of data disaggregation, shows that this is a phenomenon that cannot be explained solely by statistical aggregation.

There is no doubt that the interpretation of intra-industry trade measurement becomes more complicated with the existence of categorical aggregation. The more convenient way of facing this problem could be the reclassification of data building product categories as homogeneous as possible, (that is, according to what can be considered an "industry"). However, this regrouping is problematic due to the lack of a unique reclassification criterion, among other factors.

The election of a concrete level of data disaggregation to measure intra-industry trade is not either exempt of problems. If we select a too low level of data disaggregation most intra-industry trade registered may be due to categorical aggregation. On the other hand, when the selected level of disaggregation is too high, we run the risk of losing the economic meaning of the subgroups employed. Some products with similar factor requirements may appear in different groups and part of the recorded inter-industrial trade would be, in fact, inter-industry trade. In most empirical works on intra-industry trade it is considered that the 3-digit SITC level is a reasonable approximation to the economic concept of "industry".

With the purpose of assessing the influence of categorical aggregation on intra-industry trade measurement at a particular level of data disaggregation, several procedures have been proposed. The first of them consists of performing measurement at higher levels of statistical disaggregation. Among other shortcomings, it has the problem of dealing with the elevated volume of information needed to compute indices at high levels of data disaggregation. The second procedure, consisting of computing indices based on different classification systems, is similarly arduous. Moreover, the problem of selecting a concrete level of disaggregation to perform the measurements still persists. Finally, the third procedure involves the computation of an adjusted intra-industry trade index: B_j^*. This adjusted index is giving a more convenient measure of intra-industry trade than index B_j in the presence of categorical aggregation. Yet, if categorical aggregation is not associated with opposite sign trade imbalances in the subgroups, then B_j^* would be a downward biased intra-industry trade measure.

In the absence of information about the existence of categorical aggregation, it is not possible to know which of both measures is more suitable.

Finally, it is worthy to mention that none of the mentioned procedures gives conclusive results regarding the determination of the aggregation error's absolute relevance. However, it is convenient to employ at least one (or more) of these methods for indicative purposes, in order to reduce, in part, the arbitrary indiscriminate use of a specific level of data disaggregation to compute intra-industry trade indices.

7.4
Summary and Conclusions

In this chapter we have tried to carry out a critical review of the main indicators used for the purpose of intra-industry trade and specialisation measurement. Moreover, we have discussed the two main problems related to such measurement: trade imbalance adjustment and categorical aggregation.

The analysis performed may be summarised in the following points:

i) Two different criteria have been identified concerning intra-industry exchange, giving rise to two families of indices (not extrictly comparable): the degree of overlapping in trade flows and the degree of similarity in trade patterns (or relative structure of imports and exports). Among the indicators belonging to the first group, the indices proposed by Grubel and Lloyd (1975)[39] seem to be the more suitable. Concerning the second group of indicators, it can be concluded that the index of Michaely (1962)[40] is the most convenient measure when it comes to measuring the degree of similarity in trade patterns.

ii) Regarding the procedures aimed at correcting the distortions introduced by trade imbalance in intra-industry trade measurement, a common feature to all of them is the lack of theoretical support to justify the need for adjustment. It is thus preferable to use unadjusted indices for carefully selected periods of time.

iii) The problem of categorical aggregation remains unsolved. Although there is no definitive solution, several methods have been developed to test for the influence of categorical aggregation. With the possible exception of the product regrouping method, these tests are easy to perform and, even if not conclusive, they have an indicative character, which allows us to eliminate in part the arbitrariness of the use of a specific level of data disaggregation when measuring intra-industry trade.

iv) Two issues have dominated the literature on intra-industry trade measurement in the last years: marginal intra-industry trade and disentanglement of vertical and horizontal intra-industry trade.

The measurement of the so-called marginal intra-industry trade is related to the analysis of adjustment costs associated to trade liberalisation. The indices developed are based on the assumption that when assessing the relevance of intra-industry trade during an adjustment process, it is the proportion of intra-industry trade in new generated trade what matters, rather than the level of intra-industry trade.

On the other hand, the distinction between vertical and horizontal intra-industry trade is an important one as the determinants of both may differ. Diverse indices, which disentangle horizontal and vertical intra-industry trade, have been developed and used in empirical analysis.

Finally, it is important to mention that recent work on this subjects addresses the issue that the indicators of marginal intra-industry trade so far developed may be underestimating the extent of intra-industry trade, as they identify intra-industry trade with horizontal trade only. In other words, they cannot distinguish between inter-industry trade and vertical intra-industry trade. A method to deal with this question can be found in Thom and McDowell (1999).

---

[39] $B_j = 1 - \dfrac{|X_j - M_j|}{(X_j + M_j)}$ and $\overline{B}_j = 1 - \dfrac{\sum\limits_{j=1}^{n}|X_j - M_j|}{\sum\limits_{j=1}^{n}(X_j + M_j)}$.

[40] $\overline{H}_j = 1 - \dfrac{1}{2} \cdot \sum\limits_{j=1}^{n}\left| \dfrac{X_j}{\sum\limits_{j=1}^{n}X_j} - \dfrac{M_j}{\sum\limits_{j=1}^{n}M_j} \right|$.

References

Abd-el-Rahman, K.: Firms' Competitive and National Comparative Advantages as Joint Determinants of Trade Composition. Weltwirtschaftliches Archiv 127, 83-97 (1991)

Aquino, A.: The Measurement of Intra-industry Trade when Overall Trade is Imbalanced. Weltwirtschaftliches Archiv 117, 763-766 (1981)

Balassa, B.: Tariff Reductions and Trade in Manufactures among the Industrial Countries. The American Economic Review 56, 466-73 (1966)

Balassa, B.: Intra-industry Trade and the Integration of Developing Countries in the World Economy. In: Giersch, H. (ed.): On the Economics of Intra-industry Trade. Symposium, Tübingen 1979

Balassa, B.: The Determinants of Intra-industry Specialisation in United States Trade. Oxford Economic Papers 38, 220-233 (1986)

Bergstrand, H. J.: The Scope, Growth and Causes of Intra-Industry International Trade. New England Economic Review (Sept/Oct), 45-61 (1982)

Brülhart, M.: Marginal Intra-industry Trade: Measurement and Relevance for the Pattern of Industrial Adjustment. Weltwirtschaftliches Archiv 130-3, 600-613 (1994)

Carrera. M. G.: Comercio Intra-Industrial: Análisis del Caso Español. Ph. D. Dissertation. University of Cantabria. Department of Economics 1996

Finger, J. M. and Kreinin, M. E.: A measure of Export Similarity and its Possible Uses. The Economic Journal 89, 905-912 (1979)

Glejser, H., Goossens, K. and Vanden Eede, M.: Inter-industry versus Intra-industry specialisation in Exports and Imports (1959-1970-1973). Journal of International Economics 12, 363-369 (1982)

Greenaway, D.: The Measurement of Product Differentiation in Empirical Studies of Trade Flows. In: Kierzkowski, H. (ed.): Monopolistic Competition and International Trade. Oxford University Press 1984

Greenaway, D., Hine, R. C. and Milner, C.: Country-Specific Factors and the Pattern of Horizontal and Vertical Intra-industry Trade in the UK. Weltwirtschaftliches Archiv 130, 77-100 (1994)

Greenaway, D., Hine, R. C. and Milner, C.: Vertical and Horizontal Intra-industry Trade: a Cross-Industry Analysis For The United Kingdom. The Economic Journal 105, 1505-1518 (1995)

Greenaway, D., Hine, R. C., Milner, C. and Elliot, R.: Adjustment and the Measurement of Marginal Intra-industry Trade. Weltwirtschaftliches Archiv 130-2, 418-427 (1994)

Greenaway, D. and Milner, C.: Trade Imbalance Effects in the Measurement of Intra-industry Trade. Weltwirtschaftliches Archiv 117, 756-762 (1981)

Greenaway, D. and Milner, C.: On the Measurement of Intra-industry Trade. The Economic Journal 93, 900-908 (1983)

Greenaway, D. and Milner, C.: The Economics of Intra-industry Trade. Basil Blackwell 1986

Greenaway, D. and Milner, C.: Intra-industry Trade: Current Perspectives and Unresolved Issues. Weltwirtschaftliches Archiv 123, 39-57 (1987)

Grubel, H. G., Lloyd, P. J.: The Empirical Measurement of Intra-industry Trade. Economic Record 47, 494-517 (1971)

Grubel, H. G., Lloyd, P. J.: Intra-industry Trade: the Theory and Measurement of International Trade in Differentiated Products. London: Macmillan 1975

Hamilton, C. and Kniest, P.: Trade Liberalisation, Structural Adjustment and Intra-industry Trade: a Note. Weltwirtschaftliches Archiv 127-2, 356-367 (1991)

Kojima, K.: The Pattern of International Trade among Advanced Countries. Hitotsubashi Journal of Economics (June), 16-36 (1964)

Kol, J.: The Measurement of Intra-industry Trade. Erasmus University. Rotterdam 1988

Kol, J. and Mennes, L. B. M.: On Concepts and Measurement of Intra-industry Trade. Discussion Paper 66. Centre for Development Planning. Erasmus University, Rotterdam 1983

Kol, J. and Mennes, L. B. M.: Intra-industry specialisation: some Observations on Concepts and Measurement. Journal of International Economics 21. 173-181 (1986)

Kol, J. and Mennes, L. B. M.: Corrections for Trade Imbalance: a Survey. Weltwirtschaftliches Archiv 125, 703-717

Loertscher, R. and Wolter, F.: Determinants of Intra-industry Trade among Countries and across Sectors. Weltwirtschaftliches Archiv 116, 280-292

Menon, J., Greenaway, D. and Milner C.: Industrial Structure and Australia-UK Intra-industry Trade. The Economic Record 75-228, 19-27 (1999)

Michaely, M.: Multilateral Balancing in International Trade. The American Economic Review 52, 685-702 (1962)

Silber, J. and Broll, U.: Trade Overlap and Trade Pattern Indices of Intra-industry Trade: Theoretical Distinctions versus Empirical Similarities. Sonderforschungsbereich 178, Internationalisierung der Wirtschaft. Diskussionsbeiträge Serie II, N. 107. Fakultät für Wirtschaftswissenschafter und Statistik 1990

Thom, R. and McDowell, M.: Measuring Marginal Intra-industry Trade. Weltwirtschaftliches Archiv 135 (1), 48-61 (1999)

Verdoorn, P. J.: The Intra-block Trade of Benelux. In: Robinson, E. A. G. (ed.): Economic Consequences of the Size of Nations, 291-329. Macmillan 1960

Vona, S.: Intra-industry Trade: a Statistical Artefact or a Real Phenomenon?. Banca Nazionale del Lavoro Quarterly Review 175 (1990)

Vona, S.: On the Measurement of Intra-industry Trade: some further Thoughts. Weltwirtschaftliches Archiv 127, 678-700 (1991)

8 The Determinants of Intra-industry Trade in Spanish Manufacturing Sectors: a Cross-section Analysis

Gema Carrera-Gómez
Department of Economics
University of Cantabria (Spain)

A wide range of studies devoted to recent evolution of international trade highlights the fact that a significant and increasing proportion of flows consists of bi-directional change of products belonging to the same industry. This phenomenon is known as intra-industry trade.

Among the several interesting aspects arising from the study of this type of trade we can mention the following. On the one hand, it is difficult to find a satisfactory explanation for this phenomenon inside the traditional theoretical frame. On the other hand, it is important to analyse the factors determining this kind of trade as they differ from the conventional determinants of international trade and, consequently, the effects of trade policies and structural adjustments may be different to those obtained under the traditional assumptions. The former question has given rise to the appearance of a wide range of explanatory models, what gives an idea of the diversity of conditions under which this phenomenon may arise[1]. On the empirical side we find, on the one hand, a set of studies aimed at determining the relative importance of intra-industry trade through the use of several methods to measure it. On the other hand, we have a series of papers whose purpose is to identify the industry and country characteristics leading to intra-industry trade[2].

This paper is among the latter and it is aimed at establishing the factors explaining intra-industry trade in the Spanish economy, from an industry perspective, given the increasing relevance that this type of flows has acquired in

---

[1] A comprehensive review of this literature can be found in Greenaway and Milner (1986), Tharakan and Kol (1989) and Carrera (1996).

[2] See, for example, Greenaway and Milner (1984), Balassa and Bauwens (1988), Fariñas and Martin (1988), Bano (1991), Hugues (1993) and Montaner and Orts (1995).

Spanish foreign trade[3]. With this purpose, in section 8.1 we deal whith the measurement of Spanish intra-industry trade and calculate intra-industry trade indexes for several industrial sectors. Section 8.2 contains an analysis of the determinant factors of Spanish intro-industry trade including empirical contrast of a series of hypotheses related to industry characteristics which may influence the extent of intra-industry trade in Spanish manufacturing industrial sectors. Finally, section 8.3 synthesises the main conclusions of the paper.

8.1
Spanish Intra-industry Trade Measurement

A variety of intra-industry trade indicators have been introduced in the literature, the index proposed by Grubel and Lloyd (1975) being the more widely used for this purpose. The G-L indicator expresses the proportion of intra-industry trade in a given industry, which will be referred as i, as follows:

$$B_i = 1 - \frac{|X_i - M_i|}{(X_i + M_i)}$$

where $0 \le B_i \le 1$.

For a set of m industries an aggregated index can be constructed according to the following expression:

$$\overline{B} = 1 - \frac{\sum_{i=1}^{m}|X_i - M_i|}{\sum_{i=1}^{m}(X_i + M_i)} = \sum_{i=1}^{m} B_i \cdot \frac{(X_i + M_i)}{\sum_{i=1}^{m}(X_i + M_i)}, \tag{8.1}$$

where $0 \le \overline{B} \le 1$.

From a theoretical point of view, we can consider an industry as a group of products with similar factor requirements and a high degree of substitution. Nevertheless, this is not easy to take into practice and the available international trade classification systems contain aggregations of products that can be heterogeneous from an intra-industry trade perspective[4]. As a consequence, the main problem we face when trying to measure intra-industry trade is the difficulty of defining the industry from an operative point of view. The usual way of treating this problem consists of choosing a particular level of data aggregation, measuring and evaluating the influence of statistical aggregation, often calculating intra-industry trade indexes for higher levels of data disaggregation. Most works made on this subject use the SITC 3digit groups[5] as a reasonable approximation to the economic concept of industry, being possible to talk of a certain degree of consensus in this respect.

---

[3] See Martin (1992) and Carrera (1996).
[4] This fact causes the denominated categorical aggregation problem.
[5] Standard International Trade Classification.

Table 8.1 shows the aggregated intra-industry trade indexes for Spain for a number of sectors which have been constructed from SITC 3-digit groups. Additionally, intra-industry trade indexes have been calculated for SITC 5-digit items. The range correlation coefficient between both series of indexes is 0,96, indicating that the ranking of sectors according to their intra-industry trade intensity has practically no variations between both cases.

Table 8.1. Intra-industry trade indexes for Spain (1992)

Sector	Denomination	IIT index
1	Solid fuel, coke, hydrocarbons, radioactive minerals and petroleum refineries	0.226
2	Electric power, water supply and gas	0.430
3	Metallic mineral products	0.630
4	Non-metallic mineral products	0.675
5	Chemicals	0.616
6	Fabricated metal products (except machinery and transport material)	0.806
7	Agricultural and industrial machinery	0.632
8	Office and computing machinery, optical accuracy instruments and similar tools	0.438
9	Electrical and electronic machinery and material (except computers)	0.585
10	Automobiles, pieces and accessories	0.800
11	Other transport material	0.648
12	Food, drinks and tobacco	0.519
13	Textiles, leather and footwear	0.570
14	Wood and cork	0.541
15	Paper, graphic arts and publishing	0.716
16	Rubber and plastic products	0.734
17	Other manufacturing industries	0.563

Source: Own elaboration with foreign trade data provided by Hamburg Institute for Economic Research

8.2
Analysis of the Determinants of Intra-industry Trade in Spain

8.2.1 Hypotheses

The bulk of intra-industry trade explanatory theories conforms an analytical outline from which we can extract some basic hypotheses concerning industry characteristics influencing the degree and extent of intra-industry trade.

One of the elements the literature is emphasising as responsible of intra-industry trade share of total trade in a sector is the differentiation of product. What we could call "genuine" intra-industry trade refers to the exchange of horizontally differentiated products, where the diversity of tastes and preferences of the consumers plays a significant role[6]. On the other hand, technological differentiation of the product may lead to a specialisation of an inter-industry nature, where industries better endowed with technological knowledge produce a higher number of new products and enjoy a comparative advantage in this sense. Nevertheless, if the new products are included in international trade classifications together with the old ones, the exchange of both will appear as intra-industry trade.

Consequently, the product differentiation hypothesis may be formulated on the following terms:

• Hypothesis 1: The higher the degree of product differentiation in a particular production sector the greater the proportion of intra-industry trade in the sector.

On the other hand, the presence of scale economies is considered as an important condition for the emergence of intra-industry trade in differentiated products. It is precisely this element that causes a firm finding more profitable to produce only one or a small set of varieties of the product to export, importing meanwhile the other varieties. This way the consumers are allowed to enjoy the benefits inherent to the increase in their range of election and a certain degree of intra-industry trade is generated. These issues allow us to state the following hypothesis:

• Hypothesis 2: The share of intra-industry trade is higher in those industries with larger economies of scale.

In addition to the aforementioned, several theoretical foundations may be found that induce us to expect a positive association between the participation of multinationals in a productive sector and the degree of intra-industry trade in that sector. The diverse cost minimisation strategies employed by this type of firms under certain assumptions may generate intra-industry exchange. This makes it possible to formulate the following hypothesis:

• Hypothesis 3: The proportion of intra-industry trade in a particular industrial sector is larger the more intense the activity of multinational firms operating in that sector is.

Finally, it has been frequently noted in the literature on intra-industry trade that this type of trade is more sensitive to trade barriers than traditional inter-industry trade, what allows us to suggest the following hypothesis:

• Hypothesis 4: The share of intra-industry trade is higher in those industries facing a lower degree of trade barriers.

---

[6] On the other hand, it is often impossible to separate vertical and horizontal differentiation in empirical work (mainly because both types of differentiation can be simultaneously found in products). In any case, a positive association between both forms of product differentiation and intra-industry trade can be considered.

8.2.2 Data, Variables and Econometric Model

The set of trade and industry data used to construct the variables employed in the analysis were recorded in various classification systems or nomenclatures[7]. Therefore, and due to the lack of official tables of correspondence among such classifications, it was necessary to carry out a previous task of conversion among the different nomenclatures with the aim of having the data homogeneity required for carrying out the work. The data were finally grouped together into the industrial sectors listed in table 8.1 (see section 8.1) and the test carried out is referred to a cross-section of these industrial sectors for the year 1992.

The construction of the variables employed was made as follows:

The dependent variable used in our analysis is the level of intra-industry trade. For every sector an aggregated index has been calculated according to expression (8.1) as it is shown in table 8.2.

Table 8.2. Dependent variable

Dependent variable	Proxy
Intra-industry trade share in total sector j trade	Grubel-Lloyd (1975) aggregated index: $$B_j = 1 - \frac{\sum\limits_{i=1}^{m}\left|X_{ij} - M_{ij}\right|}{\sum\limits_{i=1}^{m}\left(X_{ij} + M_{ij}\right)} \, .$$

Notes:
$j = 1, 2, 3, ..., 17$.
i = 3-digt-SITC groups for every sector j

As regards the explanatory variables, the following have been used: horizontal product differentiation, technological product differentiation, scale economies, involvement of multinational firms in the sector and level of tariff protection. The construction of the independent variables is summarised in table 8.3.

---

[7] The following classification systems have been used:
-Stantandar International Trade Classification, Rev. 3.
-Industrial Survey 1989-1992 sectors (National Institute of Statistics).
-National Classification of Economic Activities (CNAE-74).
-Tariff sector used in Melo and Mones (1982).
-Industrial Situation Survey (Ministery of Industry and Energy).

Table 8.3. Explanatory variables

Explanatory variable	Proxy	
Horizontal product differentiation	Advertising expenditures (AE) to sales (S) ratio	$AES_j = \dfrac{\sum\limits_{l=1}^{t} AE_l}{\sum\limits_{l=1}^{t} S_l} = \dfrac{AE_j}{S_j} = \sum\limits_{l=1}^{t}\left(\dfrac{AE_l}{S_l}\cdot\dfrac{S_l}{S_j}\right)$
	Relative AE	$RAE_j = \dfrac{AE_j}{\sum\limits_{j=1}^{17} AE_j}$
Technological product differentiation	Research and development expenditure (RD) to value added (VA) ratio	$RDR_j = \dfrac{\sum\limits_{r=1}^{s} RD_r}{\sum\limits_{r=1}^{m} VA_r} = \dfrac{RD_j}{VA_j} = \sum\limits_{r=1}^{s}\left(\dfrac{RD_r}{VA_r}\cdot\dfrac{VA_r}{VA_j}\right)$
	Technological development expenditure (TD) to VA ratio	$TDR_j = \dfrac{\sum\limits_{r=1}^{s} TD_r}{\sum\limits_{r=1}^{s} VA_r} = \dfrac{TD_j}{VA_j} = \sum\limits_{r=1}^{s}\left(\dfrac{TD_r}{VA_r}\cdot\dfrac{VA_r}{VA_j}\right)$
Scale economies	Minimum efficient size (MES)* to cost disadvantage (CDR)** ratio	$SE_1 = \dfrac{MES_1}{CDR_1}$; $SE_j = \sum\limits_{l=1}^{t} SE_l \cdot \dfrac{P_l}{P_j}$
Involvement of multinational firms	Foreign direct investment (FDI)	$FDI_j = \sum\limits_{r=1}^{s} FDI_r$
	FDI to VA ratio	$FDIVA_j = \dfrac{\sum\limits_{r=1}^{s} FDI_r}{\sum\limits_{r=1}^{s} VA_r} = \dfrac{FDI_j}{VA_j}$
	FDI to total direct investment (TDI) ratio	$FDIT_j = \dfrac{FDI_j}{TDI_j}$
Level of tariff protection	Tariff protection (T)	$T_j = \dfrac{\frac{1}{m}\sum\limits_{k=1}^{m} T_k \cdot M_j^R}{M_j^R + M_j^{EU}} = \dfrac{\frac{1}{m}\sum\limits_{k=1}^{m} T_k \cdot M_j^R}{M_j}$

Notes:
$j = 1, 2, 3, …, 17$
i = 3-digt-SITC groups for every sector j
l = INE Industrial Survey sectors for every sector j
r = CNAE-74 sectors (2 digits) for every sector j. INE Research and Development Survey
k = Melo and Mones (1982) tariff sectors for every sector j
T_k = Average Common External Tariff (Melo y Monés, 1982)
M_j^{EU} = Imports from the European Union
M_j^R = Imports from the rest of the world
M_j = Total imports for sector j
*   MES is computed as the size (value of production) of the median establishment divided by the value of the sector's total production. By median establishment we mean the establishment which corresponds to the median of the accumulated distribution of the sector's production.
**   RDC is computed as the quotient whose numerator is the value added per employee in establishments smaller than the MES and whose denominator is the value added per employee in the remaining establishments.

Once the variables have been constructed, we have to associate the intra-industry trade indexes with the set of industry characteristics in table 8.3 using regression analysis. But one of the difficulties we face when doing so is the limited range of the dependent variable, which takes values inside the interval [0, 1]. Taking into account this feature, there are no guaranties that the values generated from a linear regression equation or a linear-logarithmic equation fall inside the range of the dependent variable. A Logit function will not present this problem but has the disadvantage that it cannot capture the extreme values (0 and 1), which provide relevant information. A reasonable approximation to the problem is the use of a Tobit model, which enable to incorporate this limited range characteristic of the dependent variable.

Because of the above mentioned reasons, the procedure we have employed[8] consists of estimating a standard Tobit model, which can be expressed as follows[8]:

$$y_i^* = \beta' x_i + \varepsilon_i \ ; \ \varepsilon_i \sim N(0, \sigma^2); \text{ with} \qquad \begin{array}{l} y_i = 0 \quad \text{if } y_i^* \le 0, \\[2mm] y_i = y_i^* \quad \text{if } 0 < y_i^* < 1, \\[2mm] y_i = 1 \quad \text{if } y_i^* \ge 1. \end{array}$$

where β is a vector of unknown parameters, x_i is the vector of explanatory variables containing industry characteristics and where the limited dependent variable, y_i, is the aggregated Grubel and Lloyd (1975) intra-industry trade index.

The procedure employed for estimation is the maximum likelihood method. As it is known, the estimators obtained from this method are sensitive to the assumptions of homoscedasticity and normality of the residuals and to deal with this problem several tests have been applied to check the compliance of these conditions[9]. For the assumption of homoscedasticity the BP statistic (Breusch y Pagan, 1980) has been used. With respect to the assumption of normality of the residuals, the BJL statistic (Bera, Jarque y Lee, 1984) has been employed. Additionally, the Shapiro-Wilk statistic (SW) for normality contrast has been calculated.

8.2.3 Results

Table 8.4 shows the main results of the regressions made. As it can be seen in the table the estimated coefficients have the expected sign and most of them are significant from a statistical point of view. Furthermore, the homoscedasticity and normality tests performed do not suggest evidence of the presence of these problems in any of the cases. Moreover, the contrast of the likelihood ratio. (LR) allows us to accept the hypothesis of joint significance of the parameters.

The results obtained provide, in general, support for the hypotheses formulated in 8.2.1 concerning the determinant factors of intra-industry trade.

The coefficient of the variable related to the degree of horizontal differentiation of the product, approximated as relative advertising expenditure has the expected sign and is highly significant in all the regressions, suggesting that this type of differentiation has a positive influence on the intensity of intra-industry trade.

On the other hand, the coefficient of the variable referred to technological differentiation is statistically significant in every case, revealing a positive

---

[8] See Maddala (1988) and Greene (1993).
[9] See Maddala (1993) and Greene (1993).

association between this feature of the product and the extent of intra-industry trade. Therefore, the sectors in which these activities are more intense seem to enjoy a comparative advantage provided by their specific technological knowledge, leading to inter-industry exchange of products.

The coefficient of the variable related to scale economies is also highly significant in all the regressions and points at a positive association between this characteristic and the degree of intra-industry trade. This result confirms that the existence of scale economies is an important factor in the emergence of intra-industry trade, as it is stated from a theoretical perspective.

Table 8.4. Determinants of Spanish intra-industry trade: Tobit model estimation results

Variables	(1)	(2)	(3)	(4)	(5)
Const.	0.66824 *** (12.900)	0.68151 *** (21.623)	0.66091 *** (18.332)	0.27330 * (1.872)	0.30013 * (1.828)
RDR	0.23468E-02 (1.136)				
RAE		0.66637 ** (2.316)	0.77782 ** (2.730)	0.73087 *** (3.032)	0.76309 ** (2.796)
RDR	-0.13025E-02 *** (-3.395)	-0.10736E-02 ** (-2.973)	-0.11453E-02 *** (-3.259)	-0.13255E-02 *** (-4.283)	
TDR					-0.18161E-02 *** (-3.338)
SE	1.8369 ** (2.686)	1.4700 ** (2.837)	1.6065 *** (3.105)	1.1030 ** (2.448)	1.0888 * (2.097)
FDI	0.35176E-06 (1.574)	0.24436E-06 (1.262)			
FDIVA			0.27065 (1.530)		
FDIT				0.44029 ** (2.914)	0.40696 ** (2.399)
T	-0.30198E-01 *** (-4.464)	-0.35881E-01 *** (-5.571)	-0.35389E-01 *** (-5.702)	-0.22287E-01 *** (-3.344)	-0.23631E-01 *** (-3.155)
Log-L	22.15955	23.83386	24.16422	26.44177	24.61722
BP (χ_5^2)	3.208191	1.261381	1.883921	2.327728	2.519485
BJL (χ_2^2)	0.537062	0.922578	0.001491	1.132723	1.110650
SW	0.967266	0.957539	0.948222	0.964331	0.944375
LR (χ_6^2)	17.60450	20.95310	21.61384	26.16894	22.51984
$\overline{R}^2$	0.519061	0.615289	0.631865	0.728282	0.653444

Notes:
t statistic in parenthesis
* 10% level of significance
** 5% level of significance
*** 1% level of significance

The participation of multinational firms, approximated by the share of foreign direct investment in total investment flows is again statistically significant in all the regressions in which it has been included. Furthermore, the association between this variable and the share of intra-industry trade is positive. These results give support to the hypothesis 3 in 8.2.1. The proportion of intra-industry trade in a particular industrial sector is larger when the activity of multinational firms operating in that sector is more intense.

Finally, we have to mention that tariff protection seems to play also an important role, in this case of a negative sign, in the intensity of intra-industry trade. It is true that, in principle, the existence of tariff barriers is acting as an obstacle to every type of trade. Nevertheless, we have to stress that, in the case of trade agreements among countries with similar characteristics, it may be justified an increase in the share of intra-industry trade. This is due to factors like demand similarity or cultural and geographical proximity, as well as a higher probability for the countries to belong to an economic integration scheme.

8.3
Summary and Conclusions

In this paper we have analysed the connection between sectoral intensity of intra-industry trade and a series of variables related to industry characteristics including product differentiation, scale economies, technological factors, participation of multinational firms and tariff protection. Using an econometric Tobit model a set of hypotheses concerning the determinants of the degree of intra-industry trade in an industrial sector has been tested.

Empirical evidence found support the existence of a positive association between the level of intra-industry trade and the degree of horizontal product differentiation, the existence of scale economies, and the participation of multinational firms. On the other hand, technological product differentiation and tariff protection seem to have a negative influence on the share of intra-industry trade in total trade of a sector.

References

Amemiya, T.: Advanced Econometrics. Basil Blackwell 1985

Balassa, B. and Bauwens, L.: Changing Trade Patterrns in Manufactured Goods. North Holland Publishing Company 1988

Bano, S. S. : Intra-Industry Trade. The Canadian Experience. Avebury 1991

Bera, A. K., Jarque, C.M. and Lee, L. F.: Testing the Normality Assumption in Limited Dependent Variable Models. International Economic Review 25-3, 563-578 (1984)

Breusch, T. S. and Pagan, A. R.: The Langrange Multiplier Test and its Applications to Model Specification in Econometrics. Review Of Economic Studies 47, 239-254 (1980)

Carrera, M. G.: Comercio Intra-Industrial: Análisis Del Caso Español. Ph. D. Dissertation. University of Cantabria. Department of Economics 1996

Fariñas, J.C. and Martín, C.: Determinantes Del Comercio Intra-Industrial En España. In: El Sector Exterior de la Economía Española. Colegio de Economistas de Madrid 1988

Greenaway, D. and Milner, C. R.: A cross-section Analysis of Intra-Industry Trade in the U.K.. European Economic Review 25, 319-344 (1984)

Greenaway, D. and Milner, C. R.: The Economics of Intra-Industry Trade. Basil Blackwell 1986

Greene, W.: Econometric Analysis. Prentice Hall 1993

Grubel, H. G. and Lloyd, P. J.: Intra-industry Trade: the Theory and Measurement of International Trade in Differentiated Products. John Wiley &Sons 1975

Hughes, K. S.: Intra-Industry Trade in the 1980s: a Panel Study. Weltwirtschaftliches Archiv 129-3, 561-572 (1993)

Maddala, G. S. (1988).- Limited-Dependent and Qualitative Variables In Econometrics. Cambridge University Press.

Maddala, G. S.: Contrastes de Especificación en Modelos de Variable Dependiente Limitada. Cuadernos Económicos del ICE 55, 185-223 (1993)

Martín, C.: El Comercio Industrial Español ante el Mercado Único Europeo. In: Viñals, J. (ed.): La Economía Española ante el Mercado Único Europeo. Alianza Editorial 1992

Melo, F. and Mones, M. A.: La Integración de España en el Mercado Común. Un Estudio de Protección Arancelaria Efectiva. Instituto de Estudios Económicos 1982

Montaner, J. M. and Orts, V.: Comercio Intra-Industrial en España: Determinantes Nacionales y Sectoriales. Revista de Economía Aplicada III, 45-62 (1995)

9 Economic Integration, Vertical and Horizontal Intra-industry Trade and Structural Adjustment: the Spanish Experience

Gema Carrera-Gómez
Department of Economics
University of Cantabria (Spain)

Current research in international trade suggests that intra-industry trade[1] (simultaneous imports and exports of similar products) has acquired an increasing importance in the last years, particularly in the case of transactions of manufactured products among industrialised countries.

One focus of interest to which economic literature on this subject has been addressed concentrates on the process of structural adjustment following trade liberalisation, a matter involving important implications related to economic policy. The costs of such a process may be lower when new trade flows are of an intra-industry nature. This statement is owed to the fact that, in this case, the adjustments are to take place within every industry rather than among different ones. This perception has given wide support to several integration projects, including the implementation of the Common Market or the European Community.

Furthermore, there are good reasons to believe that the adjustment implications of a given trade expansion will differ depending on the nature of IIT itself[2]. Horizontal IIT, defined as trade in different varieties of a product with similar quality but diverse attributes, is expected to give rise to less adjustment problems than vertical IIT, considered as trade in different varieties of a product that offer different levels of service[3].

Despite of the great interest arising from these questions, due to the increasing trade liberalisation, such issues are empirically underresearched. This is so, in part, because of the problems related to appropriately measure horizontal and

---

[1] From now on IIT.
[2] See Greenaway, Hine and Milner (1994, 1995).
[3] That is to say, different varieties of a product involving different qualities.

vertical IIT (as well as IIT itself) and the difficulty to incorporate to the measurement the dynamic nature of the adjustment process.

In this paper, we examine the possible connections between the nature of the newly generated trade following economic integration and the extent of structural adjustment therefore produced. For this purpose, we use Spanish trade and industry data for the time period between Spanish entrance in the European Union and the completion of the Single Market. For this purpose, we use first a marginal IIT index to measure in a *dynamic* sense changes in IIT, while changes in horizontal and vertical IIT are measured according to a methodology proposed by Greenaway, Hine and Milner (1994, 1995). Next, we measure the changes came about on several industrial characteristics during the considered time period. Finally, we test for two propositions concerning Spanish manufacturing industries. The first one assumes that structural adjustment has been lower in industries with high levels of IIT and/or where new trade was largely IIT than in industries where this trade was mainly inter-industrial. The second one says that structural adjustment has been lower in industries with high levels of horizontal IIT and/or where horizontal IIT rather than vertical IIT prevailed in newly generated trade flows. The results obtained give some support for both propositions suggesting, at the same time, the importance of disentangling vertical and horizontal IIT when dealing with structural adjustment issues.

The rest of the paper is organised as follows. Section 9.1 deals with data issues and sets out the methodology employed. Section 9.2 presents the results of the analysis. Finally, Section 9.3 provides some conclusions.

9.1
Data and Methodology

The current study covers the time period from 1985 to 1991. The first point of reference refers to the year previous to Spain's entry to the current European Union, while the second one corresponds to the year immediately previous to the completion of the European Single Market. The time period chosen is accordingly of particular relevance for the purpose at hand.

Trade and industry data are assembled for a number of 74 industries to the 4th digit of the ISIC[4]-Rev. 2 Classification. Since trade figures are published according to the SITC[5] classification, an allocation of 5th digit SITC categories into 4th digit ISIC product groups had to be performed. This reallocation was based on the preliminary table of correspondence between ISIC-based codes and SITC-based codes provided by United Nations (Department for Economic and Social Information and Policy Analysis, Statistical Division)[6]. Industrial statistics are reported by UNIDO[7]. All the statistical information used in the analysis was supplied by *HWWA-Institut für Wirtschaftsforschung*[8].

---

[4] International Standard Industrial Classification of All Economic Activities.
[5] Standard International Trade Classification.
[6] Details of the concordance are available on request from the author.
[7] United Nations Industrial Development Organization.
[8] Hamburg Institute for Economic Research (Germany).

In order to study the connections between IIT and changes in the structure of Spanish industries, it has been applied a recent methodological advance in the empirical analysis of IIT, which tends to incorporate the *dynamic* nature of the adjustment process. As it is widely agreed, the assumption that an increase in the standard Grubel-Lloyd IIT index between two points in time reflects a predominantly intra-industry change in trade flows (and thus lower adjustment costs) can be misleading and lead to erroneous conclusions[9]. It is the nature of new generated trade flows between two points in time what has to be taken into consideration when analysing the advantages of IIT associated with reduced adjustment costs rather than the final level or IIT. For this reason, a number of measures using changes in trade flows to compute the so-called marginal IIT have been proposed up to date[10].

In this study, together with the traditional Grubel-Lloyd indicator of IIT level at a particular point in time (IIT_j), we use a measure of marginal IIT, which focuses on the proportion of matched trade change relative to total trade change ($MIIT_j$)[11]. Indexes definitions are as follows:

$$IIT_j = 1 - \frac{\left| X_j - M_j \right|}{\left(X_j + M_j \right)},$$

$$MIIT_j = 1 - \frac{\left| \left(X_t - X_{t-n} \right) - \left(M_t - M_{t-n} \right) \right|}{\left| X_t - X_{t-n} \right| + \left| M_t - M_{t-n} \right|},$$

where j denotes the 4th digit ISIC industry, X and M denote exports and imports, and t and $t-n$ refer to the two points in time taken into consideration.

The former measure is the standard Grubel-Lloyd index, widely used in empirical IIT studies, while the later, proposed by Brülhart (1994) refers to two points in time (t and $t-n$) and shows the proportion of new trade which is of the intra-industry type[12].

On the other hand, as several authors point out[13], horizontal IIT is likely to lead to lower adjustment pressures than vertical IIT, since different industry and country characteristics can be associated with trade in products involving similar or different qualities (horizontal or vertical differentiation).

In this study vertical and horizontal IIT are identified using a methodology proposed by Greenaway, Hine and Milner (1994, 1995) built upon previous work of Abd-el-Rahman (1991). As these authors point out, the purpose of measuring quality differences in trade has been mainly addressed with the use of unit value

---

[9] The example provided by Shelburne (1993) illustrates this point.

[10] See Hamilton and Kniest (1991), Shelburne (1993), Brülhart (1994), Greenaway, Hine, Milner and Elliot (1994) and Thom and McDowell (1999).

[11] See Brülhart (1994) for a discussion.

[12] The $MIIT_j$ measure (like the IIT_j index) has values ranging from 0 to 1, a value of 0 indicating that new trade is entirely of the inter-industry type, and a value of 1 showing complete matching between new exports and new imports.

[13] See Greenaway, Hine and Milner (1994 and 1995).

indexes which measure the average price of a bundle of items from the same general product grouping. This approach assumes that quality is reflected in price and price can be proxied by unit values. Intra-industry trade can be thus divided into horizontal and vertical components using relative unit values of exports and imports[14].

The share of vertical and horizontal IIT in total trade is computed as follows:

$$
IIT_j^h = \left[1 - \frac{\sum_{i=1}^{n} \left| X_{ij}^h - M_{ij}^h \right|}{\sum_{i=1}^{n} \left(X_{ij}^h + M_{ij}^h \right)} \right] \cdot \frac{\sum_{i=1}^{n} \left(X_{ij}^h + M_{ij}^h \right)}{\left(X_j + M_j \right)},
$$

(9.1)

$$
IIT_j^v = \left[1 - \frac{\sum_{i=1}^{n} \left| X_{ij}^v - M_{ij}^v \right|}{\sum_{i=1}^{n} \left(X_{ij}^v + M_{ij}^v \right)} \right] \cdot \frac{\sum_{i=1}^{n} \left(X_{ij}^v + M_{ij}^v \right)}{\left(X_j + M_j \right)},
$$

(9.2)

where i refers to the 5th digit SITC products in a given 4th digit ISIC industry j.
Total IIT is then decomposed in vertical IIT and horizontal IIT as follows:

$$
IIT_j^* = IIT_j^v + IIT_j^h
$$

$$
IIT_j^* = 1 - \frac{\sum_{i=1}^{n} \left| X_{ij} - M_{ij} \right|}{\sum_{i=1}^{n} \left(X_{ij} + M_{ij} \right)}.
$$

Horizontal intra-industry trade (IIT_j^h) is given by (9.1) for the items i in commodity group j where the following condition holds:

$$
1 - \alpha \leq \frac{UV_{ij}^x}{UV_{ij}^m} \leq 1 + \alpha
$$

where UV^x and UV^m refers to unit values of exports and imports and α is a given dispersion factor.
Vertical intra-industry trade (IIT_j^v) is given by (9.2) for the items i in commodity group j where the following condition holds:

---

[14] Unit values are computed by tonne. Although there are well known problems associated with the different ways of computing unit values (see Greenaway, Hine and Milner, 1994), the use of unit value per tonne tends to be the more widely spread in trade studies.

$$\frac{UV_{ij}^x}{UV_{ij}^m} < 1 - \alpha \quad \text{or} \quad \frac{UV_{ij}^x}{UV_{ij}^m} > 1 + \alpha$$

The dispersion factor α can be given several values giving rise to different price wedges within which IIT is considered as horizontal and outside of which it is defined as vertical. Following Greenaway, Hine and Milner (1994, 1995) we have employed $\alpha = 0.15$ and $\alpha = 0.25$. The first value gives a price wedge of $\pm$ 15% meaning that when the unit value of exports related to the unit value of imports falls within a range of 0.85 to 1.15 intra-industry trade is classified as horizontal and as vertical otherwise. The second value gives a price wedge of $\pm$ 25% within which intra-industry trade is considered as horizontal and as vertical other wise.

We test for two propositions concerning Spanish manufacturing industries. The first one assumes that structural adjustment has been lower in industries with high levels of IIT and/or where new trade was largely IIT than in industries where this trade was mainly inter-industrial. For this purpose, industries are classified into two groups according to the level and increase of IIT. The second proposition assumes that structural adjustment has been lower in industries with high levels of horizontal IIT and/or where horizontal IIT rather than vertical IIT prevailed in newly generated trade flows. To test for this proposition, industries are classified into two groups depending on the level and increase of horizontal and vertical IIT.

In both cases, averages are computed for a set of industry structural characteristics for the period 1985-1991. The industry characteristics analysed are listed below:

- Number of establishments.
- Number of employees.
- Wages and salaries paid to employees.
- Output in factor values.
- Value added in factor values.
- Output per employee.
- Value added per employee.
- Wages and salaries per employee.
- Share of value added in output.
- Share of wages and salaries in value added.

Mean differences are computed next and tested for significance from a statistical point of view. The results obtained are shown in the following section.

9.2
Results

Table 9.1 shows the results obtained concerning changes in several structural characteristics for Spanish manufacturing industries according to the level and increase of IIT.

Table 9.1. Changes in structural characteristics for Spanish manufacturing industries according to the level and increase of intra-industry trade, 1985 to 1991.

Industry characteristics (Percentage changes) [a]	IIT level and increase in marginal IIT [b]		Mean difference
	Low	High	
Number of establishments	59.90	16.54	43.36 ***
	(36.20)	(-2.41)	(38.61) ***
Number of employees	15.29	15.25	0.04
	(3.07)	(5.21)	(-2.14)
Wages and salaries paid to employees	72.03	78.36	-6.33
	(72.03)	(78.36)	(-6.33)
Output in factor values	82.53	67.16	15.37
	(82.53)	(64.88)	(17.65) *
Value added in factor values	71.23	63.01	8.22
	(71.23)	(61.81)	(9.42)
Output per employee	80.44	59.68	20.76 **
	(79.70)	(57.53)	(22.17) **
Value added per employee	68.41	54.81	13.60 *
	(68.41)	(54.41)	(14.00) *
Wages and salaries per employee	66.61	70.08	-3.47
	(66.61)	(70.08)	(-3.47)
Share of value added in output	12.80	11.92	0.88
	(-4.40)	(0.33)	(-4.73)
Share of wages and salaries in value added	17.39	17.38	0.01
	(4.12)	(13.92)	(-9.80) *

Notes:

[a] Table shows averages of absolute values of percentage changes. Values in parentheses are averages of changes without taking absolute values.

[b] An industry is classified under 'high' when the share of intra-industry trade in total trade equalled or exceeded 50% in 1985 and/or the marginal intra-industry trade between 1985 and 1991 equalled or exceeded 50 %.

*** Significant at the 97,5 % level of confidence

** Significant at the 95 % level of confidence

* Significant at the 90 % level of confidence

The data shown in table 9.1 give some support for the hypothesis that structural adjustment has been lower in industries with high levels of IIT and/or where new trade was largely IIT than in industries where this trade was mainly inter-industrial. The mean difference between the industries classified under "low" and those ones classified under "high" is positive and statistically significant for the number of establishments, the output per employee and the value added per employee. When using averages of changes without taking absolute values, the mean difference is significant also for the output in factor values and the share of wages and salaries in value added. The intensity of changes after trade liberalisation in all these industry characteristics seems thus to have been higher for the group of industries with low levels of IIT and/or when the proportion of inter-industry trade in the changes in trade flows between the two time periods is higher.

Tables 9.2 and 9.3 show changes in structural characteristics for Spanish manufacturing industries according to the level and increase of horizontal and vertical intra-industry trade for the values of the dispersion factor $\alpha = 0.15$ and $\alpha = 0.25$. For both price wedges the results obtained give some support for the hypothesis that structural changes have been more intensive in industries with low levels of horizontal IIT and/or when horizontal IIT has grown more than vertical IIT for the period 1985-1991.

For the price wedge of $\pm 15\%$, the difference between the changes in the two groups of industries is statistically significant for the number of establishments, the number of employees, the wages and salaries paid to employees, the output in factor values and the share of value added in output.

When we take the price wedge of $\pm 25\%$ to classify industries under low or high horizontal IIT, all the industry characteristics considered (except for the share of wages and salaries in value added) seem to have changed more intensely for the group of industries in which vertical horizontal IIT is less important.

According to these results, we can say that the structural adjustment brought about by trade liberalisation in the Spanish manufacturing sectors seems to have been less intense for those industries in which horizontal IIT predominates than for those with high level and increase of vertical IIT.

Table 9.2. Changes in structural characteristics for Spanish manufacturing industries according to the level and increase of horizontal and vertical intra-industry trade, 1985 to 1991.

Industry characteristics (Percentage changes) [a]	Horizontal intra-industry trade [b]		Mean difference
	Low	High	
Number of establishments	47.30	15.27	32.03 *
	(22.24)	(-1.67)	(23.91)
Number of employees	17.81	13.52	4.29
	(9.95)	(1.01)	(8.94) **
Wages and salaries paid to employees	87.60	69.19	18.41 **
	(87.60)	(69.19)	(18.41) **
Output in factor values	82.11	63.95	18.16 *
	(82.11)	(61.15)	(20.96) **
Value added in factor values	71.76	60.68	10.98
	(71.11)	(59.75)	(11.36)
Output per employee	70.75	61.56	9.19
	(68.44)	(60.16)	(8.28)
Value added per employee	57.84	58.93	-1.09
	(57.53)	(58.64)	(-1.11)
Wages and salaries per employee	70.65	68.11	2.54
	(70.65)	(68.12)	(2.54)
Share of value added in output	12.55	11.89	0.66
	(-4.17)	(1.26)	(-5.43) *
Share of wages and salaries in value added	17.73	17.14	0.59
	(12.70)	(10.30)	(2.40)

Notes:

[a] Table shows averages of absolute values of percentage changes. Values in parentheses are averages of changes without taking absolute values.

[b] Intra-industry trade is classified as horizontal where the unit value of exports related to the unit value of imports (at the 5-digit level of SITC) falls within a range of 0.85 to 1.15. Outside this range, intra-industry trade is classified as vertical. An industry is classified under 'high' when the share of horizontal intra-industry trade in total trade equalled or exceeded 40% in 1985 and/or the growth of horizontal intra-industry trade was higher than the growth of vertical intra-industry trade for the period 1985 to 1991.

*** Significant at the 97,5 % level of confidence

** Significant at the 95 % level of confidence

* Significant at the 90 % level of confidence

Table 9.3. Changes in structural characteristics for Spanish manufacturing industries according to the level and increase of horizontal and vertical intra-industry trade, 1985 to 1991

Industry characteristics (Percentage changes) [a]	Horizontal intra-industry trade [b]		Mean difference
	Low	High	
Number of establishments	49.72	14.43	35.29 **
	(21.08)	(-0.39)	(21.47)
Number of employees	18.41	13.23	5.19 *
	(8.44)	(2.18)	(6.26)
Wages and salaries paid to employees	90.06	68.01	22.05 ***
	(90.06)	(68.01)	(22.05) ***
Output in factor values	87.79	60.69	27.10 ***
	(87.79)	(57.95)	(29.84) ***
Value added in factor values	77.37	57.41	19.96 ***
	(76.70)	(56.40)	(20.30) ***
Output per employee	79.64	56.04	23.61 ***
	(77.26)	(54.67)	(22.59) **
Value added per employee	66.68	53.21	13.47 *
	(66.36)	(52.93)	(13.43) *
Wages and salaries per employee	75.78	64.87	10.91 ***
	(75.78)	(64.87)	(10.91) ***
Share of value added in output	14.15	10.87	3.28 *
	(-3.48)	(0.69)	(-4.17)
Share of wages and salaries in value added	19.60	15.94	3.66
	(11.29)	(11.26)	(0.23)

Notes:

[a] Table shows averages of absolute values of percentage changes. Values in parentheses are averages of changes without taking absolute values.

[b] Intra-industry trade is classified as horizontal where the unit value of exports related to the unit value of imports (at the 5-digit level of SITC) falls within a range of 0.75 to 1.25. Outside this range, intra-industry trade is classified as vertical. An industry is classified under 'high' when the share of horizontal intra-industry trade in total trade equalled or exceeded 40% in 1985 and/or the growth of horizontal intra-industry trade was higher than the growth of vertical intra-industry trade for the period 1985 to 1991.

*** Significant at the 97,5 % level of confidence

** Significant at the 95 % level of confidence

* Significant at the 90 % level of confidence

9.3
Summary and Conclusions

It is generally assumed that the adjustment costs brought about by trade liberalisation may be different depending on the nature of changes in trade flows. Specifically, there is a greater potential for lower adjustment costs when new trade can be classified as intra-industry trade rather than inter-industry trade. These is so because in the former case reallocation is to take place within industries while the latter implies a reallocation between industries. On the other hand, it has been suggested the importance of distinguishing between horizontal IIT and vertical IIT as the determinants of both may differ. While the former affects diverse varieties of a product with similar characteristics, the latter refers to different varieties of a product involving different qualities. Reallocation of factors may differ in both cases, possibly implying less adjustment problems in the former case.

In this paper, we have examined the relationship between IIT and the adjustment consequences of trade expansion. We have tested the hypotheses that changes in industrial structural characteristics following trade expansion have been less intense for those industries with high level of IIT and/or where new trade was mainly intra-industrial and for those industries with high levels and increase of horizontal IIT.

The results obtained give some support for both propositions suggesting, on the one hand, that changes in industry structure brought about by trade liberalisation are less intense when existing and emerging trade is mainly intra-industrial and, on the other hand, that adjustment costs tend to be lower for those industries in which horizontal IIT is predominant. These results indicate the importance of intra-industry trade for the costs of the adjustment process and suggest, at the same time, the relevance of disentangling vertical and horizontal IIT when dealing with structural adjustment issues.

References

Abd-El-Rahman, K.: Firms' Competitive and National Comparative Advantages as Joint Determinants of Trade Composition. Weltwirtschaftliches Archiv 127, 83-97 (1991).

Brülhart, M.: Marginal Intra-industry Trade: Measurement and Relevance for the Pattern of Industrial Adjustment. Weltwirtschaftliches Archiv 130-3, 600-613 (1994)

Brülhart, M. and Mcaleese, D.: Intra-Industry Trade and Industrial Adjustment: The Irish Experience. The Economic and Social Review 26-2, 107-129 (1995)

Greenaway, D., Hine, R. C. and Milner, C.: Country-Specific Factors and the Pattern of Horizontal and Vertical Intra-industry Trade in the UK. Weltwirtschaftliches Archiv 130, 77-100 (1994)

Greenaway, D., Hine, R. C. and Milner, C.: Vertical and Horizontal Intra-industry Trade: a Cross Industry Analysis For The United Kingdom. The Economic Journal 105, 1505-1518 (1995)

Greenaway, D., Hine, R. C., Milner, C. and Elliot, R.: Adjustment and the Measurement of Marginal Intra-industry Trade. Weltwirtschaftliches Archiv 130-2, 418-427 (1994)

Grubel, H. G., Lloyd, P. J.: Intra-industry Trade: the Theory and Measurement of International Trade in Differentiated Products. London: Macmillan 1975

Hamilton, C. and Kniest, P.: Trade Liberalisation, Structural Adjustment and Intra-industry Trade: a Note. Weltwirtschaftliches Archiv 127-2, 356-367 (1991)

Shelburne, R. L.: Changing Trade Patterns and The Intra-Industry Trade Index: a Note. . Weltwirtschaftliches Archiv 129, 829-833 (1993)

Thom, R. and McDowell, M.: Measuring Marginal Intra-industry Trade. Weltwirtschaftliches Archiv 135 (1), 48-61 (1999)

PART IV. FAILURES OF MARKET AND INDUSTRIAL REGULATION

10 Structure, Functioning and Regulation of the Spanish Electricity Sector. The Legal Framework and the New Proposals for Reform

Francisco Javier Ramos-Real
University of La Laguna (Spain)

Eduardo Martínez-Budría
University of La Laguna (Spain)

Sergio Jara-Díaz
University of Chile (Chile)

10.1
Introduction

An electrical system consists of a series of distinct stages: generation, transmission, distribution and supply (merchandising) of electricity services to the end-users. The traditional organisational model assumes, implicitly or explicitly, the extension of a natural monopoly condition from some of these stages to others. This is a consequence of the presumptive existence of strong, vertically-integrated economies. On the other hand, an increasing number of studies have proposed the vertical disintegration of the sector, suggesting that the common ownership of the different stages of the electric sector should be replaced by the introduction of competition wherever possible. These ideas have been developed within the context of a critique of the traditional control structure, characteristic of natural monopolies, which has been emerging in the industrialised world since the 1980's. The emphasis has now shifted towards the internal efficiency of the companies involved, and to uncovering those faults in the regulatory system which do not allow the product to be obtained at minimum cost.

In this paper, we study the structure, operation and regulation of the Spanish electricity system from 1983 to 2000. This system reflected that the general trend of reform was operating in Spain in 1983. The basic aim of the regulation was to ensure both the recovery and adequate financial return on investments made in the sector at a time of economic crisis. Furthermore, the regulatory system was particularly concerned with introducing incentives as a means for efficiency. The sector began a period of transition from a traditional system of control towards competition in generation and merchandising in 1997.

This paper is organised as follows: in section 2, the structure, functioning and regulation of the sector from 1983 to 1996 is analysed. The modification and improvement process, the basic principles of regulation, the companies financial returns systems, and their influence on the behaviour of companies, are described. In section 3, we summarise the main improvements proposed in 1997. Finally, in section 4, we present the most important conclusions which can be drawn from the study.

10.2
Structure, Functioning and Regulation of the Spanish Electricity Sector between 1983-1996

The structure and operation of the electric sector after the implementation of modifications to the system in 1984, along with the financial returns system operating in the companies until 1996, meant a great change, which had important economic consequences for the Spanish electricity industry[1]. We shall now describe the operation of the Spanish electricity board during that period.

The Spanish electricity sector[2], until 1996, operated as an integrated system. The transmission of electrical power and the short term management of the capacity for generation were in the hands of an independent entity operating under the name of Red Eléctrica de España (REE) or Spanish Electricity Network. The power generation needs for the entire network were defined by the National Power Plans (Plan Energetico Nacional, PEN). Distribution, for the most part, was the responsibility of large companies vertically integrated with generation; these companies were responsible for the supply within certain geographic regions and had the exclusive right to do so. These companies were integrated into the sector's managerial group UNESA[3].

---

[1] This regulatory framework was in effect, in fact, until 1997 when the Electricity Act of 27 November 1997 came into effect, as the directions needed to apply the Ordering of the National Electricity System Act passed in December 1994 were never developed.

[2] We shall be looking only at the mainland's electricity system as the non-peninsular companies such as GESA in the Balearics and UNELCO in the Canaries operate as complete cycle systems independent of the electricity network on the mainland.

[3] Furthermore, there are some small distribution companies that acquire power generated by UNESA companies and resell it to the consumer at the end of the chain. Likewise, there also exists a series of so-called "self-producers" who produce electricity for their own industrial processes and who sell the excess to the electricity companies who, in turn, are obliged to acquire this power at prices set by the legislation. They are also obliged, under the same terms, to buy up the power from independently produced renewable energy sources.

Figure 10.1, is a simplified flowchart showing how the system works. The UNESA companies transfer their production to the transmission network. This power plus the balance arising from international transfers, form a pool where the distributors obtain electrical power to distribute to the consumer. The operational features that are peculiar to the Spanish network are in the transmission stage, which operates and is managed independently of generation and distribution.

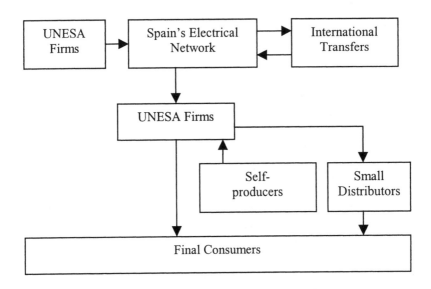

Figure 10.1. Simplified operations of the electricity system in Peninsular Spain

In 1996, the companies that constituted UNESA accounted for 88,9% of the gross production of energy and more than 90% of the distribution. UNESA was made up of ten vertically integrated companies, operating as regional distribution companies. Furthermore, a great proportion of generation was consolidated in the parent-company ENDESA , which acted only at the supply stage and which has been a public owned company for some time now. The production structure of the companies forming UNESA in 1996 is showed in Table 10.1.

Table 10.1. Production by UNESA firms in 1996

Generation.	Mill.Kwh.	%
Hydroelectric	37.694	24,1
Fossil-fueled	62.640	40
Nuclear	56.329	35,9

Source: UNESA Annual Reports

Regarding the installed capacity, the UNESA companies account for 92.65% of the total. The structure is shown in Table 10.2.

Table 10.2. Power installed in UNESA firms in 1996.

Generation	Power installed MW	% of total
Hydroelectric	16.547	36,4
Coal	10.925	24,1
Oil	8.065	17,8
Oil-Gas	2.355	5,2
Total fossils-fueled	21.345	47,1
Nuclear	7.498	16,5

Source: UNESA Annual Reports.

The generation field shows great diversification in the source of the energy. Compared with other countries, the Spanish electricity industry is characterised by a high proportion of hydroelectricity. However, there are important differences between the structure of installed capacity and the production structure. The role of coal and nuclear power in production is much higher than in capacity.

In the 1990's a rapid process of concentration took place thanks to various mergers which gave the ENDESA group (allowing for the absorption in 1996 of FECSA and SEVILLANA) 52% of the generation and 40% of the distribution market. The second group, IBERDROLA, holds a generation quota of 29% and 38% for distribution. The third and fourth producers, Union Fenosa and Hidrocantábrico, have 13% and 6% in generation and 15% and 5% in distribution, respectively.

10.2.1 The Reform Process and the Basic Principles Regulating the System's Operation (1983-1996)

The regulation until the end of 1996, which had been in effect since the early 1980's, had arisen in response to the sector's financial crisis. This crisis was the result of large investment programmes that started after the oil crisis in the 1970s. In an attempt to regulate the situation, government intervention increased during this period, setting a pattern based on negotiations between the companies and the government. In May 1983, an agreement was signed between the main companies in this sector and the Administration. The regulation and legal ordering of the Spanish electricity sector was set by law 49/84 of December 26th, which dealt with the unified administration of the sector. The Stable Legal Framework (Marco Legal y Estable, MLE) set by Royal Decree 1538/1987 regulated the economic environment in which companies should operate. The general outlines defining the Spanish regulatory framework during the period studied were three: centralised planning of the electricity systems by means of National Energy Plans, the unified control of generation and transport, and the setting of standard rates for the entire country.

The agreement made the National Network and the company, public-owned for the most part, responsible for running the Spanish electricity system. The aim of this move was to ensure optimum efficiency, to maintain the National Network, and to promote international transfers of energy. The basic running practices were regulated by law 49/1984 of December 26th. On the 28th of January 1985, Red Electrica de España S.A. (the Spanish Electricity Board) came officially into existence, and assumed the controlling role.

The second additional clause of law 49/1984 established the need for approval of a general plan for the sector regarding the transfer of assets by the Ministry of Industry and Energy, aimed at achieving greater financial-economic equilibrium as well as power equilibrium. The previous unbalance was a consequence of dissimilar investments made by the different companies in response to the oil crisis. In 1985, the negotiations regarding the transfer of assets between the main electricity companies developed and came to an end. These negotiations lasted throughout the period of 1983-1996.

10.2.2 Unified Management and Central Planning

The National Energy Plan (PEN) 1983-1992 considered, for various reasons, paralysing the construction work on five nuclear power stations being built at that time. An order from the Ministry applied an extra charge to the price of electricity in order to finance this moratorium. Simultaneously, a plan was set up, whereby the construction of coal power plants was sped up and the work on oil-gas power plants was also paralysed. The existing Oil-Gas power plants should be used to cover the peak hours demand. REE decided on the extensions to be made to the distribution network, allowing no newcomers and keeping up the local monopolies. In accordance with the aims of the PEN this network extension was carried out by these monopolies. When growth caused overlapping between the areas of two local monopolies demand, the Government assigned it to one of the distributors.

The centralised running of the Spanish electricity sector is in the hands of REE. REE decides which power plants should operate, according to the so-called order of merit, which means the increasing order of variable costs. The system of operation aimed to reduce to an absolute minimum the supply costs while maintaining them within limits set by general criteria regarding safety and energy policy[4]. The policy of unified running is carried out within a structure whereby companies involved in the generation and distribution stages, and the one parent-company ENDESA (specialised in power generation) work hand in hand. Therefore, power transfers during each timetable block become necessary so that the production planned in each company's power plants, plus the balance of exchanged power, coincides with the demand.

The assignment of energy transfers, as well as its cost, took place through a pool formed by energy surplus from firms with excess capacity, since the REE

---

[4] In this respect it is worth mentioning the restrictions resulting from quotas and limitations on the use of national coal.

programme assigned them a production that exceeded their market necessities. To the surplus of each firm, a marginal cost was assigned equal to that of the energy delivered at the highest marginal cost. From these reference values, a weighted average price was calculated with the marginal costs of all the firms' surplus. This is the price that is taken into account to calculate the standard cost[5] of transfers. In the case of firms whose variable cost was larger than that of the pool, it was supposed that they deliver energy at this price and buy again at the new average price of the resultant pool.

In Table 10.3 we summarise the reform process in the period 1983-1997.

Table 10.3. Summary of the reform process

Year	Event	Development
1983	Agreement convention signed between firms	Revision of the PEN
1984	Law 49/1984 for integrated operations of the sector	Compensation system begins.
1985	———	Development of assets exchange. January: creation of REE
1987	Legal and Stable Framework, Royal Decree 1538/1987.	
1988	———	Development of the new compensation system of firms and MLE compensations.
1994	Approval of Law Ordering the National Electricity Sector (LOSEN)	Proposal of creation of independent system.
1997	Approval of New Electricity Law	End of traditional regulation system of the MLE.

10.2.3 The Rates and Financial Return Policy of the Legal and Stable Framework (MLE)

The guidelines regulating the economic and financial returns in the sector was finalised at the end of 1987 with the promulgation of the Stable Legal Framework, which came into effect in January 1988.

Although the mechanism of the MLE is rather complicated, it basically implied that a company involved in the generation and/or distribution stages received payments equal to its standard cost. The standard costs are a value set across all the companies involved in generation and distribution, based on both the fixed and variable costs, and including sufficient return for invested capital. Income from sales, according to the methodology of the MLE, should cover the cost of the service of the entire system. This cost is calculated by finding the aggregate of all the recognised standard costs. Furthermore, a series of extra charges is added to the rates.

---

[5] In this way no firm covers its demand with energy whose variable cost is more expensive than that of the pool. This mechanism allows afterwards the compensation system that needs to identify standard costs of trade for each firm.

The Ministry of Industry and Energy, by means of the General Board of Energy, determines the standard values following particular economic and energy parameters which define each concept involved in the cost. The costs that make up the total expenses to be included in the final prices are:

1. Fixed costs of generation. These cover the investments in the infrastructure and include the depreciation charges and returns on the assets.
2. Operation and maintenance costs. One part is considered fixed and another part variable according to the power installed or energy generated.
3. Variable costs arising from fuel used and transfers. This includes the costs of fuel and other fungible materials used in generation, the net cost of transfers with the pool and other transfers such as that with self-producers and international contracts.
4. Fixed and running cost in distribution. Levels of tension above or below 36KV are distinguished. In lower levels of tension this is calculated by means of the quantity of energy circulated. For higher levels, the type of investment is used for fixed cost and physical entities are used for running costs.
5. Merchandising costs. This comprises activities related to the upkeep and development of the market. This is standardised through the number of contracts and by the power turnover in tensions larger than 1 KV.
6. Cost of distribution and generation structure. This embraces costs that are not linked to productive activity and financial expenditures of clients' accounts.
7. Miscellaneous costs. This includes the quota of the Spanish Electricity Network and other surcharges in the invoice like the nuclear moratorium, the quota of the Office of Compensation (OFICO), basic stock of uranium and research funds. These surcharges together represented 14.38% of the electrical tariff in 1989 and 13% in 1996.

The Compensation System

There is just one rate for the whole country, but the different companies have both different generation equipment and different market structures, which lead to different distribution costs and different revenue per kwh sold. The acknowledged income of the companies is not the actual sum paid by clients, but the total of the acknowledged standard costs instead. Therefore a compensation system between companies becomes necessary in order to balance out the final income received by each firm with the sum of its recognised costs.

A more detailed description of the calculation of inter-firm compensation is provided by Rodríguez and Castro (1994). The compensation system aims to even out each company's unit cost regarding generation (generation compensation) and, on the market side, the idea is to even out each company's average income as compared with the average income of the system (market compensation). The algebraic sum of the compensations equals zero.

Generation compensation is calculated as follows:

$$Z_g^i = (CF_g^i + \frac{CV_g^i}{1+\pi}) - \sum(CF_g^i + CV_g^i)\frac{D_g^i}{\sum D_g^i} + \beta_i \frac{\pi}{1+\pi}\sum CV_g^i \qquad (10.1)$$

where:

Z^i_g: generation compensation of the firm i.

CF^i_g : standard fixed cost of generation of the firm i.

CV^i_g: standard variable cost of the generation of firm i.

D^i_g: demand of the firm i in Plant[6]

π: percentage which is taken from the variable costs to reward firms with the lowest variable costs.

β_i: coefficient of efficiency in variable costs of the firm i.

The first two terms of equation (10.1) reflect the difference between the company's average generation cost and the system average, multiplied by the company's market share. The parameter π represents the percentage of the variable costs not considered in the compensation. This creates a fund (generation margin) to be redistributed among the companies, according to the coefficient β_i[7]. The third term in equation (10.1) may be interpreted as the share of the generation margin due to each company's subsystem, based on technical efficiency. Thus those companies who contribute to the reduction of the cost of the service are rewarded.

Market compensation includes compensations for distribution costs, income from sales, and other revenue.

$$Z^i_m = (\frac{D^i_d}{\sum D^i_d} \sum I^i - I^i) - (\frac{D^i_d}{\sum D^i_d} \sum C^i_d - C^i_d) \qquad (10.2)$$

where:

Z^i_m: market compensation of the firm i.

C^i_d: fixed and variable costs of distribution and commercial management of the firm i.

D^i_d: demand in Plant, obtained in each tariff from the consumption of the subscribers for the firm i.[8]

I^i: collects the net sales turnover and other incomes from each firm.[9]

---

[6] This is the sum of the energy generated in Plant from all the installations of each firm. This is standardized by a coefficient of their own consumption so that any saving in real consumption means an additional profit for the firm in question.
[7] This coefficient is calculated as being inversely proportional to variable costs.
[8] The invoiced energy declared in each tariff is multiplied by a standard coefficient of losses to convert it in demand in Plant. In this way each kwh not invoiced suppose a loss for the firm. The standard coefficient is the average value of the system for which will coincide with that of generation for all the system but not for each individual firm.

The first component in equation (10.2), if positive, means that the company receives less revenue than is due them, according to the average for the sector[10]. The second component has a similar meaning to the generation compensation in that the company is compensated for the difference between its acknowledged cost and the average for the distribution sector.

We can sum up the basic principles that make up the MLE as follows (Rodríguez and Castro, 1994):

a) The administration determines for each firm a standard cost CS, according to its generation equipment and distribution structure.

b) Each firm conducts its production activity according to the directives from the managing firm from the integrated operations, incurring a cost C, and receives from sales in its market an income R thus obtaining a gross profit:

GB=R-C.

c) Each firm receives a compensation (T) equal to the difference between the standard costs and their income (or payment if negative):

T=CS-R.

d) The net profit received (GN) by each firm will be:

GN = GB+T = (R-C) + (CS-R) = CS-C

The regulating method supposes that the aim of each company is to maximise the difference between standard and real costs. Regarding the productive efficiency of the system, it may be stated that the reduction of production costs is favoured, as any reduction in real costs benefits the company.

Effects of the MLE on Firms' Behaviour

On many occasions, the MLE has been classified as a case of yardstick competition, where the fixing of the price in any company is decided according to the average cost across the other companies. As Schleifer (1985) suggests, any improvement in efficiency in the sector becomes a modification of the 'yardstick'.

Rodríguez and Castro (1994), consider that calculation of the individual standard cost figures should be carried out in an *ad hoc* manner, arising from a specific price index (the Consumer Price Index, the Industrial Price Index or an average of the two). For this reason, the standard cost should be taken as a maximum price and updated periodically, independent of the average efficiency of the sector[11].

---

[9] Gross income is converted into net income by detracting the charge for invoicing valid in each period and adding amounts received from the Office of Compensation (OFICO) for special tariffs such as off-peak electricity provision.

[10] To give more detail, payment made by way of compensation is calculated, tariff by tariff, by comparing the average income of the company with the average income of the whole system. If the result is positive, the company keeps half, and if it is negative, it loses half. Thus the standardisation of revenue could encourage companies to increase their sale prices.

[11] The classic *price cap* formula allows for price increases equal to the rate of inflation minus a factor X which reflects the average growth of productivity of the companies.

Kühn and Regibeau (1998) consider that the regulation system of the MLE has brought about incentives to reduce costs, but they point out a series of aspects which could have a negative effect on the behaviour of the companies during this period, against the intentions of the regulator. On one hand, the incentives for cost reduction were not applied equally to all types of costs. In the case of REE, such incentives did not even exist as the standard cost established was to be the same as its income. On the other hand, the aim of maximising the difference between real and standard costs can be achieved by increasing the standard costs after complicated negotiation between the government and the companies.

Crampes & Laffont (1995) studied, within the framework of the theory of incentives, how the MLE's financial return system created incentives for efficient behaviour. The standard costs CS and real costs CR for each company i are separated into fixed F and variable V:

$$CS^i{}_{average} \equiv \frac{CS^i}{q^i} = cvs^i + \frac{FS^i}{q^i}$$

$$CR^i{}_{average} \equiv \frac{CR^i}{q^i} = cvr^i + \frac{FR^i}{q^i}$$

The standard values depend, above all, on the company's decisions regarding investments, but they also depend on the regulator's assessment of the company's fixed and operative costs. A variable e_1 will be used to refer to the effort made by the management regarding equipment or technical issues ex ante, e. g. the choice of power plant size, which is beyond the control of the regulator. The variables of the real costs depend on e_1 and on the appropriate use of the equipment, thus we will call e_2 the variable associated with the appropriate use of equipment or technical effort ex post. Although the management does not decide on the price, they do have a say in the decision of supplying to each area of the market. As each company sells different products[12], we can consider e_1, e_2 and e_3 as vectors. The optimising model that explains the behaviour of the company may be expressed as follows:

$$\max_{e1,e2,e3} \Sigma_r \left(CS^i_r - CR^i_r \right) - \psi^i (e_1, e_2, e_3))$$

$$= \Sigma_r \left[(cvs^i_r(e_{1r}) - cvr^i_r(e_{1r}, e_{2r}))q^i_r(e_{3r}) + FS^i_r(e_{1r}) - FR(e_{1r}) \right] - \psi^i(e_1, e_2, e_3))$$

where r represents each type of tariff and ψ the disutility or cost of the effort.

The technical decisions depend on e_1 and e_2, such that the first order conditions of the problem are:

$$q^i_r \left(\frac{dcvs^i_r}{de_{1r}} - \frac{\partial cvr^i_r}{\partial e_{1r}} \right) + \frac{d(FS^i_r - FR^i_r)}{de_{1r}} = \frac{\partial \psi^i}{\partial e_{1r}} \qquad (10.3)$$

$$-q_r^i \cdot \frac{\partial \, cvr_r^i}{\partial \, e_{2r}} = \frac{\partial \, \psi^i}{\partial \, e_{2r}} \tag{10.4}$$

The condition (10.4) shows that the marginal disutility of effort in variable costs coincides with the marginal profits derived from the reduction in variable costs. So, technical effort *ex post* leads to minimise costs through the compensation mechanism. From condition (10.3) it cannot be deduced that the technical effort *ex ante* is adequate, that is, the marginal disutility of effort in fixed costs does not coincide with the marginal profits derived in fixed cost reductions, for this it must be that:

$$-\frac{\partial \, CR_r^i}{\partial \, e_{1r}} = \frac{\partial \, \psi^i}{\partial \, e_{1r}} \tag{10.5}$$

We can deduce that the incentives derived from the regulatory framework can produce bias in investment decisions. As regards market effort the first order condition is:

$$(cvs_r^i - cvr_r^i)\frac{dq_r^i}{de_{3r}} = \frac{\partial \, \psi^i}{\partial \, e_{3r}} \tag{10.6}$$

This shows that the company is interested in concentrating its sales at those rates where the cost is the lowest in relation to the standard value defined by the regulator. The company does not study social welfare, measured in terms of the individual surplus of each type of consumer; nor does it find a solution to the secondary problem presented by a competitive balance whose solution would be:

$$(pr_r^i - cvr_r^i)\frac{dq_r^i}{de_{3r}} = \frac{\partial \, \psi^i}{\partial \, e_{3r}} \tag{10.7}$$

Crampes & Laffont highlight a further series of facts derived from the regulation and financial returns system, which we detail below:

1. Firms are remunerated on the basis of the equipment available encouraging the management to declare in total avoiding selective declarations.
2. The MLE determines two complementary mechanisms to correct inefficiencies. The first was a share of the margin on variable costs (generation margin) to redistribute it between the firms according to the coefficient β. This produces an incentive that approximates efficient behaviour *ex ante* although limited by the lack of weight that this margin has since it does not influence fixed costs. The second mechanism is to try to create incentives for the adequate behaviour of the market effort. For this the company only recognised half of the difference

---

[12] Considering the quantity sold in each tariff as a separate product.

in each tariff between the average sector income and that of each firm. The advantage of this mechanism allows consideration of the prices as a decision variable so that firms internalise the market structure.

3. The system resembles yardstick-competition but taking as a reference standard costs instead of the sector average. These standard costs take into account the sector's heterogeneity and avoid the production of huge profits or losses that would result from the pure application of a pure reference system.

4. From the dynamic point of view efficiency can be affected in different ways. The revision of standard costs is achieved in a discretional way[13] so that firms fear that real reductions of costs mean reductions in standard values and consequently a possible decrease in future income. This can discourage firms from investing appropriately.

5. A difficult element for the regulator to control is product quality. This is not easy to distinguish in the case of network investment if the aim is to expand or to improve the service. In the regulatory framework in force, if firms tend to minimise cost against quality, other firms will not be remunerated appropriately so that this is a problem of overall regulation. In the MLE this is a personalised problem in the context of the revision of the standard costs.

6. Another problem emerges because the system does not provide incentives to save energy since a co-ordination mechanism does not exist to reduce production. The compensation system in fixed costs means that firms have equipment ready to produce, and the mechanism of variable standard cost ensures a safe profit for any quantity that is produced.

The Evolution of Productivity

There may be certain reservations regarding incentives for efficiency present in the terms of the MLE, but the majority opinion is that considerable improvements have been made in the technical efficiency and profitability of the sector.

Kuhn and Regibeau (1998) point out certain indications that would support this opinion. For them, the prices of electricity in Spain are below the average of the surrounding countries in the majority of consumer categories. This fact, along with the high profit level in Spanish generation companies would suggest that the price of generation in Spain is somewhat lower than in many other industrialised countries.

The report produced by UNESA (1997) also tells us that, during the period that the SLF was in effect, –and more specifically from 1988-1995– utilities achieved increased efficiency which was transferred to the consumer in part through the drop in electricity rates in real terms (10.6% during that period). Equally, the report points out that the rates in Spain, both for domestic and industrial use, have been kept below the average of the main European countries.

Arocena and Rodríguez (1998) assess the consequences of the regulation on productivity in coal-based electricity generation during the period 1988-1995, using the Malmquist productivity index. The unit of analysis is the generating

---

[13] Apart from the factor depending on the Consumer Price Index or the Industrial Price Index, it is not known exactly what other adjustments are involved in the calculation of standard costs.

group and capital; work and fuel are factors considered. The main conclusions of the paper are the following:

- Productivity increases are observed for all groups during these years apart from 1989 to 1990. The annual average rate of productive growth between 1988 and 1994 is 3.2%. This productivity index can be broken down into the rate of technical efficiency and technical progress.
- The rate of technical efficiency shows its greatest increase the first year (4.7%) and the last year (2%). The first case can be explained by the immediate effects of the MLE coming into effect. In the second case, the explanation is to be found in the improvements brought into the running of the system thanks to the competitive environment created by the new Law Ordering the National Electricity System (LOSEN) in 1994.
- The rate of technical progress shows a moderate increase, except between 1991 and 1992, when it was 5.6% as a consequence of the environmental measures which required large investments and improvements in the thermal efficiency of the plants.
- This index should be modified, bearing in mind the effect of the rate of installed energy used, given that the greater use of fixed factors could explain, in part, the improvements in productivity. The new index shows improvements each year, with an average of 2.8% between 1988 and 1994.

Ramos (2000) has carried out a study of the evolution of productivity in the Spanish electricity sector, by means of the estimation of a multiproduct long run cost function, where the unit studied is the company. The results suggest that productivity has improved almost 20% during the period of 1989-1996, with an annual rate of 2.62%. The most significant improvements occurred between 1989 and 1993, during the first years of the MLE.

The improvements in productivity have, for the most part, been expressed as increased profit for the companies, as the adjustment of price rates did not take into account the possible gain in productivity.

10.3
Regulation Reform in the Spanish Electricity Sector from 1997

In this section we will deal with the most significant aspects of the renewal process undertaken in the Spanish energy sector, starting in 1997. Fundamentally, it has been a case of developing the system from a traditional control model to a market model based on the generators and on the final demand for energy. We shall detail the views and opinions of different writers about the process underway, specifically the analyses by Kühn and Regibeau (1998), Marín (1999), and Rodríguez (1999).

The reform of the regulation directed towards the market was discussed initially in 1993, and was started by the promulgation of the Law Ordering the National Electricity Sector (LOSEN) in 1994. This legislation permitted the gradual introduction of competition in the sector without totally dismantling the system established by the MLE. The idea was to create a competitive energy market parallel to the existing system. The National Commission for the Electricity System (CNSE), which was a regulatory institution independent of the Ministry of Industry and Energy, was created although the latter retained the power of final decision. The problems arising from the system designed by the LOSEN, in combination with the change of government in 1996 accelerated the reform process. The companies reached an agreement with the government at the end of 1996, called the Electricity Protocol, which provided the basis for the new Electricity Law of November 27th, 1997.

The Electricity Law of 1997 (LSE)

The 1997 Electricity Law (LSE) extended the liberalisation brought about by the LOSEN and created the electricity wholesale market, with an initial transition period to deregulate prices and re-structure the market. This liberalising process has to meet the standards laid out in European Guidelines 96/92 EC on the community rules governing the internal energy market. The liberalising process suggested in the EU guidelines has been, however, slower than that followed in Spain.

The final aim is to completely deregulate generation and merchandising. Transmission and distribution, networks by definition, will continue to be regulated, as will be the tolls applied for their use. The law only specifies, within the areas of these regulated activities, that the tolls should be related in some way to the costs and should be uniform across the State. Third party access to the network will be guaranteed, assuming available capacity.

The agents who will take part in the electricity market are the generators who produce the electricity, the companies whose high-voltage wires carry the electricity, the distributors who serve the non-eligible customers, the customers eligible because of the volume of energy they consume, and the new marketing companies. The market will be overseen by two operating companies: the system operator who physically manages both the network and the delivery of power, and the market operator who directs the energy transfer system to determine the market price. The CNSE will inspect the system.

A company with sufficient financial and technological means will be allowed to enter the generation segment; any agent with sufficient financial resources will be able to sell energy to any type of consumer. The income of these marketing agents will depend solely on the contracts signed with their customers. The prices obtained by the generating companies will be decided by the market or bilateral contracts.

The spot market functions as a double auction where there are sales and purchase offers on the demand side. A regulatory surcharge, known as the power guarantee, is added to the spot market price, to avoid insufficient supply. The initial amount was fixed at 1.3 pesetas/kwh and corresponds to all the capacity available during the 4,500 peak demand hours of a year. At the end of 1998, the average charge was around 1.26ptas/kwh.

The merchandising segment will be liberalised gradually, so that, in year 2001, all high voltage customers will be able to choose their supplier, (which represents 50% of the power consumed). The customers who cannot choose freely will still be within the influence area of particular distributors; the rate will be set by the government, and will be standard across the country. This rate will be based on the permanent costs of the system (operators and CNSE), the purchase price of the electricity, distribution and transmission costs, and two types of financial returns from transition costs: the nuclear moratorium and the expenses incurred by transition to competition.

The regulating regime imposes some type of vertical separation of activities in relation to property and accounting regulations. The operators will be private companies. Companies and consumers operating on the spot market will be allowed to participate, though with a maximum limit to the number of shares. The companies taking part in any of the regulated activities will not be allowed to participate directly in the non-regulated areas. Although there may be a legal separation, the presence of holding companies operating in both fields will be permitted. The accounting regulations require keeping separate accounts in the case of firms with shares in more than one regulated area; this is required from those companies that only participate in the areas subject to competition.

The Nuclear Moratorium and the Costs of Transition to Competition (CTC)

The payments to the firms affected by the nuclear moratorium have been extended indefinitely. The companies receive compensation by means of a surcharge on the price of electricity, which cannot exceed 3.54% of the income obtained. The Transition to Competition Costs (CTC) are aimed at compensating the loss of capital of the companies constituting the MLE on December 31st 1997, due to the introduction of competition. This payment will be expressed in pts/kwh and will reflect the difference between the average revenue obtained by these companies under the previous system and that obtained in the spot market. If the average price on the market exceeds 6 ptas/kwh, the difference will be deducted from the discounted value of the compensation. These payments will be made during a period of ten years and will increase the utility rates.

The discounted value of the compensation will not exceed 1,988,561 million pesetas (including the incentives related to coal). These coal-related incentives have been a load on the sector, since the national coal cost is twice as much as coal on the international market. These incentives will last throughout the transition period, as the law explicitly permits the authority's interference in the rules so that the use of national sources of primary energy may reach 15%.

Controversies

The CTC has been very controversial since the start of the liberalisation process. The calculations noted in the Protocol were widely criticised by the CNSE and consumer associations. For some existing assets, the price obtained on the market may suppose a loss in value (the remuneration through market price being lower than the costs acknowledged under the previous remuneration system); however, the opposite may also occur[14]. The controversy has reappeared with the claim on part of the CTC (worth 1.3 billion pesetas) by the power firms, a claim backed by the government. There is a debate regarding the exact final quantity of money to be paid. Moreover, the European Commission's intervention considering the CTC as a disguised grant system to favour national companies, places the whole process in question.

The opinion that the sector is highly concentrated on a few firms seems fairly unanimous, as is the opinion that these companies operate following the vertical integration structure in the area of generation and distribution. The privatisation of ENDESA could have been carried out segregating the assets beforehand, but the opposite route was chosen. The government allowed ENDESA to acquire other companies and create a larger group. Rodríguez (1999) has pointed out that this can be analysed from two different angles. In the national context, and bearing in mind the scarce capacity for international connection, the level of concentration could be considered excessively high for the market to function efficiently. If, on the other hand, we consider the international market and adopt a mid-term and long-term perspective, any policy of de-concentration could have an influence on the future competitive ability of the Spanish companies. Ramos (2000) noted the existence of moderate economies of vertical integration between generation and distribution and, to a greater extent, the presence of economies of horizontal integration between the different types of generation and distribution. The existence of savings obtained from undertaking different activities together should be kept in mind when restructuring the sector, but it is not incompatible with the vertical disintegration of the sector as long as the markets allow effective competition in each area.

Another problem is the distortion that the CTC can bring about in the spot market. The control of the spot market price by the same companies that receive the CTCs generates unethical incentives. The established companies could try to keep the prices in this market down, in order to claim maximum compensation and, at the same time, make it difficult for other companies to enter the field of generation. Rodríguez (1999) notes that the average price of the market in 1998 has settled to around 6 pts/kwh, thus maximising the income derived from the market without affecting the maximum quantity recoverable through the CTC.

The regulatory effort is insufficient to introduce competition into the sector in Spain, according to Kühn and Regibeau (1998). We now detail the opinion offered by these authors, who compare the Spanish situation with that of the United Kingdom. Basically, they analyse three issues: the concentration of the generation field, the slow liberalisation of merchandising and the high level of vertical integration.

---

[14] One illustrative example is that of the Austrian regulator. In Austria, as in Spain, hydroelectric energy is remunerated according to costs, independent of when it was generated. However, liberalisation allows it to be remunerated at the price of the pool, which at peak times is much higher, providing extra revenue for the companies. The Austrian regulator considered that this improvement in the remuneration system more than compensated for the CTCs and so did not award any further compensation. Each European country has followed different criteria in their liberalisation process, regarding this type of compensation for transition costs. In England and Wales, for example, it has been incorporated into the company sale price.

1. In the United Kingdom, the high level of concentration on the supply side allowed only a few companies the control of marginal supplies on the spot market; the gains obtained in productivity were not felt by the consumer. In Spain, only two companies (ENDESA & IBERDROLA) control the majority of the assets that determine the marginal price of the market: the coal power plants and the hydroelectric plants. The problems of market structure are worsened by other characteristics of the Spanish sector. In Great Britain, the larger companies' share began to deteriorate with the introduction of combined-cycle technology. In Spain, there was a greater capacity surplus in the sector and the primary energy source, natural gas, is practically a monopoly. These companies make agreements with the existing generators to keep new firms from entering the field.

2. The extended period of transition for the liberalisation of the merchandising allows the distribution monopolies already in existence to set up barriers protecting themselves from competition in distribution. The manipulation of the final price for consumers is possible given that it is set by an implicit agreement between the government and the companies. Although the government and the firms have committed themselves to annual price reductions of 3%, the high margins in generation allow greater price reductions.

3. The high level of vertical concentration does not seem appropriate, nor does the delay in the freedom to choose the supplier by final consumers. These two circumstances could make the price hardly vulnerable to competition pressure, given that the same companies will bid on demand as distributors and/or merchandising agents.

Finally, the regulating institutions have been designed to give MIE greater control over the CNSE. Moreover, the government has certain prerogatives for the fixing of tolls and for other important decisions.

10.4
Conclusions

The organisation structure of the electricity sector between 1983 and 1996 drew together the features of a vertically integrated and a non-integrated structure. The transmission stage operated separately from the generation and distribution stages, and its management was also separated from those two stages. The regulation system assumed that the aim of the company was to maximise the difference between standard and real costs, in order to favour the reduction of production costs, given that any decrease in real costs supposed an increase in gains for the company. The studies carried out by different analysts suggest that, while the Stable Legal Framework was in effect, the electricity companies achieved increased productivity mainly thanks to management improvements, which had positive repercussions on the efficiency of the companies.

The reform of the sector that got underway in 1997 had as its goal the complete deregulation of the areas of generation and merchandising. The new scheme for operating and regulating will be developed gradually. Some experts express specific doubts about the future of the liberalisation, basing their opinion on the point of departure of this process. The factors that encourage this opinion are largely focussed on four issues: the low capacity for international connection, the excessive concentration in the area of generation, the slow liberalisation of the marketing area, and a high degree of vertical integration.

References

Arocena, P. and Rodríguez, L.: Incentivos en la regulación del sector eléctrico español (1988-1995) (Incentives for regulation in the Spanish Electric Sector, 1988-1995). Revista de Economía Aplicada 18, 61-84 (1998)

Crampes, C. and Laffont, J. J.: Transfers and Incentives in the Spanish Electricity Sector. Revista Española de Economía. Monográfico Regulación, 117-140 (1995)

Kühn, K. and Regibeau, P.: ¿Ha llegado la competencia?. Un análisis económico de la reforma de la regulación del sector eléctrico en España (Has competition arrived? An economic analysis of the regulatory reform in the Spanish Electric Sector). Instituto de Análisis Económico 1998

Marín, P. L.: Liberalización y competencia en el sector eléctrico (Liberalisation and competition in the electric sector). Economistas 80, 62-71 (1999)

Ramos Real, F. J.: Economías de integración y productividad en el sector eléctrico español en el periodo 1983-1996. Un enfoque multiproductivo (Economies of Integration and Productivity in the Spanish Electric Sector. A Multiproduct Approach). Ph. D. Thesis, Departamento de Analisis Economico, Universidad de La Laguna, 2000

Rodríguez Romero, L.: Regulación, estructura y competencia en el sector eléctrico español (Regulation, structure and competition in the Spanish Electric Sector). Economistas 82, 121-132 (1999)

Rodríguez Romero, L. and Castro Rodríguez, F.: Aspectos económicos de la configuración del sector eléctrico en España: ¿ Una falsa competencia referencial? (Economic aspects of the electric sector in Spain. A false yardstick competition?). Cuadernos económicos de I.C.E. nº 57, 161-183 (1994)

Shleifer, A.: A theory of yardstick competition. Rand Journal of Economics 16-3, 319-327 (1985)

UNESA: Evolución económico-financiera del sector eléctrico 1988-1995 (Financial-Economic Evolution of the Electric Sector). UNESA 1997.

11 Effects of a Reduction of Standard Working Hours on Labour Market Performance[*]

Carlos Pérez-Domínguez
Department of Economics
University of Valladolid (Spain)

In recent years many people have proposed a general reduction of the number of working hours as an effective measure to reduce unemployment rates in the European countries. This proposal has had a strong effect on public opinion, since the "working-less-for-everyone-to-be-able-to-work" assumption seems to be a self-evident truth. But there is a fallacy involved in this assumption: the labour market is rather dynamic and neither the jobs available nor the number of applicants have to remain fixed when the standard working hours are reduced by legal means.

This paper will develop a theoretical model that will enable us to ascertain how a reduction of the standard working hours affects the labour market performance.

The first section of this paper studies the expected effects of a reduction of standard working hours on employment. The second section analyses the effects of this measure on labour force participation. The third section combines the results of the previous sections in order to evaluate the effects of such a reduction on the unemployment rate. The fourth and final section summarises the main results of the present paper.

---

[*] I am grateful to José Miguel Sánchez-Molinero for helpful comments and suggestions. I acknowledge financial support for Spanish Ministry of Labour.

11.1
Effects on Employment

11.1.1 The Basic Model

We shall start by assuming that the labour demand function for an individual firm is given by the following expression

$$w = f(H); \quad f(h) > 0; \quad f'(H) < 0 \tag{11.1}$$

where H stands for the total number of hours demanded and w is the real wage per hour.

We assume that the length of the working day, h, is legally fixed. The firm has to decide how many workers, N, is going to hire, so that the total number of working hours, H, is optimal. We assume that overtime is not allowed.

The previous assumptions allow us to write

$$W/h = f(h \ N) \tag{11.2}$$

where W is the wage per person. We assume that W is fixed either by the law or by collective bargaining. Taking logarithms and reordering this equation, we have

$$\log W = \log h + \log f(h \ N) \tag{11.3}$$

Taking differentials on both sides of this equation, we obtain

$$\dot{W} = \dot{h} + \frac{d\log f}{dH}(h \cdot dN + N \cdot dh) \tag{11.4}$$

where the dotted variables indicate logarithmic derivatives (that is, growth rates). If we now multiply and divide the right hand side by H, we obtain

$$\dot{W} = \dot{h} - \frac{1}{\varepsilon}\left(\dot{h} + \dot{N}\right) \tag{11.5}$$

where ε accounts for the elasticity of the working hours with respect to the hourly wage in absolute value.

Regrouping and solving for $\dot{N}$ we have

$$\dot{N} = (\varepsilon - 1)\dot{h} - \varepsilon \dot{W} \tag{11.6}$$

This expression tells us how the number of employees varies in response to changes in the standard working hours and in the wage per person.

Next, we shall analyse the effects of a reduction of the standard working hours ($\dot{h} < 0$) on the number of workers demanded under two extreme theoretical assumptions: first, the wage per worker does not change ($\dot{W} = 0$); and second, the wage per worker falls in the same proportion as the working hours.

If the wage per worker is not altered, the effects of a measure that reduces the standard working hours on employment is given by

$$\dot{N} = (\varepsilon - 1) \cdot \dot{h} \tag{11.7}$$

This means that employment could increase, decrease or remain constant depending on whether the working-hours elasticity (in absolute value) is lower, higher or equal to one.

Some economic works on the Spanish economy have found that the most feasible values for ε are those close to one[1]. In the case $\varepsilon = 1$, a reduction of the number of working hours would not cause any effect on employment, unless it included some wage cutting measures.

In the case the wage per worker is adjusted in such a way that payment per hour remains constant, $\dot{w} = 0$, expression (11.6) implies that[2]

$$\dot{N} = -\dot{h} \tag{11.8}$$

regardless of the value of ε. In this particular case, the decrease in the number of working hours would increase employment in the same proportion.

When $\varepsilon > 1$, we already know that cutting the standard working hours causes a negative effect on employment unless a wage reduction takes place. Hence, we may ask the following: in what proportion should the wage per worker fall in order to avoid the negative effect on employment?

We want $\dot{N} = 0$; hence, expression (11.6) implies

$$\dot{W} = \left(1 - \frac{1}{\varepsilon}\right)\dot{h} \tag{11.9}$$

Given that $\varepsilon > 1$, the term within brackets must be positive and lower than one. Therefore, the wage per worker falls in order to keep the employment level constant.

To sum up, the conclusion of the previous argument can be stated as follows:

If the wage rate does not vary, a reduction of the standard working hours increases employment, provided that the elasticity of the working hours with respect to wages, ε, is less than one, and reduces employment when $\varepsilon > 1$. When $\varepsilon = 1$, the effect of the reduction of working hours on employment is null.

The negative effects of this type of measure on employment are, then, constrained to the case where $\varepsilon > 1$. But these effects can be alleviated if the reduction of the working hours is accompanied by a wage cut. In order to avoid a decrease in the employment level, the wage per worker should fall (although in a lower proportion than that of the working hours).

11.1.2 The Role of Fixed Labour Costs

To extend the basic model, we must consider the existence of fixed costs associated to the hiring of workers. These costs do not vary when the number of working hours (given a particular number of workers) diminishes. Such costs have to do with employee screening expenditures, as well as with worker training, monitoring, and welfare expenditures.[3]

---

[1] Dolado J.J. (1991, p. 675).
[2] Note that, given the wage per hour $w = W/h$, a constant w requires that $\dot{W} = \dot{h}$.
[3] For a complete classification of this costs, see Hamermech (1993, p. 47).

When such costs exist, the total hourly wage (w) can be written as the sum of two components: a variable component (w^V), and a fixed component (w^F), that is

$$w = w^V + w^F = (W^V + W^F) / h \qquad (11.10)$$

where W^V and W^F are the variable and fixed hiring costs per employee.

Let us define w^F as a proportion α $(0 < \alpha < 1)$[4] of w^V. The demand function of working hours can be written as

$$w = w^V + \alpha\, w^V = (1 + \alpha)\, w^V = (1 + \alpha)\, W^V / h = f(h\,N) \qquad (11.11)$$

Taking logarithms in both sides of the above equation and reordering terms we obtain

$$\log W^V = \log h - \log(1 + \alpha) + \log f(h\,N) \qquad (11.12)$$

and fully differentiating

$$\dot W = \dot h - d\log(1+\alpha) + \frac{d\log f}{dH}(h \cdot dN + N \cdot dh) \qquad (11.13)$$

This expression allows us to write

$$\dot N = (\varepsilon - 1) \cdot \dot h - \varepsilon \cdot \dot W^V - \varepsilon \cdot d\log(1+\alpha) \qquad (11.14)$$

If we use the following approximation

$$\log(1 + \alpha) \approx \alpha \qquad (11.15)$$

expression (11.14) becomes

$$\dot N = (\varepsilon - 1) \cdot \dot h - \varepsilon \cdot (\dot W^V + \alpha \cdot \dot\alpha) \qquad (11.16)$$

We may now assume that the flexible part of the wage per worker adjusts to the variation in the working hours, so that w^V does not vary; that is

$$\dot W^V = \dot h \qquad (11.17)$$

We may also assume that the fixed part of the wage per worker is not altered in spite of the fact that the working hours are being reduced; that is

$$\dot W^F = 0 \qquad (11.18)$$

Given that $W^F = \alpha \cdot W^V$, expression (11.18) implies that

$$0 = \dot W^F = \dot\alpha + \dot W^V = \dot\alpha + \dot h \qquad (11.19)$$

This means that, when h falls and W^F remains constant, α must increase in the same proportion as the standard working hours fall; that is

$$\dot\alpha = -\dot h \qquad (11.20)$$

Substituting expressions (11.17) and (11.20) into (11.16), we obtain

---

[4] This assumption can be justified on the basis of experience. Experience suggests that training costs, monitoring costs, etc. are, on the whole, less than total variable wage costs over the entire period during which the worker remains attached to the firm.

$$\dot{N} = (\alpha \cdot \varepsilon - 1) \cdot \dot{h} \qquad (11.21)$$

In the case there were no hiring costs, α would become zero and the above expression would boil down to

$$\dot{N} = -\dot{h}$$

This coincides with (11.8), and we already know the meaning of this expression.

If hiring costs are positive, $\alpha > 0$, provided that $\dot{h} < 0$, it must be true that

$$\dot{N} < -\dot{h}$$

This means that the existence of hiring costs reduces the potential increase of employment caused by a reduction of the working hours, when this reduction is matched by a wage cut in the same proportion.

When the reduction of the working hours is not matched by any wage cut, $\dot{W}^V = \dot{W}^F = 0$, (meaning that $\dot{\alpha} = 0$), expression (11.16) becomes

$$\dot{N} = (\varepsilon - 1) \cdot \dot{h}$$

This means that changes in N adjust to changes in h according to the value of ε. This is exactly the same situation that we met before and does not need any further comments.

In sum, we may conclude that the potential positive effect on employment of a reduction of the working hours will be lower in industries where hiring costs represent a higher proportion of the wage bill.

11.1.3 Effort Effect and Organisational Effect

So far, we have not distinguished between the number of working hours really hired by employers ($H = h \cdot N$) and the effective working hours (H^e).

This distinction arises when the "productivity" of an hour's work varies[5] depending on the level of effort, and this effort is nor always the same. Organisational factors, such as the size of the working team or the efficiency of monitoring may be affected by the reduction of the working hours, which, in turn, might have some influence on the efficiency of labour.

When the efficiency of labour varies due to a change in effort, we shall speak about an "effort effect". When the efficiency of labour changes due to the organisational factors above mentioned, we shall speak about an "organisational effect".

In principle, the effort effect would have a permanent character, whereas the organisational effect appears to be essentially temporary. The reduction of the working hours reduces work weariness, and this is a permanent effect. The organisational effect, however, can be regarded as a short-term distortion in the firm's organisational plans.

---

[5] Nickell, S.J. (1996, p. 634) also distinguishes between actual and effective working hours. Fallon and Verry (1988, p. 118) also analyse the role of work weariness and the length of the working day on labour productivity.

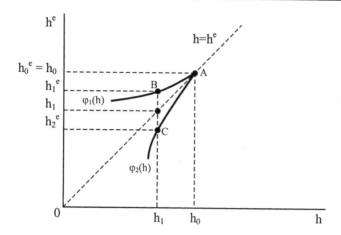

Fig. 11.1

In order to model these two effects, we are going to assume that the firms' effective working hours are defined as

$$H^e = N \; h^e = N \; \varphi(h) \tag{11.22}$$

where the number of effective hours, h^e, is a function φ of the actual number of hours, h. Function φ behaves as shown in figure 11.1. This figure can be explained as follows:

1. Prior to the reduction of the working hours, the working day has a length h_0. In such a situation we assume that $h^e_0 \equiv \varphi \; (h_0) = h_0$. This basically implies that production processes have been designed for a working day such as h_0.
2. The effort effect is reflected in the $\varphi_1(h)$ function. This function is defined for $h \leq h_0$, is increasing ($\varphi'_1 > 0$), and strictly convex ($\varphi_1'' > 0$). It also lies above the 45° line, meaning that, when the working hours are reduced by legal means (h becomes less than h_0) work weariness decreases and labour becomes more productive. Thus, the effective number of working hours can be expected to decrease less than the actual working hours ($h^e \equiv \varphi_1(h) > h, \; \forall \; h < h_0$), (point B of figure 11.1).
3. The organisational effect is reflected in the $\varphi_2(h)$ function. This function is defined for $h \leq h_0$, is increasing ($\varphi'_2 > 0$) , and strictly concave ($\varphi_2'' < 0$). It also lies below the 45° line, meaning that, when the working hours are reduced by legal means, the firm has to readjust its production processes to a shorter working day, and that implies a reduction in the efficiency of labour. Thus, the effective number of working hours can be expected to decrease more than the actual working hours ($h^e \equiv \varphi_2(h) < h, \; \forall \; h < h_0$), (point C of figure 11.1).

According to the above assumptions, the demand for working hours would be expressed by

$$w = f \, (H^e) \Rightarrow W \, / \, h = f \, [N \; \varphi(h)]; \; f \, (H^e) > 0; \; f' \, (H^e) < 0 \tag{11.23}$$

Taking logarithms in both sides of this equation and fully differentiating, we obtain

$$\dot{W} = \dot{h} - \frac{1}{\varepsilon^c}\left[\dot{N} + \frac{h \cdot \varphi'(h)}{\varphi(h)} \cdot \dot{h}\right] \qquad (11.24)$$

If we compare this expression with (11.5), we can observe that the only difference between them lies in the elasticity term, $h.\varphi'(h) / \varphi(h)$, that multiplies $\dot{h}$ in the right hand side of (11.24). This elasticity (from now on represented as χ) measures the sensitivity of the effective working hours with respect to changes in the standard working hours.

According to the above, expression (11.24) can be rewritten as

$$\dot{N} = (\varepsilon - \chi)\cdot\dot{h} - \varepsilon\cdot\dot{W} \qquad (11.25)$$

This expression is very similar to (11.6). However, our conclusions will be different depending on the value of χ.

In those industries where the effort effect prevails, the χ term (now called χ_1) is positive but lower than one. This situation is represented in point B in figure 11.1. On the contrary, in those industries where the organisational effect prevails, the χ term (now called χ_2) is higher than one (as shown by point C in figure 11.1).

If the wage per person were to fall in the same proportion as the working hours ($\dot{W} = \dot{h}$), expression (11.25) would become

$$\dot{N} = -\chi\cdot\dot{h} \qquad (11.26)$$

If the effort effect prevailed, $(0 < \chi < 1)$, employment would increase, but at a lower rate than that of the fall of the working hours. This effect would be permanent. If, on the contrary, the organisational effect prevailed ($\chi > 1$), the reduction of the working hours would increase employment in a greater proportion than that of the fall of the working day. Nevertheless, in this case, the effect is likely to be temporary and may disappear as firms readjust to the new standard working hours.

As a general conclusion of this part of the paper, we may state the following:

The effect on employment of a reduction of the standard working hours depends on the relative strength of the effort and the organisational effects. When the former prevails, the potential increase of employment is proportionally less than the reduction of the working hours. This effect is likely to be permanent. On the contrary, if the latter prevails, the effects on employment are proportionally greater than the reduction of the working hours. In this case, the effects are likely to be temporary.

The organisational effect is probably stronger in large firms, with complex work structures, whereas in small and medium-size firms the effort effect is likely to be the most relevant.

11.2
Effects on Labour Market Participation

11.2.1 Labour Market Participation with Compulsory Working Hours[6]

The traditional choice model between income and leisure enables us to obtain the optimum number of working hours supplied by a utility maximising individual. However, in the present model, the individual's decision becomes a discrete variable: the individual must choose between working the standard hours or not working.[7] Figure 11.2 illustrates this situation.

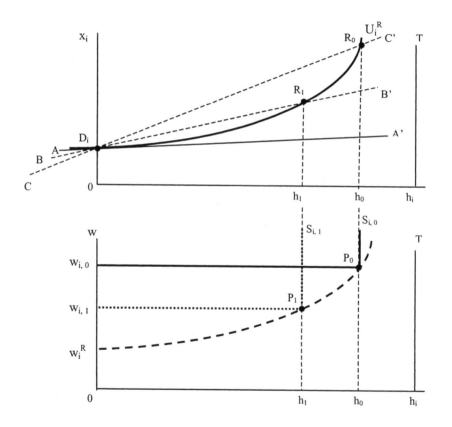

Fig. 11.2

6 I thank Angel Martin-Roman's comments and suggestions on this section.
7 Zabalza, Pissarides and Barton (1980) use a similar model but with a budget restriction consisting of three points.

Let us assume an individual, i, who derives utility from consumption, x_i, and from leisure, $T - h_i$, where T represents total available time and h_i the working hours. The individual has a non-labour income which allows him to consume D_i if he chooses not to work ($h_i = 0$). The level of utility at that particular point is represented by the U_i^R indifference curve in the upper graph. The slope of the AA' line would be his reservation wage, w_i^R. Only when the wage rate is above that level, the individual would be willing to work.

Assuming that the length of the working day, h_0 ($h_0 > 0$), is fixed by the law, the reservation wage would be $w_{i,0}$ (the slope the CC' line). For any wage below that level the individual would be better off, if he chose not to work. This individual would only improve his situation by working the standard hours at wages higher than $w_{i,0}$. The individual's labour supply would now be represented by the broken solid line $S_{i,0}$ in the lower graph. This supply is described by the following function

$$h_i(h_0) \begin{cases} 0 & \forall w \leq w_{i,0}(h_0) \\ h_0 & \forall w > w_{i,0}(h_0) \end{cases} \tag{11.27}$$

If the number of working hours were reduced to h_1 ($h_1 < h_0$), the new reservation wage would be $w_{i,1}$ (the slope of the BB' line), which is lower than $w_{i,0}$. Therefore, the reduction of the working hours would imply a new labour supply for the individual such as that represented by the broken dotted line in the lower graph of figure 11.2, $S_{i,1}$.[8]

If we assume that there are several workers and that each worker has a different reservation wage, we could build an aggregate labour supply "curve" (for any given length of the working day) such as the solid broken line $S_0(h_0)$ or the dotted broken line $S_1(h_1)$ in figure 11.3. If the number of workers is large enough, these broken lines could be approximated by continuous curves.

The labour supply function in this model can be expressed in terms of hours (hours of labour supplied at each particular wage, given the length of the working day) or in terms of persons (number of individuals available for work at each

---

[8] It can be easily shown that there is a positive relationship between the individual's reservation wage and the standard working hours. This reservation wage is a value of w such that:

$$U_i^R(T, D_i) = U_i(T - h_i, D_i + w \cdot h_i)$$

Let us call $w_{i,0}$ the w value that satisfies the above equation for a length of the working day such as h_0; and let us assume that the working hours are exogenously reduced ($dh_0 < 0$). Then, it follows that:

$$0 = \partial U_i^R / \partial h_0 = -\partial U_i / \partial (T - h_0) + \partial U_i / \partial x_i \cdot [w_{i,0} + h_0 \cdot \partial w_{i,0} / \partial h_{0i}]$$

which implies that:

$$\pi_{i,0} = (RMS_{i,0} / w_{i,0}) - 1 > 0$$

where $\pi_{i,0}$ is the elasticity of the reservation wage with respect to the working hours, and $RMS_{i,0}$ is the Marginal Rate of Substitution between income and leisure. Given any positive value of the working hours, and given the strict convexity of the indifference curves, it must be true that $RMS_{i,0} > w_{i,0}$. Hence, $\pi_{i,0}$ must be strictly positive, which means that changes in the working hours give rise to changes of the reservation wage in the same direction.

particular wage, given the length of the working day). The graphical representation would be identical in both cases. We would only need to take into account that each block of h hours represents an additional worker.

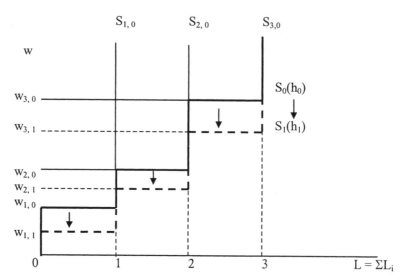

Fig. 11.3

Aggregate labour supply, measured in terms of people available for work, can be written as $L=L(w, h)$. If the number of workers is large enough and there is enough diversity among them, such function could be regarded as continuous. This would allow us to express the effects of changes in w or in h on L in terms of derivatives. In sum, the aggregate labour supply function can be written as

$$L = L (w, h); \qquad L_w > 0; \qquad L_h < 0; \tag{11.28}$$

11.2.2 Effects of a Reduction of the Working Hours on Aggregate Labour Supply

The full differential of (11.28) is

$$dL = L_w \, dw + L_h \, dh$$

which allows us to write

$$\dot{L} = \sigma_w \cdot \dot{w} - \sigma_h \cdot \dot{h} \tag{11.29}$$

where σ_w is the elasticity of labour supply with respect to the hourly wage and σ_h is the elasticity of labour supply with respect to the length of the working day (taken in absolute value). If we now take into account that $\dot{w} = \dot{W} - \dot{h}$ and substitute this expression into the previous one, we obtain

$$\dot{L} = \sigma_w \cdot \dot{W} - (\sigma_w + \sigma_h) \cdot \dot{h} \tag{11.30}$$

If the wage per worker is not altered after reducing the number of working hours, the resulting effect on participation is given by

$$\dot{L} = -(\sigma_w + \sigma_h) \cdot \dot{h} \qquad (11.31)$$

When the working day becomes shorter ($\dot{h} < 0$), labour supply increases due to two reasons. One reason is that a shorter working day with a constant wage per man implies a higher hourly wage and that tends to increase participation, as measured by σ_w. Another reason is that a shorter working day has a direct effect on participation as measured by elasticity σ_h.

When the reduction of the working hours is accompanied by a fall in the wage per person such that the hourly wage remains constant, ($\dot{w} = 0$), the effect of such a measure on participation can be calculated from expression (11.29) and is given by

$$\dot{L} = -\sigma_h \cdot \dot{h} \qquad (11.32)$$

The basic conclusion of the last two sections is that a reduction of the working hours increases participation both directly and indirectly (through changes in the hourly wage).

11.3
Effects on the Unemployment Rate

11.3.1 The Basic Case

This section analyses the effects of a reduction of the working hours on the economy's unemployment rate (u). Our scenario will be an economy where firms do not have to face any fixed costs when hiring their workers. We shall also ignore, for the moment, the possible influence of the length of the working day on work efficiency.

The unemployment rate (u) is defined as

$$u \equiv U/L \equiv 1 - N/L; \text{ hence: } N/L = 1 - u \qquad (11.33)$$

and given that

$$\log(1 - u) \approx -u \qquad (11.34)$$

we may write

$$\log(N/L) \approx 1 - u$$

which implies

$$du \approx \dot{L} - \dot{N} \qquad (11.35)$$

If we replace $\dot{L}$ with expression (11.30) and $\dot{N}$ with expression (11.6), we have

$$du \approx \sigma_w \dot{W} - (\sigma_w + \sigma_h)\dot{h} - (\varepsilon - 1)\dot{h} + \varepsilon \dot{W} \qquad (11.36)$$

Reordering terms, the above expression becomes

$$du \approx (\varepsilon + \sigma_w)\dot{W} + (1 - \varepsilon - \sigma_w - \sigma_h)\dot{h} \tag{11.37}$$

This expression allows us to make some predictions about the effect of a shorter working day on the unemployment rate.

If the wage per worker does not vary when the working day becomes shorter, expression (11.37) boils down to

$$du \approx [1 - (\varepsilon + \sigma_w + \sigma_h)] \cdot \dot{h} \tag{11.38}$$

which means that, when the working hours are reduced, the unemployment rate increases, provided that the sum of the hour elasticity of labour demand and the two labour supply elasticities (all of them in absolute value) is higher than one; that is, provided that $(\varepsilon + \sigma_w + \sigma_h) > 1$. This condition will be true as long as $\varepsilon > 1$.

If we assume that the wage per person falls in the same proportion as the working hours ($\dot{W} = \dot{h}$), the hourly wage remains unchanged, and expression (11.37) becomes

$$du \approx (1 - \sigma_h) \cdot \dot{h} \tag{11.39}$$

which means that the reduction of the working hours will reduce the unemployment rate, provided that σ_h is less than one.

Finally, we may calculate the wage reduction required to prevent the unemployment rate from being affected when the working hours are reduced, under the assumption that $(\varepsilon + \sigma_w + \sigma_h)$ is higher than one. Assuming $du=0$, expression (11.37) allows us to write

$$\dot{W} = \frac{(\varepsilon + \sigma_w) + (\sigma_h - 1)}{(\varepsilon + \sigma_w)} \cdot \dot{h} \tag{11.40}$$

This means that the effects of a shorter working day on the unemployment rate could be alleviated by decreasing the wage per person. If σ_h is lower than one, the required reduction in the wage per person will be proportionately smaller than that of the working hours. If $\sigma_h > 1$, the required change in W will be proportionately greater.

As a general conclusion of this section we may state the following:

The effect of a reduction of the working hours on the unemployment rate depends on the changes of the wage per person that accompany that measure. If the wage per person does not change at all, the reduction of working hours is likely to increase the unemployment rate, given that the sum of the three elasticities (the elasticity of labour demand -ε-, plus the two elasticities of labour supply -σ_w and σ_h-) is likely to be greater than one. Only in the case of a rigid labour demand ($\varepsilon < 1$) and a quite rigid labour supply ($\sigma_w + \sigma_h < 1$), it could occur that $\varepsilon + \sigma_w + \sigma_h < 1$, which is the condition required for the unemployment rate to go down when the working day becomes shorter and the wage per man does not change. In any case, the positive effect of the reduction of the working hours on the unemployment rate could be mitigated if such reduction were accompanied by a fall in the wage per person.

11.3.2 Effects on the Unemployment Rate under a More General Model

This section analyses the effects caused by a reduction of the working hours on the unemployment rate within a context different from that considered in the previous section. Here, we shall take into account the existence of fixed as well as variable wage costs, as described in section 11.1.2. The influence of the length of the working day on work efficiency will also be taken into account, following the lines established in section 11.1.3.

First of all, we must take into account that the fixed component of the wage (either per hour or per person) does not enter the labour supply function. Hence, this function must be rewritten as

$$L = L\,(w^v, h)$$

which means that

$$\dot{L} = \sigma_w \cdot \dot{W}^v - (\sigma_w + \sigma_h) \cdot \dot{h} \tag{11.41}$$

It must be observed that the elasticity σ_w is now referred to the variable component, w^v, of the hourly wage. For simplicity, we have kept the same notation as before.

As regards the labour demand function, some changes must be made in order to take into account (a) the existence of hiring costs; and (b) the fact that the length of the working day may influence the efficiency of labour.

When both (a) and (b) are considered, the labour demand function can be rewritten as

$$(1 + \alpha)\,w^v = f(H^e) \Rightarrow [(1 + \alpha)\,W^v] / h = f[N \cdot \varphi(h)]; f(H^e) > 0; f'(H^e) < 0;$$

which means that

$$\dot{N} = (\varepsilon - \chi) \cdot \dot{h} - \varepsilon \cdot (\dot{W}^v + \alpha \cdot \dot{\alpha}) \tag{11.42}$$

If we substitute (11.41) and (11.42) into (11.35), we obtain

$$du \approx (\varepsilon + \sigma_w) \cdot \dot{W}^v + (\chi - \varepsilon - \sigma_w - \sigma_h) \cdot \dot{h} + \varepsilon \cdot \alpha \cdot \dot{\alpha} \tag{11.43}$$

If the working hours go down and the wage per man remains constant ($\dot{W}^v = 0$, which implies $\dot{\alpha} = 0$), the variation of the unemployment rate is given by

$$du \approx [\chi - (\varepsilon + \sigma_w + \sigma_h)] \cdot \dot{h} \tag{11.44}$$

Comparing this expression with (11.38), we observe that the only difference between them lies in elasticity χ, which measures the sensitivity of the effective working hours with respect to changes in the standard working hours. We would like to compare the effect of a reduction of the working hours according to (11.44) and according to (11.38). In order to do so, we rewrite (11.44) as

$$du^* \approx [\chi - (\varepsilon + \sigma_w + \sigma_h)] \cdot \dot{h} \tag{11.45}$$

By subtracting (11.38) from (11.45), we obtain

$$[du^* - du] \approx (\chi - 1) \cdot \dot{h} \tag{11.46}$$

Hence, when the working day becomes shorter ($\dot{h} < 0$), if the effort effect prevails (χ <1), du* > du. This means that the effect of a shorter working day on the unemployment rate is stronger now than in the basic case: the unemployment rate increases now *more* than before. The previous statement assumes that a shorter working day increases the unemployment rate; but we already know that this may not be so. In some presumably rare cases, a shorter working day can reduce unemployment. In such cases, the above expression tells us that du* is *less negative* than du, meaning that the unemployment rate falls *less* (as a result of a shorter working day) than in the basic case.

The opposite will happen when the organisational effect prevails (χ >1). Nevertheless, this effect will only be temporary, following the interpretation given in section 11.1.3.

Now, let us suppose that the flexible part of the wage per person falls in the same proportion as the working hours ($\dot{w}^V = \dot{h}$), which means that the flexible part of the hourly wage remains unchanged. On the other hand, since the fixed part of the wage per worker (hiring costs) does not change, α must increase in the same proportion as the standard hours fall; that is, $\dot{\alpha} = -\dot{h}$. In this case, expression (11.43) becomes

$$du \approx [\chi - (\sigma_h + \varepsilon \cdot \alpha)] \cdot \dot{h} \tag{11.47}$$

If we rewrite du in expression (11.47) as du**, and subtract (11.39) from (11.47), we obtain

$$[du^{**} - du] \approx [(\chi - \varepsilon \cdot \alpha) - 1] \cdot \dot{h} \tag{11.48}$$

We want to know whether this expression is positive or negative, when the working hours fall ($\dot{h} < 0$). If the effort effect prevails (χ < 1), given that $\varepsilon \cdot \alpha$ is always positive, [($\chi - \varepsilon \cdot \alpha$) – 1] is necessarily negative. Hence, du** > du. This means that the effect of a shorter working day on the unemployment rate is stronger than in the basic case. We must also notice that that effect is also stronger the higher the proportion of hiring costs over total labour costs (the higher α).

As a general conclusion of this section we may state the following:

When there are hiring costs and when the reduction of the working day reduces work weariness, it becomes more difficult to reduce the unemployment rate through a reduction of the working hours.

11.4
Conclusions

In this paper, we have analysed the effects of a legal measure reducing the standard working hours on employment, participation, and unemployment rates. Our basic conclusions are the following:

1. If the wage rate does not vary, a reduction of the standard working hours increases employment, provided that the elasticity of the working hours with respect to wages (ε) is less than one and reduces employment when ε >1. When ε =1, the effect of the reduction of working hours on employment is null.

The negative effects of this type of measure on employment are, then, constrained to the case where $\varepsilon > 1$. But these effects can be alleviated if the reduction of the working hours is accompanied by a wage cut. In order to avoid a decrease in the employment level, the wage per worker should fall (although in a lower proportion than that of the working hours).

2. The potential positive effect on employment of a reduction of the working hours will be lower in industries where hiring costs represent a higher proportion of the wage bill. Such costs have to do with employee screening expenditures, as well as with worker training, monitoring, and welfare expenditures.

3. The effect on employment of a reduction of the standard working hours depends on the relative strength of the effort and the organisational effects. The former takes place when the reduction of the working hours reduces work weariness. The latter occurs when factors such as the size of the working team or the efficiency of monitoring are affected by the reduction of the working day.

   When the effort effect prevails, the potential increase of employment (provided the wage rate falls in the same proportion as the working day) is proportionally less than the reduction of the working hours. This effect is likely to be permanent. On the contrary, if the organisational effect prevails, the effects on employment are proportionally greater than the reduction of the working hours. In this case, the effects are likely to be temporary.

4. When the working day becomes shorter, labour supply increases due to two reasons. One reason is that a shorter working day with a constant wage per man implies a higher hourly wage and that tends to increase participation. Another reason is that a shorter working day has a direct effect on participation (it induces people to participate more).

5. The effect of a reduction of the working hours on the unemployment rate depends on the changes of the wage per person that accompany that measure. If the wage per person does not change at all, the reduction of working hours is likely to increase the unemployment rate. Only in the case of a rigid labour demand and a quite rigid labour supply, the unemployment rate is likely to decrease when the working day becomes shorter and the wage per man does not change. In any case, the positive effect of the reduction of the working hours on the unemployment rate could be mitigated if such reduction were accompanied by a fall in the wage per person.

6. When there are hiring costs and when the reduction of the working day reduces work weariness, it becomes more difficult to reduce the unemployment rate through a reduction of the working hours.

References

Dolado, J.J.: Valoración Crítica de las Estimaciones Econométricas Disponibles de la Relación entre los Precios Relativos y el Empleo en la Economía Española. In: Bentolila, S., Toharia, L., Estudios de Economía del Trabajo en España, III El Problema del Paro, C. 20. MTSS 1991

Fallon, P., Verruy, D.: The Economics of Labour Markets. Phillip Allan 1988

Hamermesh, D.: Labour Demand. New Jersey, Princeton University Press 1993

Nickell, S.: Dynamic Models of Labour Demand. In: Ashenfelter,O., Layard, R., Handbook of Labour Economics, Chapter 9. North-Holland 1987

Zabalza, A., Pissarides, C., Barton, M.: Social Security and the Choice Between Full-Time Work, Part-Time Work and Retirement. Journal of Public Economics 14 (1980)

12 Dynamic Adjustments in a Two-Sector Model

Francisco Galera
University of Navarra (Spain)

Pablo Coto-Millán
University of Cantabria (Spain)

This paper presents a simple dynamic model in which only one resource is used entirely in order to produce two goods. Technology displays constant returns in both cases. The resource is owned by a few individuals who must choose between the two activities in which to use it. Here we analyse the decisions of change of activity in which the resource is to be used taking into account the different profitability per time unit of the activities directed to produce both goods. We show that, under certain conditions, it is possible to reach cyclic, or chaotic, dynamics so that the returns per factor may never be equal in both sectors.

The basic instrument for the analysis is a difference equation. It is common knowledge that the behaviour of this type of equation essentially depends on the values taken by certain parameters, and that, using simple assumptions, the solutions may behave in a cyclic or chaotic manner. This fact has led to applications in economic models and justifies apparently random behaviours in an analytical manner. See, for example, the mentioned papers by Kelsey, Lichtenberg A.H. & Ujihara, A. and Dwyer, G. P. Jr.

This paper is framed within this type of literature but its main contribution is not only to illustrate a possible example of chaotic behaviour but also, and more importantly, to state that this behaviour is more likely in certain conditions than in others.

12.1
The Formal Model

Let us assume an economy constituted by N equal individuals in which each one of these individuals owns 1/N amount of a productive resource – either labour or any other type – at each time period. The total amount of the resource is 1. This resource may be used to produce two types of goods called C and D. The activity dedicated to produce C is named the first sector while the remaining activity is the second sector. At each time unit, the individuals decide whether they use their resource in goods C or D. We let x_t represent the amount of the resource used in the first sector during the period t, which coincides hypothetically with the amount of individuals who dedicate the resource to that sector. $1-x_t$ will be the amount of resource dedicated to the production of D.

The returns in the production of C and D are constant so that the amount produced of C will be $d(1-x_t)$. From here we will assume that d=1. There will be one price for each good, taking the price of goods D as numerary, the expression used will be

$$p_t = p_t^C$$
$$p_t^D = 1$$

In order to establish the demand functions for each goods, we will assume that all the individuals have the same tastes and these are expressed in a utility function such as the Cobb-Douglas function:

$$U = a \ln C_t^n + (1 - a) \ln D_t^n \qquad (12.1)$$

where C_t^n is the amount demanded for goods C during the period t by the n individual and D_t^n has an analogous meaning. With this assumption, the demand for each one of the economic agents are given by the following equations:

$$C_t^n = a/p_t \cdot I_t^n$$
$$D_t^n = (1 - a) \cdot I_t^n \qquad (12.2)$$

where I_t^n is the individuals' incomeduring the period t.

In this economy, the individuals' income available comes entirely from their resource income. With this assumption, we have the following equation:

$$\sum_{n=1}^{N} I_t^n = p_t c x_t + 1 - x_t \qquad (12.3)$$

Therefore, the aggregated demand of goods C in the period t will be:

$$C_t = \sum_{n=1}^{N} C_t^n = \sum_{n=1}^{N} \frac{a}{p_t} I_t^n = \frac{a}{p_t}(p_t c x_t + 1 - x_t) \qquad (12.4)$$

The demand for goods D will be similarly obtained. By equating the aggregated demand and supply for each goods, we will have the following equation:

$$c x_t = \frac{a}{p_t}(p_t c x_t + 1 - x_t), \quad 1 - x_t = (1-a)(p_t c x_t + 1 - x_t) \qquad (12.5)$$

From any of these equations we can reach the equilibrium price:

$$p_t = \frac{a(1 - x_t)}{(1-a)c x_t} \qquad (12.6)$$

In fact, by substituting p_t in the above equation, we can observe that this is the equilibrium price.

Taking into account the fact that workers assign the amount of factor according to their own individual interest, to avoid a transfer of resources from one sector to another, it must hold that the returns per time unit are the same in both activities.

$$p_t c = 1 \qquad (12.7)$$

In other words, if an individual employs his resources in the first sector, he will get the same income – per time unit – as in the second sector.

When this condition is not given, the factor will be re-assigned with the corresponding changes in prices. We will assume that the number of agents who want to change the assignment of the factor from the second to the first sector is proportional to the difference – or quotient, which is the same in this case since the returns value of the second factor is 1 - between the returns of both activities:

$$\Delta x_t = r (p_t c - 1) \qquad (12.8)$$

From this, and from the equilibrium prices in equation (12.6), we obtain the dynamic equations of the model we are studying:

$$x_{t+1} = x_t + r \frac{a - x_t}{(1-a)x_t} \qquad (12.9)$$

We are basically interested in the stability conditions as well as in the possible evolutions of the variable x_t, which represents, as already said, both the amount of resource and the proportion of individuals who assign their resource to the first sector. Now, we must solve the recurrence defined in equation (12.9). To see in a simple manner how this type of recurrences are studied, see chapter 11 in Peitgen et al.

12.2
Basic Results

To make the reading of this exposure less complex, we will summarise the essential results and technical data and will include them in the annex in a simplified form.

We would like to answer some questions about the equilibrium stability of the equilibrium, the possibility of chaotic dynamics and the stability of the system itself. In particular:

I) What conditions must be imposed to parameters "r" and "a" in order to reach a stable equilibrium? How do those restrictions depend on parameter "a", in other words, on the relative size of the first sector?

II) Under what conditions may a chaotic dynamics appear? Do those conditions depend on parameter "a"?

III) What values of "r" and "a" guarantee that a negative number of producers does not appear in the second sector? What about the first sector? What conditions provoke the disappearance of a sector in a particular period?

These questions are answered as follows:

I) The system is stable if $r < U(a) = 2a(1-a)$.

II) The system enters in the so-called chaotic zone when $r \geq Y(a) \approx 2.63626a(1-a)$.

III) A negative number of producers does not appear in the first sector when

$$V(a) = \begin{cases} 4a(1-a) & \text{if } a \leq \frac{1}{2} \\ 1 & \text{if } a > \frac{1}{2} \end{cases}$$

A negative number of producers does not appear in the second sector if $r \leq W(a)$, as defined in the annex.

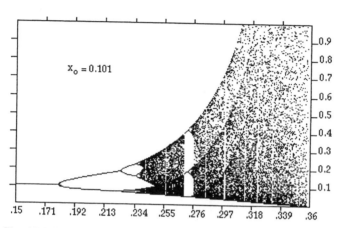

Fig. 12.1. Bifurcation diagram of x with respect to r with a=0.1

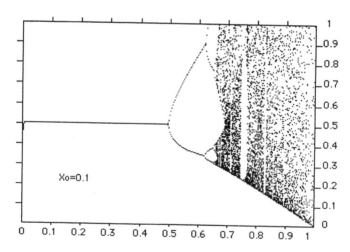

Fig. 12.2. Bifurcation diagram of x with respect to r with a=0.5

Figures 12.1 and 12.2 present the bifurcation diagrams of the variable x with respect to the parameter r with a=0.1 and a=0.5 values. For those who are not familiarised with these diagrams, an interpretation of them can be seen in the works by Peitgen et al, Collet & Eckmann, Devaney or in any other work dealing with chaos from an elementary point of view.

12.3
Conclusions

The dynamic possibilities of the model essentially depend on parameters "r" and "a". As indicated, parameter r measures the response of the agents to the differences in the profits. The higher "r", the greater the amount of individuals and resources moving form one sector to another and, initially, that mobility should make the system more stable since any desequilibrium would be more rapidly corrected. However, we can observe that, if the value of r exceeds a certain limit, the only equilibrium presented by the dynamic system becomes unstable, which generates a cyclic, or even chaotic, behaviour in some cases. If the value of r becomes even higher, any of the sectors may disappear from the economy.

Moreover, parameter "a" basically measures the individuals' tastes. The higher "a", the greater the relative weight of the first sector within the economy. This relative weight affects the dynamic features of the system. To be precise, if the sectors of economy have a similar relative weight (that is to say, if $a \cong 0.5$), the system proves more stable since, as seen in figure 1, the value of r must be higher to produce both instability and a chaotic situation. In fact, when a=0.5 a chaotic situation is not possible because, before entering the chaotic zone, one of the sectors disappears and the dynamics become pointless. On the other hand, if the volume of a sector is much lower than that of another sector, it is more likely that unstable dynamic and even chaotic behaviour appears.

In my opinion, this fact is significant since it suggests –taking into account all the restrictions of a model with so simple assumptions and only two sectors – that, when the productive resources are assigned and the size of the production sectors are similar, we may expect a more stable and calm dynamics of factor transfer from one activity to the other. However, when the sectors have different sizes, it would be more likely that unstable dynamics appear permanently without ever equalling the factor returns in the different activities and also that some productive sectors disappear.

Annex

In order to justify the answers to questions I), II) and III) formulated above, we will study the interaction in the function:

$$y = f(x) = x + r\frac{a-x}{(1-a)x}$$

where we have that the only fixed point $f(x^*) = x^*$ is found in $x^* = a$.

Let us see the basis for these answers:

I) The derivative of f is:

$$f'(x) = 1 - \frac{ra}{(1-a)x^2}$$

Therefore,

$$f'(a) = 1 - \frac{r}{a(1-a)}$$

And, since $r > 0$ and $0 < a < 1$, the equilibrium point is locally stable if and only if

$$R < 2a(1-a) = U(a)$$

II) From the above result, we have that the first bifurcation appears in $r=2a(1-a)$. In order to establish condition II), firstly, we will find where the second bifurcation appears. Here, we are making the same study as in I) but this time applied to function $g(x) = f(f(x))$. This means that we have to get the values for which this function is satisfied, x^* being a fixed point of g different from a that verifies:

$$-1 < g'(x^*) < 1.$$

In this case, solving the equation:

$$g(x) = f(f(x)) = x$$

we obtain the following three values:

$$x_1 = a$$

$$x_2 = a(5 + \sqrt{5})/4$$

$$x_3 = a(5 - \sqrt{5})/4$$

and, solving the equation:

$$g'(x^*) = f'(f(x^*))\, f'(x^*) = -1,$$

taking for x^* the x_2 or x_3 values – the same result is obtained for both of them – and omitting the estimations, we obtain the value of the parameter in which the second bifurcation is located: $r = 2.5a(1-a)$.

Secondly, in order to find the entry into the chaotic zone, we will use the Feigenbaum constant [see Peitgen (1992)]: assuming that $r_1, r_2, r_3, \ldots$ are parameter r values for which the successive bifurcations appear, then:

$$\lim \frac{r_n - r_{n-1}}{r_{n+1} - r_n} = d = 4.669201$$

Moreover, assuming that not only the limit but also all these quotients are equal to the Feigenbaum constant (d) and, taking into account that we already know the value at which the two first bifurcations appear, we have that:

$$\lim r_n \cong 2.63626a(1-a),$$

which is the chaotic zone. This bifurcation has been previously represented as $Y(a)=2.63626a(1-a)$ and, even though it is approximated, it very much coincides which the bifurcation diagrams experimentally obtained.

III)   The f function always has a minimum value.

Let x_{min} be the minimum of f in the $[0,1]$ interval, it i obtained that:

$$x_{min} = \sqrt{\frac{ra}{1-a}} \qquad \text{when } r \le (1\text{-}a)/a$$

or we have $x_{min} = 1$ in the opposite case.

Therefore,

$$f(x_{min}) = \begin{cases} 2\sqrt{ra/(1-a)} - [r/(1-a)] & \text{if } r = (1\text{-}a)/a \\ 1\text{-}r & \text{if } r > (1\text{-}a)/a \end{cases}$$

The $f(x_{min}) \ge 0$ condition is equivalent to: $r \le 4a(1\text{-}a)$ if $r \le (1\text{-}a)/a$. However, when this condition is not satisfied we have that $1\text{-}r \ge 0$. In this case, if we define the following function:

$$V(a) = \begin{cases} 4a(1-a) & \text{if } a \le \tfrac{1}{2} \\ 1 & \text{if } a > \tfrac{1}{2} \end{cases}$$

we can express the results obtained as follows: with the dynamics generated by this system, the first sector shall always have a positive resource number if and only if $r \le V(a)$.

There is a much more complicated result when a negative number of resources does not appear in the second sector. Here we can also distinguish two cases. When the minimum of the function is located in the significant zone, the equation to be solved is:

$f^2(x_{min}) = 1$

which is equivalent to

$$2\sqrt{\frac{ra}{1-a}} - \frac{2r}{1-a} + \frac{ra}{(1-a)\cdot[2\sqrt{ra/(1-a)} - r/(1-a)]} = 1$$

which is also equivalent to the following cubic equation:

$$4r^3 + 4(1\text{-}a)(1\text{-}4a)r^2 + (1\text{-}a)^2(25a^2 - 14a + 1)r - 4(1\text{-}a)^3 a = 0$$

This, after undergoing the corresponding transformations, has a solution equivalent to the following expression:

$$(1-a)\cdot\left\{\frac{4a-1}{3} + \frac{1}{6}\sqrt[3]{1-a}[\sqrt[3]{388a^2 + 43a + 1 + (45a+3)\sqrt{a(75a+6)}} + \right.$$

$$\left. \sqrt[3]{388a^2 + 43a + 1 - (45a+3)\sqrt{a(75a+6)}}]\right\}$$

which, to abbreviate, we shall call f(a).

When the minimum is located outside the significant zone (as said before, this happens when $r > (1-a)/a$), the condition we want to get is that $r < (2-2a)/(2-a) = y(a)$. Therefore, this condition is satisfied when:

1) if $r < (1-a)/a$ then, $r < f(a)$;
2) if $r > (1-a)/a$ then, $r < y(a)$.

However, if it is verified that 2), then $(1-a)/a < r < y(a) = (2-2a)/(2-a)$, which is only true if $2/3 < a < 1$. Therefore, the function which expresses a behaviour in which no negative number of resources appears in the second sector, is the following:

$$W(a) = \begin{cases} f(a) & \text{if } a \leq 2/3 \\ y(a) & \text{if } a > 2/3 \end{cases}$$

In order to check this results, we can see that if $a = 2/3$, it must be satisfied that: $f(a) = y(a) = (1-a)/a$; which, in fact, is so.

Basic References

Chiarella, C.: The Elements of a Nonlinear Theory of Economics Dynamics. Lecture Notes in Economics and Mathematical Systems. Springer Verlag, Berlin 1990

Collet, P., Eckmann, J.P.: Iterated Maps on the Interval as Dynamical Systems. Progress in Physics, Vol. I. Birkhäuser, Boston 1980

Devaney, R.L.: An Introduction to Chaotic Dynamical Systems. 2nd Ed. Addison-Wesley, California 1989

Dwyer, G. P. Jr.: Stabilization Policy Can Lead to Chaos. Economic Inquiry, vol. XXX, 40-46 (1992)

Kelsey, D.: The Economics of Chaos or the Chaos of Economics. Oxford Economic Papers 40, 1-31 (1988)

Lichtenberg A.H., Ujihara, A.: Application of Nonlinear Mapping Theory to Commodity Price Fluctuations. Journal of Economic Dynamics and Control 13,225-246 (1989)

Peitgen, H.O., Jürgens, H., Saupe, D.: Chaos and Fractals. Springer Verlag, New York; 1992

Other References

Baumol, W.J., Benhabib, J.: Chaos: Significance, Mechanism, and Economic Applications. The Journal of Economic Perspectives, Vol. 3-1, Winter, 77-105 (1989)

Chiarella, C.: The Elements of a Nonlinear Theory of Economics Dynamics, Lecture Notes in Economics and Mathematical Systems, Springer Verlag, Berlin 1990

Collet, P., Eckmann, J.P.: Iterated Maps on the Interval as Dynamical Systems. Progress in Physics, Vol. I.. Birkhäuser, Boston 1980

Deneckere, R., Pelikan, S. : Competitive Chaos. Journal of Economic Theory 40, 13-25 (1986)

Devaney, R.L.: An Introduction to Chaotic Dynamical Systems. 2nd Ed. Addison-Wesley, California 1989

Gumowski, I., Mira, C.: Recurrences and Discrete Dynamical Systems. Lecture Notes in Mathematics 809. Springer 1980

Kelsey, D.: The Economics of Chaos or the Chaos of Economics. Oxford Economic Papers 40, 1-31 (1988)

Lakshmikantham, V., Trigiante, D.: Theory of Difference Equations, Numerical Methods and Applications. Academic Press, London (1988)

Lorenz, H.W.: Nonlinear Dynamical Economics and Chaotic Motion. Lecture Notes in Economics and Mathematical Systems, 334. Springer Verlag, Berlin 1989

Mirowski, P.: From Mandelbrot to Chaos in Economic Theory. Southern Economic Journal, October, vol. 57-2 (1990)

Preston, C.: Iterates of Piecewise Monotone Mappings on an Interval. Lecture Notes in Mathematics, 1347. Springer Verlag, Berlin-Heidelberg 1988

Rasband, S.N.: Chaotic Dynamics of Nonlinear Systems. John Wiley & Sons, New York 1989

Wiggins, S.: Introduction to Applied Nonlinear Dynamical Systems and Chaos. Texts in Applied Mathematics 2. Springer Verlag, New York 1990

Contributions to Economics

Stefan Traub
Framing Effects in Taxation
1999. ISBN 3-7908-1240-4

Pablo Coto-Millán
Utility and Production
1999. ISBN 3-7908-1153-X

Frank Riedel
**Imperfect Information
and Investor Heterogeneity
in the Bond Market**
2000. ISBN 3-7908-1247-1

Kirsten Ralf
Business Cycles
2000. ISBN 3-7908-1245-5

Michele Bagella/
Leonardo Becchetti (Eds.)
**The Competitive Advantage
of Industrial Districts**
2000. ISBN 3-7908-1254-4

Frank Bohn
**Monetary Union and
Fiscal Stability**
2000. ISBN 3-7908-1266-8

Jaime Behar
**Cooperation and Competition in a
Common Market**
2000. ISBN 3-7908-1280-3

Michael Malakellis
**Integrated Macro-Micro-Modelling
Under Rational Expectations**
2000. ISBN 3-7908-1274-9

Stefan Baumgärtner
**Ambivalent Joint Production and
the Natural Environment**
2000. ISBN 3-7908-1290-0

Henri Capron, Wim Meeusen (Eds.)
**The National Innovation System
of Belgium**
2000. ISBN 3-7908-1308-7

Tobias Miarka
**Financial Intermediation and
Deregulation**
2000. ISBN 3-7908-1307-9

Chisato Yoshida
**Illegal Immigration and Economic
Welfare**
2000. ISBN 3-7908-1315-X

Nikolaus Thumm
Intellectual Property Rights
2000. ISBN 3-7908-1329-X

Max Keilbach
**Spatial Knowledge Spillovers and
the Dynamics of Agglomeration and
Regional Growth**
2000. ISBN 3-7908-1321-4

Alexander Karmann (Ed.)
Financial Structure and Stability
2000. ISBN 3-7908-1332-X

Joos P. A. van Vugt/Jan M. Peet (Eds.)
**Social Security and Solidarity in the
European Union**
2000. ISBN 3-7908-1334-6

Johannes Bröcker/Hayo Herrmann
(Eds.)
**Spatial Change and Interregional
Flows in the Integrating Europe**
2001. ISBN 3-7908-1344-3

Kirstin Hubrich
**Cointegration Analysis
in a German Monetary System**
2001. ISBN 3-7908-1352-4

Nico Heerink et al. (Eds.)
**Economic Policy
and Sustainable Land Use**
2001. ISBN 3-7908-1351-6

Friedel Bolle/Michael Carlberg (Eds.)
Advances in Behavioral Economics
2001. ISBN 3-7908-1358-3

Volker Grossmann
**Inequality, Economic Growth, and
Technological Change**
2001. ISBN 3-7908-1364-8

Thomas Riechmann
Learning in Economics
2001. ISBN 3-7908-1384-2

Miriam Beblo
Bargaining over Time Allocation
2001. ISBN 3-7908-1391-5